THE

CRITTENDEN COMMERCIAL ARITHMETIC

AND

Business Manual.

DESIGNED FOR THE USE OF

MERCHANTS, BUSINESS MEN,

ACADEMIES, AND COMMERCIAL COLLEGES.

BY

JOHN GROESBECK,

CONSULTING ACCOUNTANT,

PRINCIPAL OF CRITTENDEN'S PHILADELPHIA COMMERCIAL COLLEGE.

ABRIDGED EDITION.

PHILADELPHIA:

E. C. & J. BIDDLE, 508 MINOR ST.

1867.

"Knowledge is the guide of practice."

"If a man's wits be wandering, let him study arithmetic."—BACON.

"Washington studied the intricate forms of business. He copied out bills of exchange, notes of hand, bills of sale, receipts, and all the varieties of the class, with a precision and elegance that were remarkable."

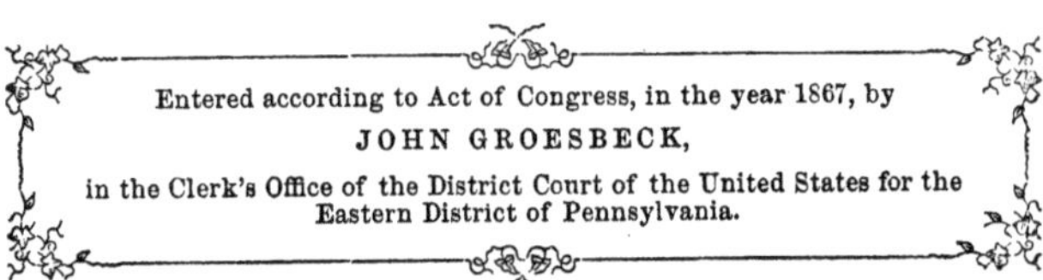

STEREOTYPED BY MACKELLAR, SMITHS & JORDAN,
PHILADELPHIA.
PRINTED BY J. B. RODGERS.

Second Edition.

PREFACE.

THE object of this book is to impart that practical knowledge which is daily required in business life.

Business is based upon comprehensible principles and facts, and a knowledge of them will promote efficiency in actual transactions. Practice only can impart skill in application; but practice enlightened by knowledge sooner acquires proficiency, and saves from many errors and much useless drudgery.

Among the qualifications necessary in mercantile pursuits, none are more essential than a thorough acquaintance with the methods of calculation employed, and a familiarity with the various forms and uses of business papers.

The calculations presented in the following pages have been selected as the best in actual use among business men; and several of them, it is believed, are now published for the first time. The forms are those with which every person should be familiar, and include a greater variety than has yet appeared in any one collection. They are accompanied by explanations which will be of service to those of limited experience in business affairs.

The author has been connected for the last ten years with Crittenden's Commercial College, for which this manual was primarily prepared; and, in addition to his knowledge of the wants of the student, he has been frequently consulted by merchants and others upon difficult questions that have occurred in their practice. These difficulties have been carefully noted, and many of their intricacies are here solved and explained. The student of book-keeping will also find much to aid him in his attempts to master that science.

The author takes this opportunity to acknowledge his indebtedness to numerous friends for their valuable assistance in the preparation of the work, and to render them his sincere thanks. He would also express his obligations to the officers of numerous banks and mercantile houses, of the Mint, the Custom-House, and of various public and private establishments, for the opportunities afforded him for obtaining reliable information on many subjects of interest and value.

In the first edition of a work of this nature, though prepared with much care, perfection is not to be expected; and the author will esteem it a special favor if business men, teachers, and others, will communicate any suggestion, new or improved method of calculation, or any useful information on business topics that will add to its completeness.

CONTENTS.

COMMERCIAL ARITHMETIC.

BUSINESS FORMS AND INFORMATION.

CHARACTERS AND ABBREVIATIONS

USED IN BUSINESS.

@	At.
a/c	Account.
¢	Cents.
%	Per cent.
#	Number.
1^1	One and one-quarter.
1^2	One and one-half.
1^3	One and three-quarters.

15 doz. $\frac{5}{\$12}$, $\frac{5}{\$15}$, $\frac{5}{\$18}$. Fifteen doz., 5 of which are $12 per doz., 5 doz. @ $15, and 5 doz. at $18 per doz.

1 hhd. Sugar.
1100
155 945lbs., 1100 pounds gross weight, 155 lbs. tare, or weight of hhd., 945 lbs. net weight.

4 ps. 42, 36, 28, 32 } 138 yds. The numbers in the bracket are the number of yds. in each piece respectively.

10 doz. $\frac{4}{5}$ @ 2/– $\frac{6}{8}$ @ 3/6. 4 doz. No. 5 @ 2 shillings per doz.; 6 doz. No. 8 @ 3*s.* 6*d.* per doz.

7 × 9, or 7 by 9 in. 7 in. wide, 9 in. long.

◇A W.W., and similar characters and letters, are placed on packages to designate a particular lot or shipment.

(Goods are numbered and marked, that they may be distinguished without minute description.)

Acc't.	Account.
Adv.	Adventure.
Am't.	Amount.
Ass'd.	Assorted.
Bal.	Balance.
Bbl.	Barrel.
Blk.	Black.
Bo't.	Bought.
B. L., or B. of L.	Bill of Lading.
Co.	Company.
Cr.	Creditor.
Com.	Commission.
Cons't.	Consignment.
Dft.	Draft.
Disc't.	Discount.
Do. or ditto.	The same.
Doz.	Dozen.
Dr.	Debtor.
Ea.	Each.
E.E.	Errors excepted.
E. & O.E.	Errors and omissions excepted.
Exch.	Exchange.
Exps.	Expenses.
Fig'd.	Figured.
Fol.	Folio.
Forw'd, or fwd.	Forward.
fr.	From.
Fr.	French.
Fr't.	Freight.
Guar.	Guarantee.
Gal.	Gallon.
Hhds.	Hogsheads.
Ins.	Insurance.
Insol.	Insolvency.
Inst. (instant)	This month.
Invt.	Inventory.
Int.	Interest.
Mdse.	Merchandise.
Mo.	Month.
Net.	Without deduction.
No.	Number.
Pay't.	Payment.
Pd.	Paid.
Pk'gs.	Packages.
Per, or pr.	By.
Per cent.	By the hundred.
Prem.	Premium.
Prox. (proximo)	The next month.
Ps.	Pieces.
Rec'd.	Received.
Ship't.	Shipment.
S. S.	Steamship.
Sunds.	Sundries.
Ult. (ultimo)	The last month.
Yds.	Yards.
Yr.	Year.

COMMERCIAL ARITHMETIC.

METHODS OF ADDITION.

1. Addition constitutes the greater part of all the calculations of business and common life; and the ability to add with rapidity and accuracy is of more practical utility than all the other arithmetical operations combined. This ability, however, can be readily acquired by the exercise of memory and the right kind of practice. A regular method should be pursued; encumbering the mind with amounts to be carried from one operation to another should be avoided; and a practical familiarity with the sums of combinations of numbers should be cultivated as much as possible. Any thing which lessens the number of operations to be performed promotes rapidity. By closely adhering to the following methods, a short time only will be required for acquiring considerable proficiency.

2. In writing numbers, care should be taken to make the figures clear and plain, so that a 3 will not be mistaken for a 5, or a 7 for a 9; and also that the figures in one line do not run into those in the line below, and that all the figures of a column be placed directly under each other.

3. Commence at the foot of the column and add upward, and, if the column is long, always set down the carrying figure. This relieves the mind from apprehension of loss of time, from being compelled, by interruptions which often occur in business, to leave the work when nearly through the addition of several columns of figures; and then, if necessary, any column may be re-added without the trouble of adding the preceding.

Always add the carrying figure to the next column *on commencing.*

4. The following methods of retaining the carrying figure are adopted by most accountants :—

FIRST METHOD.	SECOND METHOD.
	15
$13213.30	15
25342.13	27
12468.31	27
1143.13	20
35321.34	23
13476.21	10
2113.13	
103077.55	103077.55
2222.11	

In the first method, the figure to be carried is written *small* immediately under the figure to which it belongs.

In the second method, the whole result of each column is set down by itself, the sum of each column being written one place to the left under the sum of the column preceding it; then, when all the results are written, the right-hand figures, including all the footing of the last column, will give the total result.

5. *If the figures are not set down in regular order under each other*, instead of trying to follow the column upward, take the figure which is the same number of places from the right hand as the figure with which you started, not regarding whether it is below tens or hundreds, or very near the right-hand figure, or at some distance from it. For instance, if you wish to add a column of hundreds which have been set down irregularly, instead of looking for the next figure above, look for the next figure which is three places from the right. This method will save time, and avoid perplexity and uncertainty.

6. To secure accuracy, the addition should be performed twice,—in different directions: this gives new combinations, and, if there has been a mistake, is a preventive of its repetition, which is likely to occur, especially when the mind has been too long engaged.

7. If the columns of figures are long, it is generally better to place the footings on a separate piece of paper and test their correctness, before placing them in ink on the book; as mistakes can then be corrected without defacing the page by erasures.

8. Familiarity with the totals of combinations should be the object of all practice. Counting is not adding. It is quite as easy, and considerably quicker, to say at once, 8 and 7 are 15, than to count 8, 9, 10, 11, 12, &c., up to the result 15; and also to say, 3, 6, 10, 15, than to say, 3 and 3 are 6, 6 and 4 are 10 10 and 5 are 15.

COUNTING-HOUSE DRILL TABLES.

Drill Table No. 1.

20	20	20	20	20	20	20	20	20	20
19	19	19	19	19	19	19	19	19	19
18	18	18	18	18	18	18	18	18	18
17	17	17	17	17	17	17	17	17	17
16	16	16	16	16	16	16	16	16	16
15	15	15	15	15	15	15	15	15	15
14	14	14	14	14	14	14	14	14	14
13	13	13	13	13	13	13	13	13	13
12	12	12	12	12	12	12	12	12	12
11	11	11	11	11	11	11	11	11	11
10	10	10	10	10	10	10	10	10	10
9	9	9	9	9	9	9	9	9	9
8	8	8	8	8	8	8	8	8	8
7	7	7	7	7	7	7	7	7	7
6	6	6	6	6	6	6	6	6	6
5	5	5	5	5	5	5	5	5	5
4	4	4	4	4	4	4	4	4	4
3	3	3	3	3	3	3	3	3	3
2	2	2	2	2	2	2	2	2	2
1	1	1	1	1	1	1	1	1	1
2	3	4	5	6	7	8	9	10	11

Drill Table No. 2.

20	21	22	23	24	25	26	27	28	29	30
19	20	21	22	23	24	25	26	27	28	29
18	19	20	21	22	23	24	25	26	27	28
17	18	19	20	21	22	23	24	25	26	27
16	17	18	19	20	21	22	23	24	25	26
15	16	17	18	19	20	21	22	23	24	25
14	15	16	17	18	19	20	21	22	23	24
13	14	15	16	17	18	19	20	21	22	23
12	13	14	15	16	17	18	19	20	21	22
11	12	13	14	15	16	17	18	19	20	21
10	11	12	13	14	15	16	17	18	19	20
9	10	11	12	13	14	15	16	17	18	19
8	9	10	11	12	13	14	15	16	17	18
7	8	9	10	11	12	13	14	15	16	17
6	7	8	9	10	11	12	13	14	15	16
5	6	7	8	9	10	11	12	13	14	15
4	5	6	7	8	9	10	11	12	13	14
3	4	5	6	7	8	9	10	11	12	13
2	3	4	5	6	7	8	9	10	11	12
1	2	3	4	5	6	7	8	9	10	11

The above columns should be added until the addition can be easily performed and without hesitation.

9. In the following columns, add all the figures enclosed in each bracket as *one number*, and name only results in the same manner as when the figures are taken separately. Thus, in adding column No. 4, say 7, 11, 16, &c.

10. When a figure is repeated several times, count the number of times it occurs, and multiply by the figure. Thus, if the figure 8 occurs seven times in a column, multiply 7 by 8 for the result, instead of adding seven 8's together.

11. When three figures occur in regular order,—as 4, 5, 6, or 6, 7, 8,—three times the middle figure will be their sum; when five figures occur, take five times the middle figure. When there are four figures in regular order, take twice the sum of the extremes; when there are six, take three times the sum of the extremes.

(1.)	(2.)	(3.)	(4.)
324	678	3 3 4	1 1 2
235	789	3 4 5	1 2 3
143	976	4 6 3	2 6 4
421	899	3 7 7	4 1 1
312	989	7 8 4	2 5 5
234	988	4 6 6	3 1 2
343	878	2 8 1	5 3 3
423	673	8 3 7	3 2 4
225	789	2 9 3	2 6 5
123	968	3 0 5	2 8 1
334	887	4 5 5	0 4 4
212	987	5 5 1	1 2 2
324	798	2 3 9	0 4 1
123	976	3 7 5	1 2 1
431	687	7 6 5	2 0 4
212	997	3 4 2	4 1 3
4419	13959	72 1 2	

ADDITION OF SEVERAL COLUMNS AT ONE OPERATION.

12. To add two or more columns at one operation.

To the lower number add first the units of the next number above, then the tens, then the hundreds; and so continue.

	OPERATION.
23	
31	$22 + 5 = 27,\ 27 + 10 = \ 37$
24	$37 + 4 = 41,\ 41 + 20 = \ 61$
15	$61 + 1 = 62,\ 62 + 30 = \ 92$
22	$92 + 3 = 95,\ 95 + 20 = 115$ Ans.
115	

	OPERATION.
234	
112	$322 + 3 = 325 + 20 = 345 + 400 = \ 745$
423	$745 + 2 = 747 + 10 = 757 + 100 = \ 857$
322	$857 + 4 = 861 + 30 = 891 + 200 = 1091$ Ans.
1091	

Practice will enable a person to add amounts of two or more figures at one operation: thus, $22 + 15 = 37$, $37 + 24 = 61$, $61 + 31 = 92$, $92 + 23 = 115$ Ans. As soon as the combinations become familiar, addition by this method can be performed without difficulty; but, for ordinary purposes, one column at a time is sufficient. In Ledger accounts, when the last two or three columns are not all filled, they may be added at one operation with advantage.

13. Very long columns of figures are sometimes added in the following manner:—

FIRST METHOD.	SECOND METHOD.	
247	247	
362	362	
228	228	
436	436	1273
1273	128	
128	326	
326	121	575
121	121	
1848	316	
121	405	842
316		2690 Ans.
405		
2690 Ans.		

BALANCING ACCOUNTS.

14. It is frequently of advantage to the accountant to find the difference between two sums by addition, instead of by subtraction. For example, if he wishes to find the difference between 2427 and 1235, instead of taking the trouble of placing the smaller number under the larger, he will add, mentally, to 1235 a sum that will make the whole equal to 2427, writing the figures as he proceeds under 1235.

2427	1235
	1192—balance.

When both sides of an account contain several amounts, first add the larger side in the usual manner; *then commence at the top of the columns, on the smaller side of the account, and add downwards, inserting the necessary figures to make the required balance.* Thus, to find the balance of the following account:

Dr.		V. I. Andrews.			Cr.
1867.			1867.		
Jan. 3.	To Mdse.	$84.00	Jan. 10.	By Cash,	$45.00
" 10.	" "	72.00	" 17.	" "	67.00
" 24.	" "	43.00		*Balance,*	*87.00*
		$199.00			

First, add the larger side; then say, $5+7=12$, and 7, *the figure required to make the balance*, $=19$. Set down 7 and carry 1. $1+4+6=11$, and the remaining figure of the balance $=19$. To test the accuracy of the work, add the whole of the smaller side, and include the balance.

EXAMPLE II.

Dr.		George L. Burtis.			Cr.
1867.			1867.		
Feb. 9.	To Mdse.	$187.37	Feb. 15.	By Cash,	$150.00
" 26.	" "	37.42	Mar. 10.	" "	437.75
Mar. 4.	" "	260.38			
Apr. 9.	" "	720.16			
May 6.	" "	132.50			

EXAMPLE III.

Dr.		Thomas Wallace.			Cr.
1867.			1867.		
Jan. 9.	To Cash,	$375.00	Jan. 2.	By Mdse.	$375.00
" 15.	" Mdse.	270.50	Feb. 2.	" Cash,	200.00
" 17.	" "	320.75	" 15.	" "	275.50
" 26.	" "	175.23	" 18.	" Bills Pay.	116.25
Mar. 3.	" "	315.85			

FRACTIONS.

RULES FREQUENTLY USED.

15. To multiply whole numbers by fractions.

RULE.—*Multiply by the numerator, and divide the product by the denominator.*

EXAMPLES.

1. Multiply 464 by $\frac{3}{4}$.

$464 \times 3 = 1392$; $1392 \div 4 = 348$ Ans.

2. Multiply 12672 by $18\frac{3}{4}$.

```
  12672
    18¾
 ______
4)38016—product by 3.
   9504—product by ¾.
 101376    "    " 8.
 12672     "    " 1.
 ______
 237600—product by 18¾.
```

16. To multiply a fraction by a fraction.

Rule.—*Multiply the numerators together for a new numerator, and the denominators together for a new denominator.*

1. Multiply $\frac{2}{5}$ by $\frac{4}{7}$.

$2 \times 4 = 8$
$5 \times 7 = 35$ Ans. $\frac{8}{35}$.

2. Multiply $\frac{4}{5}$ by $\frac{6}{11}$.
3. " $\frac{18}{29}$ " $\frac{3}{4}$.
4. " $\frac{7}{17}$ " $\frac{12}{31}$.

17. To divide by a fraction.

Rule.—*Invert the divisor, and multiply as in the previous rules.*

1. Divide $\frac{5}{9}$ by $\frac{3}{4}$.

$\frac{3}{4}$ inverted $= \frac{4}{3}$
$5 \times 4 = 20$
$9 \times 3 = 27$ Ans. $\frac{20}{27}$.

2. Divide $\frac{8}{15}$ by $\frac{2}{3}$.
3. " $\frac{1}{4}$ " $\frac{1}{2}$.
4. " $\frac{1}{2}$ " $\frac{1}{4}$.

18. To divide by a mixed number.

Rule.—*Multiply the whole number in the divisor by the denominator of the fraction, and to the product add the numerator. Multiply the dividend by the denominator of the fraction; then divide as usual. The remainder, if any, must be divided by the denominator of the fraction to obtain the true remainder.*

1. Divide 480 by $5\frac{1}{2}$.

```
 5½   480
 2      2
 __   ___
11)   960
      _____
      87 3/11
```

2. Divide 2675 by $18\frac{3}{4}$.
3. " 18992 by $133\frac{1}{3}$.
4. " 425 by $31\frac{1}{4}$.
5. " 341 by $7\frac{1}{3}$.

CONTRACTIONS

IN

MULTIPLICATION AND DIVISION.

The following contractions are useful for imparting readiness and dexterity in the mechanical processes of multiplication and division. If thoroughly mastered, they will be found to be of great service, and will amply repay the time and labor expended in acquiring them. They include, in a condensed form, nearly all of practical value that has yet been published, together with some methods which, it is believed, now appear in print for the first time.

The labor of making out bills and invoices, entering sales, taking account of stock, and many similar operations, may be much lessened by their use; as extensions can be made without writing out the operations, while the liability to mistakes is diminished, because there is less labor, and fewer figures are employed.

CONTRACTIONS IN MULTIPLICATION.

19. To multiply two numbers of two places each when the units or tens are alike.

RULE.—*Multiply units by units; then,* IF THE UNITS ARE ALIKE, *multiply the sum of the tens by the units, and the tens by tens.* IF THE TENS ARE ALIKE, *multiply the sum of the units by the tens, and the tens by tens; in all cases carrying as usual.*

EXAMPLES.

1. Multiply 34 by 54.

34	$4 \times 4 = 16$
54	$5 + 3 = 8 \times 4 = 32 + 1$ (carried) $= 33$
1836	$3 \times 5 = 15 + 3$ (carried) $= 18$

2. Multiply 45 by 43.

45	$5 \times 3 = 15$
43	$5 + 3 = 8 \times 4 = 32 + 1$ (carried) $= 33$
1935	$4 \times 4 = 16 + 3$ (carried) $= 19$

3. Multiply 44 by 64.
4. " 32 " 72.
5. " 28 " 18.
6. " 45 " 35.
7. " 123 " 33.
8. " 65 " 55.
9. " 124 " 34.
10. Multiply 36 by 34.
11. " 64 " 64.
12. " 35 " 34.
13. " 72 " 73.
14. " 37 " 35.
15. " 45 " 45.
16. " 66 " 66.

$45 \times 45 = 5 \times 4$ with the square of 5 annexed.
$75 \times 75 = 8 \times 7$ " " 5 "

20. This rule includes the multiplication of two numbers whose units or tens are ones, the squaring of numbers, multiplying when the units are alike and the sum of the tens is ten, &c.

As it is capable of several hundred applications, its value is obvious. A little practice will give the ability to write the products without setting down the figures to be multiplied. It is believed that this is the first time the above rule has appeared in print.

21. To multiply by numbers, the half, third, or fourth of which is a convenient multiplier.

RULE.—*Multiply the half of one number by twice the other, or one-third of one number by three times the other, &c.*

EXAMPLES.

1. Multiply 28 by 16.

$28 \times 2 = 56$
$16 \div 2 = 8$ $\qquad 56 \times 8 = 448.$

2. Multiply 35 by 27.

$27 \div 3 = 9$
$35 \times 3 = 105$ $\qquad 105 \times 9 = 945.$

22. This rule is well adapted for mental operations, and is especially applicable to numbers which can easily be changed to tens, hundreds, &c.

3. Multiply 42 by 15.

$42 \div 2 = 21$
$15 \times 2 = 30$ $\qquad 21 \times 30 = 630.$

4.	Multiply	76	by	15.	9.	Multiply	48	by	$13\frac{1}{3} = 16$ by 40.
5.	"	134	"	35.	10.	"	36	"	$22\frac{1}{2}$.
6.	"	43	"	24.	11.	"	24	"	$23\frac{1}{3}$.
7.	"	182	"	18.	12.	"	136	"	45.
8.	"	56	"	28.	13.	"	28	"	$17\frac{1}{7}$.

$56 \times 4 = 224,\ 28 \div 4 = 7,\ 224 \times 7 = 1568.$

23. To multiply when one part of the multiplier is a factor or multiple of the other.

RULE.—*Multiply by the smaller part of the multiplier; then multiply the product so obtained by the number which shows how many times this smaller part is contained in the other, placing the right-hand figure of the second product under the right-hand figure of that part of the multiplier to which it belongs.*

EXAMPLES.

1. Multiply 285 by 164.

$16 \div 4 = 4$

```
  285
  164
 ----
 1140  product by 4.
 4560  4 times the product
-----
46740    by 4 = 285 × 16.
```

2. Multiply 654 by 436.

```
   654
   436
   ---
 2616    product by 4.
 23544 9 times the prod.
------
285144     by 4 = 654 × 36.
```

3. Multiply 364 by 126.
4. " 387 " 279.

5. Multiply 4267 by 142.
6. " 276 " 357.
7. " 812 " 426.
8. " 373 " 369.
9. " 235 " 424.
10. " 644 " 321.
11. " 342 " 535.
12. " 822 " 642.
13. " 545 " 927.

14. The custom-house value of a franc is 18.6 cents: what is an invoice amounting to 32165 francs worth in United States currency?

15. What is an invoice of cassimeres, valued at £3225, worth, the custom-house value of a pound sterling being $4.84?

24. To multiply by any number ending with 9.

RULE.—*Multiply by the next higher number, and subtract the multiplicand.*

EXAMPLES.

1. Multiply 42 by 39.

$39 + 1 = 40$
$42 \times 40 = 1680$
$1680 - 42 = 1638$ Ans.

2. Multiply 45 by 99.

3. Multiply 432 by 59.
4. " 125 " 699.
5. " 175 " 290.
6. " 325 " 999.
7. " 424 " $9\frac{1}{2}$.
8. " 36 " $68\frac{3}{4}$.

25. To multiply by two figures at once.

RULE I.—*Multiply both figures in the multiplier by each figure in the multiplicand separately.* Or,

RULE II.—*Multiply units by units; then to the product of each succeeding figure in the multiplicand by the units of the multiplier, add the product of the figure preceding it by the tens, and carry as usual. Multiply the last figure of the multiplicand by the tens of the multiplier.*

NOTE.—When large numbers are to be multiplied, for the purpose of remembering which figure has been used, place a dot over each figure of the multiplicand as soon as multiplied.

EXAMPLE UNDER RULE I.

Multiply 3265 by 24.

$$\begin{array}{r} 3265 \\ \underline{24} \\ 78360 \end{array}$$

$24 \times 5 = 120$, $24 \times 6 = 144 + 12$ (carried) $= 156$.
$24 \times 2 = 48 + 15$ (carried) $= 63$, $24 \times 3 + 6$ (carried) $= 78$.

EXAMPLES UNDER RULE II.

1. Multiply 34 by 43.

$$\begin{array}{r} 43 \\ \underline{34} \\ 1462 \end{array}$$

$3 \times 4 = 12$, write 2.
$4 \times 4 = 16 + 1$ (carried) $= 17$ to carry.
$3 \times 3 = 9 + 17$ " $= 26$, write 6.
$4 \times 3 = 12 + 2$ " $= 14$.

2. Multiply 212121 by 23.

$$\begin{array}{r} 212121 \\ \underline{23} \\ 4878783 \end{array}$$

	2	1	2	1	2	1
						23
	2×3	1×3	2×3	1×3	2×3	1×3
2×2	1×2	2×2	1×2	2×2	1×2	
Ans. 4	8	7	8	7	8	3

With a little practice, the products may be written without the trouble of writing the numbers under each other, which often, as in making out invoices, entering sales, &c., effects a considerable saving of time. When thoroughly understood, the liability to mistakes is less than by the ordinary method, because there are fewer operations.

3. Multiply 42 by 14.
4. " 36 " 16.
5. Multiply 63 by 31.
6. " 26 " 51.

Find the answers to the following by multiplying the numbers as they stand:—

24 yards calico	@ 14c. per yd.	Ans. $3.36.
52 lbs. sugar	@ 17c. per lb.	"
36 bus. oats	@ 51c. per bus.	"
48 bus. corn	@ 63c. per bus.	"
362 yds. carpeting	@ 77c. per yd.	"
28 lbs. tea	@ 74c. per lb.	"
72 yds. muslin	@ 42c. per yd.	"
34 gross pens	@ 85c. per gross.	"

26. To multiply when the multiplier is a convenient or aliquot part of 10, 100, 1000, &c.

RULE.—*Annex as many ciphers to the multiplicand as there are in the number of which the multiplier is an aliquot part; then*

Take such part of the multiplicand so increased, as the multiplier is of the number of which it is an aliquot part.

EXAMPLES.

1. Multiply 424 by 25.

$25 = \frac{1}{4}$ of 100. $42400 \div 4 = 10600$.

2. Multiply 4936 by $12\frac{1}{2}$.

$12\frac{1}{2} = \frac{1}{8}$ of 100. $493600 \div 8 = 61700$.

ALIQUOT PARTS OF 10.	ALIQUOT PARTS OF 100.		ALIQUOT PARTS OF 1000.
$2\frac{1}{2} = \frac{1}{4}$	$6\frac{1}{4} = \frac{1}{16}$	$18\frac{3}{4} = \frac{3}{16}$	$83\frac{1}{3} = \frac{1}{12}$
$3\frac{1}{3} = \frac{1}{3}$	or $\frac{1}{4}$ of $\frac{1}{4}$	or $\frac{1}{8} + \frac{1}{2}$ of $\frac{1}{8}$	$125 = \frac{1}{8}$
$1\frac{2}{3} = \frac{1}{6}$	$8\frac{1}{3} = \frac{1}{12}$	$31\frac{1}{4} = \frac{5}{16}$	$166\frac{2}{3} = \frac{1}{6}$
$1\frac{3}{7} = \frac{1}{7}$	or $\frac{1}{3}$ of $\frac{1}{4}$	$37\frac{1}{2} = \frac{3}{8}$	$250 = \frac{1}{4}$
$1\frac{1}{4} = \frac{1}{8}$	$12\frac{1}{2} = \frac{1}{8}$	$62\frac{1}{2} = \frac{5}{8}$	$333\frac{1}{3} = \frac{1}{3}$
$1\frac{1}{9} = \frac{1}{9}$	$14\frac{2}{7} = \frac{1}{7}$	$66\frac{2}{3} = \frac{2}{3}$	$375 = \frac{3}{8}$
	$16\frac{2}{3} = \frac{1}{6}$	$75 = \frac{3}{4}$	$625 = \frac{5}{8}$
	$25 = \frac{1}{4}$	$83\frac{1}{3} = \frac{5}{6}$	$833\frac{1}{3} = \frac{5}{6}$
	$33\frac{1}{3} = \frac{1}{3}$	$87\frac{1}{2} = \frac{7}{8}$	$875 = \frac{7}{8}$

27. *This table can also be used to show the value of an aliquot part. For example,* $\frac{5}{8}$ *of* 1000 *equal* 625; $\frac{5}{6}$ *of* $100 = 83\frac{1}{3}$.

3. Multiply 48 by $2\frac{1}{2}$.
4. " 18 " $3\frac{1}{3}$.
5. " 384 " $12\frac{1}{2}$.
6. " 486 " $16\frac{2}{3}$.
7. " 165 " $33\frac{1}{3}$.
8. " 96 " $1\frac{2}{3}$.
9. Multiply 320 by $6\frac{1}{4}$.
10. " 840 " $8\frac{1}{3}$.
11. " 225 " $14\frac{2}{7}$.
12. " 648 " 125.
13. " 726 " $166\frac{2}{3}$.
14. " 2456 " $37\frac{1}{2}$.

15. What is the cost of $12\frac{1}{2}$ yds. cloth @ $18\frac{3}{4}$c. per yd.?

$12\frac{1}{2} = \frac{1}{8}$; changing $18\frac{3}{4}$ to a decimal, $18.75 \div 8 = \$2.34\frac{3}{8}$.

28. Aliquot parts may be conveniently used when the multiplier is but little more or less than an aliquot part.

EXAMPLES.

1. Multiply 24 by $17\frac{2}{3}$.

$17\frac{2}{3} = 16\frac{2}{3} + 1$; $16\frac{2}{3} = \frac{1}{6}$.

$$\begin{aligned} 24 \times 16\tfrac{2}{3} &= 400 \\ 24 \times 1 &= 24 \\ \hline &\ 424 \text{ Ans.} \end{aligned}$$

2. Multiply 36 by $18\frac{2}{3}$.
3. " 48 " $13\frac{1}{2}$.
4. " 33 " 35.
5. " 36 " $34\frac{1}{3}$.

29. To multiply mixed numbers in which the fractions are alike.

Rule.—*To the product of the whole numbers add that part of their sum which is expressed by the fraction, and the product of the fraction multiplied by itself.*

Note.—Perform the operation mentally whenever it can be done.

EXAMPLES.

1. Multiply $6\frac{1}{2}$ by $4\frac{1}{2}$.

$$\begin{aligned} 6 \times 4 &= 24 \\ \tfrac{1}{2} \text{ of } (6+4) &= 5 \\ \tfrac{1}{2} \times \tfrac{1}{2} &= \underline{\tfrac{1}{4}} \quad 29\tfrac{1}{4} \text{ Ans.} \end{aligned}$$

2. Multiply $8\frac{1}{4}$ by $4\frac{1}{4}$.
3. " $6\frac{1}{3}$ " $9\frac{1}{3}$.
4. " $8\frac{1}{3}$ " $4\frac{1}{3}$.
5. " $7\frac{1}{5}$ " $8\frac{1}{5}$.
6. " $4\frac{1}{2}$ " $4\frac{1}{2}$.
7. " $6\frac{3}{4}$ " $6\frac{3}{4}$.
8. Multiply $12\frac{1}{4}$ by $3\frac{1}{4}$.

$\frac{1}{4}$ of $15 = 3\frac{3}{4}$

$\frac{3}{4} + \frac{1}{16} = \frac{13}{16}$. Ans. $39\frac{13}{16}$.

9. Multiply $16\frac{2}{3}$ by $9\frac{2}{3}$.
10. " $8\frac{1}{3}$ " $6\frac{1}{3}$.

30. When the whole numbers are alike, and the fraction is one-half, the half of the sum of the whole numbers equals one of the numbers, and the operation can be shortened by multiplying the whole number by itself plus 1, and annexing $\frac{1}{4}$:—

$$4\tfrac{1}{2} \times 4\tfrac{1}{2} = 5 \times 4 + \tfrac{1}{4} = 20\tfrac{1}{4}.$$

31. This rule will apply to whole numbers, by taking the units as so many parts of ten, and the tens as so many parts of one hundred. Thus, to multiply 45 by 45: 40 equals 4 tens, 5 equals one-half of ten, and one-fourth of one hundred equals 25; then, $5 \times 4 = 20$, to which annex $\frac{1}{4}$ of 100, that is, 25, and we have 2025.

11. Multiply 65 by 65.
12. " 35 " 35.

12. Multiply 650 by 650.
13. " 450 " 450.

32. To multiply mixed numbers when the whole numbers are alike.

RULE.—*To the product of the whole numbers add that part of one of them which is expressed by the sum of the fractions, and the product of the fractions.*

EXAMPLES.

1. Multiply $12\frac{1}{4}$ by $12\frac{1}{2}$.

$$12 \times 12 = 144$$
$$\tfrac{1}{4} + \tfrac{1}{2} = \tfrac{3}{4}$$
$$\tfrac{3}{4} \text{ of } 12 = 9$$
$$\tfrac{1}{4} \times \tfrac{1}{2} = \tfrac{1}{8}$$
$$144 + 9 + \tfrac{1}{8} = 153\tfrac{1}{8} \text{ Ans.}$$

2. Multiply $8\frac{1}{3}$ by $8\frac{1}{6}$.
3. " $9\frac{1}{4}$ " $9\frac{1}{12}$.
4. " $8\frac{1}{5}$ " $8\frac{1}{20}$.
5. " $6\frac{1}{2}$ " $6\frac{3}{4}$.
6. " $12\frac{1}{3}$ " $12\frac{1}{6}$.
7. " $7\frac{1}{7}$ " $7\frac{3}{7}$.
8. " $8\frac{1}{4}$ " $8\frac{3}{4}$.

NOTE.—*When the sum of the fractions equals one, and the whole numbers are alike, that part of one of them which is expressed by the sum of the fractions is equal to itself, and the operation can be shortened by multiplying the whole number by itself plus 1, and annexing the product of the fractions.*

Thus, to multiply $8\frac{1}{4}$ by $8\frac{3}{4}$:—

$\frac{3}{4} + \frac{1}{4} = \frac{4}{4}$, or 1; $\frac{4}{4}$ of $8 = 8$

$9 \times 8 = 72$ $\frac{1}{4} \times \frac{3}{4} = \frac{3}{16}$ $72\frac{3}{16}$ Ans.

10. Multiply $4\frac{2}{3}$ by $4\frac{1}{3}$.
11. " $12\frac{1}{6}$ " $12\frac{5}{6}$
12. " $7\frac{1}{5}$ " $7\frac{4}{5}$.
13. " $6\frac{1}{4}$ " $6\frac{3}{4}$.
14. " $8\frac{1}{3}$ " $8\frac{2}{3}$.

15. Multiply 4.25 by 4.75.

$4.25 = 4\frac{1}{4}$ $4.75 = 4\frac{3}{4}$

$5 \times 4 = 20$ $\frac{1}{4} \times \frac{3}{4} = \frac{3}{16}$

$\frac{3}{16} = .1875$

20.1875 Ans.

33. To multiply any mixed numbers.

RULE.—*Multiply by the fraction of the multiplier, then by the whole number;*—or, *Reduce both multiplier and multiplicand to improper fractions, and then proceed as in multiplication of fractions.*

EXAMPLE.

Multiply $6\frac{1}{3}$ by $9\frac{1}{2}$.

$6\frac{1}{3}$
$9\frac{1}{2}$

$3\frac{1}{6}$ prod. by $\frac{1}{2}$.
3 " of $\frac{1}{3}$ by 9.
54 " " 6 " 9.

Ans. $60\frac{1}{6}$.

Or, $6\frac{1}{3} = \frac{19}{3}$ $9\frac{1}{2} = \frac{19}{2}$

$\frac{19}{3} \times \frac{19}{2} = \frac{361}{6} = 60\frac{1}{6}$.

34. To multiply by numbers which are from 1 to 12 less than 100, 1000, &c.

RULE.—*Multiply the multiplicand by the difference between the multiplier and 100, 1000, &c., and subtract the product from the product of the multiplicand by 100, 1000, &c.*

EXAMPLES.

1. Multiply 35 by 98.

$98 = 100 - 2$
$35 \times 2 = 70$
$35 \times 100 = 3500$
$3500 - 70 = 3430$ Ans.

2. Multiply 125 by 198.
3. " 205 " 96.
4. " 375 " 89.
5. Multiply 215 by 98.

NOTE.—When from 1 to 12 more than 100, add the product of the multiplicand by the unit figure, after annexing the required number of ciphers.

$325 \times 102 = 32500 + 650 = 33150$ Ans.

6. Multiply 475 by 101, 103, 106.

35. To multiply two numbers which are equidistant from any number which may be squared mentally.

RULE.—*From the square of the mean number subtract the square of the difference between the mean number and one of the given numbers.*

EXAMPLES.

1. Multiply 98 by 102.

100, the mean number between 98 and 102;
Square of $100 = 10000$; $4 =$ the square of the difference;
$10000 - 4 = 9996$ Ans.

2. Multiply 32 by 28.

Square of 30 = 900;
900 — 4 = 896.

3. Multiply 41 by 39.

4. Multiply 88 by 92.
5. " 37 " 43.
6. " 46 " 34.
7. " 73 " 87.
8. " 41 " 59.

When the sum of the units equals ten, and one of the tens is an odd number and the other is an even number, the numbers are equidistant from some number of tens, which is obtained by taking half of the sum of the tens plus 1.

9. Multiply 45 by 95.

10. Multiply 35 by 65.

36. This rule includes multiplying by numbers of two places each, *when the sum of the units is 10 and the difference of the tens is 1;* by numbers *the sum of whose units equals 10, and whose tens are alike;* mixed numbers, in which *the sum of the fractions equals 1, and the difference of the whole numbers is 1.*

11. Multiply $12\frac{1}{2}$ by $11\frac{1}{2}$. Ans. $143\frac{3}{4}$.

12. Multiply $7\frac{1}{3}$ by $6\frac{2}{3}$.

13. Multiply $4\frac{1}{4}$ by $3\frac{3}{4}$.
14. " 61 " 59.
15. " 126 " 114.

37. To square any number of 9's instantaneously.

RULE.—*Beginning at the left, write 9 as many times less 1 as there are 9's in the given number, an 8, as many ciphers as 9's, and 1.*

The square of 999 = 998001; square of 9999 = 99980001. The square of any number of 3's equals $\frac{1}{9}$ the square of the same number of 9's.

CONTRACTIONS IN DIVISION.

38. Multiplying or dividing both the dividend and divisor by the same number does not alter the quotient.

39. To divide by any number ending in 5, or an aliquot part of 10, or any number of tens.

RULE.—*Multiply both the dividend and divisor by any number that will make the divisor equal some number of tens or hundreds; then divide as usual.*

NOTE.—*If there is a remainder, it must be divided by the number by which the dividend was multiplied, to obtain the true remainder.*

EXAMPLES.

1. Divide 4480 by 35.
   $35 \times 2 = 70$
   $4480 \times 2 = 8960$
   $8960 \div 70 = 128$ Ans.
2. Divide 3644900 by 175.
   $175 \times 4 = 700$
   $3644900 \times 4 = 14579600$
   $14579600 \div 700 = 20828$ Ans.
3. Divide 6785 by 45.
4. " 3725 " 75.
5. " 628750 by 55.
6. " 2628000 " 225, by $22\frac{1}{2}$, $17\frac{1}{2}$, $23\frac{1}{3}$, $17\frac{1}{7}$, $18\frac{1}{3}$, or $18\frac{2}{6}$.

40. To divide by an aliquot part of 100, 1000, &c.

RULE.—*Multiply the dividend by the number which expresses how many times the given divisor is contained in 100, 1000, &c., and point off as many places as there are ciphers in the number divided by the given divisor.*

EXAMPLES.

1. Divide 485 by 25.
   $100 \div 25 = 4$
   $485 \times 4 = 19.40$ Ans.
2. Divide 8480 by $12\frac{1}{2}$.
   $100 \div 12\frac{1}{2} = 8$
   $8480 \times 8 = 678.40$ Ans.
3. Divide 69600 by $16\frac{2}{3}$.
4. Divide 4762000 by $33\frac{1}{3}$.
5. " 2875 " $62\frac{1}{2}$.
   $62\frac{1}{2} = \frac{5}{8}$ of 100
   2875
   8
   5)23000
   46.00 Ans.

$62\frac{1}{2} = \frac{5}{8}$ or $\frac{10}{16}$: therefore, if the number is multiplied by 4 and the product by 4, and *three* places be pointed off, the same result will be obtained.

41. To divide by numbers greater or less than 10 or 100 by an aliquot part

RULE.—*Find what part of the given divisor the difference between it and 10 or 100 equals;* then

Increase the dividend by this aliquot part of itself, if the divisor is less, but diminish it if the divisor is more than 10 or 100, and point off as many decimals as there are ciphers in the number of tens taken.

EXAMPLES.

1. Divide 3165 by $7\frac{1}{2}$.

$10 - 7\frac{1}{2} = 2\frac{1}{2}$
$2\frac{1}{2} = \frac{1}{3}$ of $7\frac{1}{2}$

To 3165
Add $1055 = \frac{1}{3}$ of 3165

422.0 Ans. 422.

2. Divide 6345 by 15.

$15 = 10 + 5$
$5 = \frac{1}{3}$ of 15

From 6345
Subtract $2115 = \frac{1}{3}$ of 6345

423.0 Ans. 423.

3. Divide 18764 by $66\frac{2}{3}$.
4. " 2465 " 75.
5. " 42736 " $83\frac{1}{3}$.
6. " 37254 " $88\frac{8}{9}$.
7. Divide 18992 by $133\frac{1}{3}$.
8. " 7462 " $166\frac{2}{3}$.
9. " 4265 " $116\frac{2}{3}$.
10. " 3256 " $87\frac{1}{2}$.

42. To divide by any number but little less than 100, 1000, &c.

RULE.—*Cut off from the right of the dividend as many figures as the divisor contains.*

Multiply the figures on the left of the point by the difference between the divisor and 100, 1000, &c. Point off as many figures as there are in the divisor, and write the product under the dividend.

Multiply the part of this product on the left of the point, if any, by the same multiplier, cut off, and set down as before.

Continue so until the number of figures in the product do not exceed those in the divisor; then add the several results, and to the sum add the product of the number of units carried to the left of the point, if any, by the number used as a multiplier.

The part on the left of the point will be the quotient; that on the right, the remainder.

If the remainder exceeds the divisor, carry one to the quotient, and take the difference between the divisor and remainder for the true remainder.

EXAMPLES.

1. Divide 5532 by 98.

```
98)55|32
    1|10
     | 2
   ------
   56|44
```

$100 - 98 = 2$
$55 \times 2 = 110$
$1 \times 2 = 2$

$56\frac{44}{98}$ Ans.

2. Divide 485 by 95.

```
95)4|85
    |20
   —|——
   5|05
    | 5, the product of 1 (the number carried
   —|——      across the point) by 5.
   5|10
```

3. Divide 11201 by 98.
4. " 3267 " 97. Ans. $33\frac{66}{97}$.
5. Divide 4268 by 93.
6. " 4264 " 88.
7. " 2487 " 91.

CALCULATIONS USED IN PARTICULAR BRANCHES OF BUSINESS.

43. To find the value of tons and hundred-weight without the use of fractions.

RULE.—*Multiply the number of hundred-weight by 5, and annex the product to the tons, as so many hundredths of tons; then multiply by the given price per ton, and point off two decimals.*

EXAMPLES.

1. What is the cost of 18 tons, 17 cwt. coal @ $4 per ton?
   $17 \times 5 = 85$ $18.85 \times 4 = 75.40$. Ans. $75.40.
2. What is the cost of 35 tons, 15 cwt. hay at $12 per ton?
3. What is the cost of 48 tons, 17 cwt. coal, at $6.50 per ton?

44. To find the value of shillings and pence in the decimals of a pound sterling.

RULE.—*Multiply the shillings by 5, and call the product hundredths.*

Multiply the pence by $4\frac{1}{6}$, and call the product thousandths.

The sum of these two values will be the decimal required.

EXAMPLES.

1. Reduce 12*s.* 6*d.* to the decimal of a pound.

$$12 \times 5 = .60$$
$$6 \times 4\tfrac{1}{6} = .025$$
$$.625$$

2. Reduce £187 13*s.* 3*d.* to the decimal of a pound.

$$13 \times 5 = .65$$
$$3 \times 4\tfrac{1}{6} = .0125$$
$$.6625$$

Ans. £187.6625.

45. To change aunes to yards.

NOTE.—An aune is a French measure, equal to $1\frac{1}{4}$ yards.

RULE.—*Annex a cipher, and divide by 8.*

EXAMPLES.

1. In 484 aunes, how many yards?

$$4840 \div 8 = 605 \text{ Ans.}$$

2. In 3848 aunes, how many yards? In 1265? In 1847?

NOTE.—$1\frac{1}{4} = \frac{5}{4}$, or $\frac{10}{8}$. This rule can easily be applied to numerous other calculations. The contents of boards $1\frac{1}{4}$ inches thick, &c., may be computed in this manner; the selling price of goods in order to gain 25% on the cost; and others.

3. What is the selling price of goods, which cost 64 cents per yard, to gain 25%?

$$640 \div 8 = 80$$

$$64$$
$$16 = 25\% \text{ of } 64$$
$$80$$

46. To find how many gallons of linseed oil in a given number of pounds, at $7\frac{1}{2}$ lbs. per gallon.

RULE.—*Add one-third of the number of pounds to itself, and point off one decimal.*

EXAMPLES.

1. How many gallons in 675 lbs.?

$$675$$
$$225 = \tfrac{1}{3} \text{ of } 675$$
$$90.0$$

Ans. 90 gals.

2. In 1846 lbs. how many gallons? in 675, in 339 lbs.?

47. To find the number of piculs in a given number of pounds.

NOTE.—A picul is a Chinese weight of 133⅓ lbs.

RULE.—*Subtract one-quarter of the given number of pounds, and point off two decimals.*

EXAMPLES.

1. In 18992 lbs. tea, how many piculs?

$$\begin{array}{r} 18992 \\ 4748 = \frac{1}{4} \text{ of } 18992 \\ \hline 142.44 \end{array}$$

Ans. 142.44.

PERCENTAGE.

48. Percentage is a method of computing by means of a fraction whose denominator is 100.

The term *per cent.* is an abbreviation of the Latin *per centum*, which signifies *by the hundred.*

49. The **Rate** per cent. is the number of hundredths. Thus, 8 per cent. is eight-hundredths, and may be expressed $\frac{8}{100}$, or .08, or 8%.

Per cent. is simply the proportion of a hundred, and is not any of the denominations of Federal money: 10 per cent. is not 10 cents, nor 10 dollars, but $\frac{10}{100}$; 10 per cent. of \$50 = \$5; 10 per cent. of 85 bbls. = 8½ bbls.

Percentage is used in most commercial calculations, such as Interest, Commission, Insurance, Profit and Loss, &c.

50. CASE I.—To find the percentage of any number or quantity, the rate per cent. being given.

RULE.—*Multiply the given number by the rate per cent., and divide by 100* (i.e. *point off two decimals*).

EXAMPLES.

1. What is 8% of \$640?

$640 \times 8 = 5120.$ Ans. \$51.20

$8\% \text{ of } 640 = \frac{8}{100} \text{ of } 640 = \frac{5120}{100} = 51.20.$

The percentage on sterling money and denominate numbers is found after reducing the numbers to the lowest denomination given, or to the decimal of the highest, and then proceeding as in simple numbers.

2. What is 6 per cent. of £15 9*s*. 6*d*.?

By Art. 44. 9*s*. 6*d*. = £.475

$$
\begin{array}{r}
15.475 \times 6 = .92850 \\
20 \\
\hline
18.57000 \\
12 \\
\hline
6.84000
\end{array}
$$

Ans. 18*s*. $6\frac{84}{100}d$.

£15 9*s*. 6*d*. = 3714*d*. 3714 × 6 = 22284

222.84*d*. = 18*s*. $6\frac{84}{100}d$.

51. CASE II.—To find what rate per cent. one number is of another.

RULE.—*Annex two ciphers to the percentage, and divide by the number on which the percentage is reckoned.*

EXAMPLE.—What per cent. of 40 is 8?

800 ÷ 40 = 20. 8 = $\frac{8}{40}$ of 40; $\frac{8}{40}$ of 100 = 20.

52. CASE III.—To find a number when the value of a certain per cent. of it is known.

RULE.—*Annex two ciphers to the percentage, and divide by the rate per cent.*

EXAMPLE.—42 is 25% of what number?

4200 ÷ 25 = 168.

53. CASE IV.—To find what number is a certain per cent. *more* or *less* than a given number.

RULE.—When the given number is MORE than the required number, *annex two ciphers to the given number, and divide by 100* PLUS *the rate per cent.*

When the given number is LESS than the required number, *annex two ciphers to the given number, and divide by 100* LESS *the rate per cent.*

EXAMPLES.

1. What amount of gold, at a premium of 25 per cent., can I buy for $720 in currency?

$100 + 25 = 125$; $72000 \div 125 = 576$. Ans. $576.

2. Purchased merchandise and sold it for $1680, thereby losing 20 per cent. What did the merchandise cost?

$100 - 20 = 80$; $168000 \div 80 = 2100$. Ans. $2100.

INTEREST.

54. Interest is compensation for the use of money or value. The sum for the use of which interest is paid is called the Principal; the sum of the Principal and Interest is called the Amount.

55. Legal Interest is the rate established by law. Usury is interest greater than the legal rate, and is prohibited by law. In some States, however, parties are allowed to give and receive higher than legal rates by special contract. All interest in ancient times was called usury.

56. When no rate is mentioned, the legal rate is always understood. Debts of all kinds draw interest from the time they become due, but not before, unless specified. Interest on interest remaining unpaid is considered illegal.

57. The legal rate in most of the States, and on debts due the United States, is 6% per annum. In New York, Michigan, South Carolina, Wisconsin, Georgia, and Minnesota, it is 7%; in Alabama and Texas, 8%; Louisiana, 5%; California and Kansas, 10%; and in Oregon, 12½%.

58. The legal rate in England and France is 5%; in Canada, Nova Scotia, and Ireland, 6%.

59. In Pennsylvania, commission merchants and agents of parties not residing in the State are authorized to enter into an agreement to pay a rate not exceeding 7% on balances of money remaining in their hands, and to receive a rate not exceeding that amount, for advances of money made by them on consignments from persons living and transacting business beyond the limits of the State.

60. In Arkansas, Illinois, Iowa, Michigan, Mississippi, Missouri, and Tennessee, interest as high as 10% can be taken by special contract; in Louisiana and Florida, as high as 8%; in Minnesota, Texas, and Wisconsin, as high as 12%; in California, any per cent.

61. Most merchants settle their accounts semi-annually, or oftener, and the interest is calculated for days. The interest on Notes and Bonds which have some time to run, is generally calculated for months and days.

COMPUTING TIME.

62. To find the time between two dates, omit the day of the date and include the day of maturity.

For instance, if Tuesday is the tenth day of the month, to the next Tuesday, the seventeenth, is seven days; but if both Tuesdays are included, we have eight days, if both are omitted, only six days.

63. When months are mentioned, they are construed to mean calendar months, by which is meant the time from one day in one month to the same day in another month.

Notes or securities falling due on the 30th or 31st of any month which has only 28, 29, or 30 days in it, are considered to be nominally due on the last day of the month, and therefore legally due on the 3d of the following month. For instance, a note dated November 30th, payable 3 months after date, falls due on the last day of February, and three days of grace make it payable on March 3d. Less than a month is reckoned at the rate of 30 days to the month.

64. When it is required to find the difference between two dates in years, months, and days, it may be done as in Subtraction of Compound Numbers.

EXAMPLE.

What is the difference in time between July 15th, 1865, and September 19th, 1862?

The earlier date is placed under the later, and the numbers of the months are written instead of their names.

Yr.	mo.	da.
1865	7	15
1862	9	19
2	9	26

65. As the number of days in the different months varies, counting time by days is the only exact method, when the dates are less than a year apart.

From Jan. 1, 1867, to July 1, 1867, is 6 mos., containing 181 days.
" Sept. 1, " " Mar. 1, 1868, " 6 " " 182 "
" Apr. 1, " " Oct. 1, 1867, " 6 " " 183 "
" Mar. 1, " " Sept. 1, " " 6 " " 184 "

66. The number of days between two given dates may be found as in the following example :—

What is the number of days between January 5th and July 3d?

Add the number of days in January after the 5th to the days in the intervening months, and the three days in July.

In	Jan.	26 days.
"	Feb.	28 "
"	Mar.	31 "
"	Apr.	30 "
"	May	31 "
"	June	30 "
"	July	3 "
	Total,	179

67. Or, call each month 30 days, and correct by adding one for every month intervening which contains 31 days, and subtract two for February, except in leap-years; then but 1. In the example already given, from Jan. 5th to July 3d, there are five whole months, two of which contain 31 days, and one, February, contains but 28. They consequently average 30 days each, making 150, which, with 26 days in January and 3 days in July, make a total of 179.

Time Tables will be found useful for ascertaining the time between different dates.

68. It is sometimes desirable to know for what time to draw a note so that it will not fall due on a Sunday or a holiday. After finding the number of days, divide by 7 to obtain the number of weeks and days, then count the odd days from the day of the week on which the note is dated. In the example given, 179 days = 25 weeks and 4 days. If January 5th was on Monday, then July 3d will be four days from Monday, or on Thursday.

69. The following may be useful to those who have frequent occasion to draw notes:—

33 days = 4 weeks and 5 days, 63 days = 9 weeks, 93 days = 13 weeks and 2 days: therefore,

A note at *thirty* days will fall due *five* days later than the day of the week on which it was given.

A note at *sixty* days will fall due on the *same day* of the week.

A note at *ninety* days will fall due *two* days later.

70. It is customary among business men, in reckoning interest, to consider the year as consisting of 12 months of 30 days each, or 360 days. As there are 365 days in a year, this gives $\frac{5}{365}$, or $\frac{1}{73}$, too much. The difference is so small, however, that in ordinary transactions it is not noticed. The mercantile custom has in many cases been sanctioned by law. In New York, the law on this subject (Rev. Stat. vol. ii. p. 182) reads as follows:—

"For the purpose of calculating interest, a month shall be considered the twelfth part of a year, and as consisting of thirty days; and interest for any number of days less than a month shall be estimated by the proportion which such number of days shall bear to thirty."

INTEREST AT 6 PER CENT.

71. The interest on $1 for one year or

12 months	=	6 cents.
2 "	=	1 cent.
1 month or 30 days	=	½ cent, or 5 mills.
6 "	=	1 mill.

Therefore, *one-half* the number of months equals the interest on 1 dollar, in *cents;* and *one-sixth* the number of days equals the interest on 1 dollar, in *mills.*

72. To compute interest at 6 per cent.

If the time is in months or years.

RULE.—*Multiply the principal by one-half the number of months, and point off two decimals. If there are cents in the principal, point off four decimals; the remaining figures will be the interest, in dollars.*

If the time is in days.

RULE I.—*Multiply the principal by one-sixth the number of days, and in the product point off three decimals. If there are cents in the principal, point off five; the remaining figures will be the interest, in dollars.*

Or, to avoid multiplying by fractions:—

RULE II.—*Multiply the principal by the number of days, and divide the product by 6; then point off as in the preceding rule.*

73. When the time is less than 1 month, the cents in the principal may be disregarded; when less than 2 months, all under 50c.; when less than 3 months, all under 33c.

EXAMPLES.

1. What is the interest on $1875 for 7 months?
   $1875 \times 3\frac{1}{2} = 6562\frac{1}{2}$ Ans. $65.62½.
2. What is the interest on $4250 for 24 days?
   $4250 \times 4 = 17000$ Ans. $17.
3. What is the interest on $5650.37 for 27 days?
4. " " $7250.45 " 3 mos. 29 days?
5. " " $364.50 " 1 yr. 4 mos. 12 da.?
6. " " $1575.25 " 9 mos. 17 days?

The notes, accounts-current, interest accounts, in another part of the book, will afford additional examples for practice.

74. To compute interest at any given rate.

RULE I.—*Find the interest at six per cent., and divide it by 6; the quotient will be the interest at one per cent.; then multiply this interest by the given rate.* Or,

RULE II.—*Find the interest at six per cent., and add to it or subtract from it in the same ratio as the given rate is greater or less than 6.*

For 7% add $\frac{1}{6}$.
" 8% " $\frac{1}{3}$.
" 9% " $\frac{1}{2}$, or divide by 4 instead of 6.
" 10% take $\frac{10}{6}$ by annexing one cipher and dividing by 6.
" 12% multiply by 2, or divide by 3 instead of 6.

For 3% take $\frac{1}{2}$, or divide by 12 instead of 6.
" 4% subtr. $\frac{1}{3}$, or divide by 9 instead of 6.
" 4½% " $\frac{1}{4}$.
" 5% " $\frac{1}{6}$.
" 5½% " $\frac{1}{12}$.

EXAMPLES.

1. Find the interest on $1285. for 33 days at 7%.
2. " " $4825.60 " 90 " " 9%.
3. " " $2726.35 " 3 mos. 18 da. " 10%.

ACCURATE INTEREST.

75. To compute accurate interest.

RULE.—*Find the interest as in the preceding rules, and subtract from it $\frac{1}{73}$ part of itself; in leap-year subtract $\frac{1}{61}$.*

NOTE.—$\frac{1}{73}$ *equals a little less than 1½ cents for each dollar of interest.*

Or, Multiply the interest on the given sum for 1 year by the number of days for which interest is required, and divide by 365. The quotient will be the required interest. This rule is equivalent to the following formula:—

As 365 : {The number of days for which int. is required} :: {The int. on the given sum for 1 year} : {The required int.}

INTEREST ON GOVERNMENT BONDS.

76. By the ordinary method of computing interest at 6%, the interest on $6000 is $1 per day, and the principal will double itself in 200 months. The difference to the United States Government between paying interest at the rate of 360 days to the year, and paying accurate interest, or at the rate of 365 days to the year, is $5 per year for every $6000.

The *Five-Twenty* Loan is over $950,000,000, and the interest on it more than $155,000 per day. The difference, on this loan, between usual interest and accurate interest, is nearly $2250 per day. The formula under the preceding rule is employed in the Treasury Department at Washington.

EXAMPLES.

1. What is the interest on U. S. Bonds of $15000 from May 1st to July 17th, at 6% ?

From May 1st to July 17th = 77 days.
Int. on $15000 for 1 year = $900; 900 × 77 = 69300.
69300 ÷ 365 = $189.86 Ans.

2. What is the interest on a Five-Twenty U. S. Bond of $1000 from Nov. 1st to Feb. 3d?

3. What is the interest on a Ten-Forty U. S. Bond of $1000, bearing 5% interest, from March 1st to Aug. 10th?

INTEREST IN ENGLAND.

77. The legal rate of interest in England is 5 per cent., and parts of a year are counted in days at the rate of 365 days to the year. To compute English interest:—

RULE.—*Reduce the shillings and pence, if any, to the decimal or fraction of a pound (see Art. 44); then—*

FOR YEARS—*Multiply the principal by the number of years, and the product will be the interest, in shillings.*

FOR MONTHS—*Multiply the principal by the number of months, and the product will be the interest, in pence.*

FOR DAYS—*Multiply the principal by the number of days, divide the product by 73, and point off two decimals: the quotient will be the interest, in the denomination of the principal.*

EXAMPLE.—What is the interest on £425 for 1 year, 3 months, and 10 days, at 5% ?

425*s.*, interest for 1 year.
106.25 " " 3 months.
11.64 " " 10 days.
542.89*s.* = £27 2*s.* 11*d.* Ans.

PROBLEMS IN INTEREST.

78. To find the *principal*, when the time, rate per cent., and interest are given.

RULE.—*Divide the given interest by the interest on* ONE DOLLAR *for the given rate and time.*

EXAMPLES.

1. What sum invested at 6% for one year will produce $360?

Interest on $1, for 1 year, at 6% = .06.
.06)360.00 = 6000 Ans. $6000.

2. What principal in 2 years at 7% will give $3556?
3. " " 3 " 6 mos. at 6% will give $470?
4. " " 6 " 8 " " 8% " $540?
5. " " 3 " 4 " " 6% " $540?
6. What must I pay for real estate, producing $750 per year, that I may receive 6% on my investment?
7. What must I pay for stocks, paying a dividend of $345 yearly, that I may gain 9%?
8. What reduction must I obtain that I may purchase stocks of the par value of $8000, paying 6% dividend yearly, to receive 8% on what I invest?

79. To find the *rate* per cent., when the principal, time, and interest are given.

RULE.—*Divide the given interest by the interest on the principal at* ONE *per cent.*

EXAMPLES.

1. A house which cost $4800 rents, above expenses, for $264 per year. What per cent. does it pay on the investment?

Interest on 4800 at 1% = 48.
264 ÷ 48 = 5½ Ans. 5½%.

2. If I invest $3650 for 1 year, 2 months, and receive $480, what rate do I receive per year?

80. To find the *time*, when the principal, rate, and interest are given.

RULE.—*Divide the given interest by the interest on the principal for* ONE DAY; *the quotient will be the required time, in days.*

EXAMPLES.

1. In what time will $5530.42 produce $30.42 interest at 6% ?

Interest on $5530.42 for 1 day = .921+

```
.921)30.42(33+.
     2763
     ----
      2790
      2763          Ans. 33 days.
      ----
```

2. How long will it take a sum of money to double itself at 6% simple interest? At 7%? At 8%?

3. Invested $6000 at 6%, for which I received $750.42. How long was it invested?

81. To find the principal, when the time, rate per cent., and amount are given.

RULE.—*Divide the given amount by the amount of* ONE DOLLAR *for the given rate and time.*

EXAMPLES.

1. What principal will amount to $1120 in 2 years, at 6% ?

Amount of $1 for 2 years at 6% = $1.12.
1120 ÷ 1.12 = 1000 Ans. $1000.

2. What principal will amount to $1500 in 1 year, 3 mos., at 5% ? At 7%?

TRUE DISCOUNT.

82. Discount, as usually calculated, is the same as Simple Interest; but *true discount* is a deduction from an amount which is equal to the interest on the remainder at the same rate and for the same time for which the deduction was made.

83. The **Present Worth** is the sum paid, or the value of the note, or debt, after the discount has been deducted.

84. To find the Present Worth.

RULE.—*Divide the given sum by the amount of* ONE DOLLAR *for the given rate and time.*

To find the discount, subtract the present worth from the given sum.

EXAMPLES.

1. What is the present worth of $1360, due 6 years hence, @ 6%?

Int. on $1 for 6 yrs. = .36
1.00

Amount, 1.36)1360.00(1000

Ans. $1000.

2. What is the present worth of $1248, due 8 months hence, @ 6%? What is the true discount?

3. What is the present worth of $162.50, due 6 months hence, @ 7%, and what the discount?

BANKING.

85. Bank Discount is computed in the same manner as simple interest. It is deducted from the amount or face of the note when the note is discounted, and the remainder, called the proceeds, is placed to the credit of the person for whom the note is discounted. As the person offering the note can obtain the money immediately, and the note may remain unpaid until three o'clock on the day of its maturity, banks, generally, in reckoning time, include the day on which the note is discounted, as well as the day on which it matures. This, with the *three days of grace*, for which discount is also taken, makes *four* more days than the time mentioned in the note.

See, also, TRANSACTIONS WITH BANKS.

86. To compute Bank Discount.

RULE.—*Multiply the amount by* $\frac{1}{6}$ *the number of days, including the day of discount and the three days of grace, and in the product point off three decimals.*

The above will give the interest at 6%. For any other rate, add or subtract in proportion as the given rate is greater or less than 6%, as in Art. 74.

EXAMPLES.

1. Robert F. Hay, on May 2d, offered the following note, properly indorsed, for discount:—

$525. PHILADELPHIA, March 29, 1867.

Sixty days after date, I promise to pay to Robert F. Hay, or order, at the Union National Bank, Five Hundred and Twenty-Five Dollars, without defalcation. Value received. R. J. BIRNEY & Co.

How much will he receive as the net proceeds of the note?

60 days from March 29th is May 28th, which, with the three days of grace added, gives May 31st. From May 2d to May 31st, including the day of discount, is 30 days.

Interest on $525 for 30 days = 26.25 discount.
525 — 26.25 = 498.75 net proceeds.

Face of the note, $525.00

2. On Nov. 4th, offered for discount a note for $350, dated Oct. 15th, payable 3 months after date. How much cash will I receive?

Find the time, discount, and proceeds of the following notes:—

3. Discounted Nov. 4th, at 6%.

$750. PITTSBURGH, Oct. 15, 1866.

Three months after date, I promise to pay to the order of Jas. Dunlap & Co. Seven Hundred and Fifty Dollars, at the Citizens' National Bank, without defalcation. Value received. JOHN F. CHASE.

---

4. Discounted Jan. 12th, at 7%.

$1250.$\frac{75}{100}$. NEW YORK, Dec. 10, 1865.

Sixty days after date, I promise to pay to S. H. Crittenden & Co., or order, Twelve Hundred and Fifty $\frac{75}{100}$ Dollars, for value received. HENRY T. STEWART.

---

5. Discounted July 6th, at 6%.

$450.$\frac{50}{100}$. TRENTON, N.J., May 10, 1866.

Four months after date, I promise to pay at the First National Bank, to the order of Samuel T. Brown, Four

Hundred and Fifty $\frac{50}{100}$ Dollars, without defalcation or discount. Value received.

HAYWARD, GLEASON & CO.

---

6. Discounted Sept. 18th, at 6%.

$1875. CHICAGO, Aug. 15, 1866.

Ninety days after date, we promise to pay to the order of Charles Manning & Co. Eighteen Hundred and Seventy-Five Dollars, for value received.

H. EVANS & CO.

---

87. To find how large a draft, at a given premium, may be purchased for a certain amount.

RULE.—*Divide the given amount by $1, increased by the rate of premium.*

NOTE.—To find how large a draft may be purchased, when sold at a discount, divide the given amount by $1, less the rate of premium.

EXAMPLES.

1. How large a draft may be purchased for $2020, at a premium of 1%?

1.01)2020(2000. Ans. $2000.

2. What is the face of a draft on New York to cost $18500, at 1½% premium?

3. For what amount may a draft on Cuba be purchased with $6430.77, at a premium of 4½%?

4. A commission merchant wishes to invest the proceeds of a sale, amounting to $4840, in a draft on St. Louis, which can be purchased at a discount of ¾%. How large a draft can he obtain?

88. To find the amount of a note that shall produce a given sum when discounted at bank.

RULE.—*Divide the sum required by the proceeds of $1 for the given rate and time.*

EXAMPLES.

1. For what sum must a note be drawn so that the discount for 63 days at 6% may be deducted and the proceeds will be $1295?

Interest on $1 for 63 days = .0105.

$$\begin{array}{r} \$1.0000 \\ .0105 \\ \hline .9895)1295(1308.74 \text{ Ans.} \end{array}$$

2. Required the amount of a note that may be discounted for 33 days, at 6%, and $5500 received as the proceeds.

3. How large must a note be made to obtain $425.50 from a bank, for 42 days; discount @ 6%?

89. Banks, by deducting the interest in advance, obtain a larger rate per cent. than they would by taking true discount; and this rate increases in proportion to the time for which the discount is taken. The advantages of short credits, however, are generally considered to be more than an equivalent for any such excess that might be gained by extending the time.

The following table shows the rates of interest obtained by banks, including the advantage from compounding the interest, when they discount notes at 6 and at 7 per cent., for any number of months from one to twelve. It will be seen that when the time is less than two months—the usual limit for which notes are discounted in cities—the excess is inconsiderable.

RATE.	1 mo.	2 mos.	3 mos.	4 mos.	5 mos.	6 mos.	7 mos.	8 mos.	9 mos.	10 mos.	11 mos.	12 mos.
6 per cent.	6.200	6.216	6.232	6.248	6.264	6.281	6.298	6.315	6.332	6.349	6.366	6.383
7 " "	7.272	7.295	7.317	7.339	7.362	7.385	7.408	7.402	7.456	7.480	7.503	7.527

At the nominal rate of 6 per cent., a bank receives, when it discounts a note for 1 month, $\frac{5}{995}$, or $.5\frac{25}{995}$ of 1 per cent. ($\frac{25}{9950}$ of 1 per cent. more than 6 per cent. per annum = $\frac{1}{4}$ of ONE CENT on $99.50); when for 2 months, $\frac{1}{99}$, or $1\frac{1}{99}$ per cent.; when for 1 year, $\frac{6}{94}$, or $6\frac{18}{47}$ per cent.

INTEREST ACCOUNTS.

90. In the settlement of mercantile accounts, interest is calculated or not, according to custom or the agreement of the parties. Amounts are considered due at the time they should be paid in cash, or when they are equivalent to cash.

91. Bankers, Saving Funds, &c., charge and allow interest on dealers' accounts according to regulations which vary in different places. After the time is adjusted, interest is generally calculated by one of the following methods:—

FIRST METHOD.

By Interest on each amount to the time of settlement.

SECOND METHOD.

By Product of Days.

THIRD METHOD.

By Daily Balances.

92. By the FIRST METHOD, interest is reckoned on each amount from the day it is due to the day of settlement, and the balance between the debit and credit interest is added to that side of the account on which the amount of interest is the largest.

When an amount is not due until after the day of settlement, a discount is allowed, and entered on the opposite side of the account in the interest column.

The labor of making out such accounts is much lessened by the use of Interest Tables, such as Price's and others.

FIRST METHOD.—BY INTEREST ON EACH AMOUNT TO THE TIME OF SETTLEMENT.

JOHN C. BENNETT & Co. *in Account Current and Interest Account with* GEORGE D. PATTEN & Co. *to January 1, 1867.*

Date.	When due.		Amt.	Days.	Int.	Date.	When due.		Amt.	Days.	Int.
1866. July 31	1866. Oct. 31	To Mdse. at 3 mos., as per bill rendered, . . .	1200 00	62	12 40	1866. July 31	1866. Sept. 29	By Invoice of Coffee, at 60 days, shipped per Str. "Wm. P. Clyde," . .	1575 00	94	24 68
Aug. 5	Nov. 5	" Mdse. at 3 mos., as per bill rendered, . . .	1542 00	57	14 65	Oct. 15	Nov. 12	" Net Proceeds of sales of Sugar and Rice, as per Acc't Sales rendered, ...	1256 00	50	10 47
Sept. 10	Sept. 10	" Mdse. (Net), as per bill rendered, ...	750 00	113	14 13	" 23	" 25	" Draft on P. R. Brown & Co. at 30 days, . .	1000 00	37	6 17
Oct. 15	1867. Feb. 15	" Net Proceeds of sales of Flour, as per your Account Sales.	1830 00			Nov. 30	1867. Mar. 3	" Note of H. Y. King & Co. at 3 months, your favor, ...	500 00		
Nov. 20	1866. Nov. 20	" Cash paid your Draft on us at sight, favor J. Grant & Co., ...	640 00	42	4 48	1867. Jan. 1		" Discount on $1830, per contra, ...		45	13 73
1867. Jan. 1		" Discount on $500, per contra, ...		61	5 08						
		Credit Bal. of Interest,			*4 31*						
			5962 00		55 05				4331 00		55 05
								Add Bal. of Interest, .	4 31		
						July 1		*Bal. carried down,* . .	*1626 69*		
			5962 00		55 05				5962 00		55 05
1867. Jan. 1		To Balance due, ...	1626 69					E. E.			
		NEW YORK, Jan. 1, 1867.						GEO. D. PATTEN & Co.			

93. By the SECOND METHOD, each amount is multiplied by the number of days from the time it is due to the day of settlement. The interest on the sum of the products for *one day* equals the sum of the interest on each amount taken separately. The interest on the balance of products for one day equals the balance of interest.

When an amount is not due until after the day of settlement, it is multiplied by the number of days from the day of settlement to the day when it becomes due, and the product is placed in the column of products on the opposite side, in the same manner as discount is treated in the first method.

94. By the THIRD METHOD, the balance existing at any time is multiplied by the number of days it remains unchanged. The interest on the product for *one day* equals the interest on the balance for the number of days it continues; and the interest on the difference between the total daily balances for one day equals the balance of interest between the debit and credit sides of the account, calculated on each amount separately, as by the first method.

When the rate of interest on one side of the account is different from the rate on the other, the interest is calculated on the total daily products of each side separately for one day, and the balance of interest is taken. If the rate of interest on both sides of the account is the same, the difference between the footings of the debit and credit sides of the total daily balances may be taken first, and the interest reckoned on that for one day.

This method is used by many bankers. Besides saving much labor, the total daily balances may be entered without delaying for any particular day, and can therefore be kept in readiness, and the account completed with very little additional trouble, whenever the day of settlement is determined.

For practice, all the accounts given may be made out in each of the different methods, and may also be averaged by Compound Average with the same results as above.

SECOND METHOD.—BY PRODUCT OF DAYS.

MESSRS. L. & B. CURTIS *in Account Current and Interest Account with* MESSRS. FIELD & COGLEY *to July 1, 1867.*

Date.	When due.		Amt.	Days.		Date.	When due.		Amt.	Days.	
1867. Jan. 1	1867. Jan. 1	To Bal. due from old acc't	375 00	181	67875	1867. Feb. 5	1867. Feb. 5	By Cash, ...	300 00	146	43800
Feb. 10	May 10	" Mdse. @ 3 mos., as per bill rendered, . . .	450 00	52	23400	May 10	May 23	" Draft on Drexel & Co. at 10 days' sight, . .	500 00	39	19500
Mar. 25	" 24	" Mdse. @ 60 days, as per bill rendered, . . .	268 00	38	10184	June 2	July 5	" Note at 30 days, . . .	250 00		
May 24	Aug. 24	" Mdse. @ 3 mos., as per bill rendered, . . .	150 00			July 1		" Discount on $150, per contra, ...		54	8100
July 1		" Discount on $250, per contra, ...		4	1000						
			1243 00		102459				1050 00		71400
		Add Bal. of Interest,	5 18					*Balance of Products,*			*31059*
								31059÷6=5.176 Bal. of Int.			
								Balance of Account,	*198 18*		
			1248 18		102459				1248 18		102459
1867. July 1		To Balance due, ...	198 18								
								E. E.			
								FIELD & COGLEY.			
		PHILADA., July 1, 1867.									

THIRD METHOD.—BY DAILY BALANCES.

THE WESTERN SAVING FUND

In account with HENRY J. RODGERS.

Interest to Feb. 28th, 1867.

1867.					1867.				
Jan.	2	To Cash,	100	00	Jan.	7	By Check,	50	00
"	12	" "	250	00	"	22	" "	100	00
Feb.	11	" "	30	00	Feb.	1	" "	40	00
"	21	" "	200	00	"	21	" "	50	00
					"	28	" Int. to Feb. 28, '67,	1	62
					"	"	" Cash on settlement of acct.	338	38
			580	00				580	00

Balances.						Time.		
100,	from Jan. 2	to Jan. 7,	5	days	=	500	for 1	day.
50,	" " 7	" " 12,	5	"	=	250	"	"
300,	" " 12	" " 22,	10	"	=	3000	"	"
200,	" " 22	" Feb. 1,	10	"	=	2000	"	"
160,	" Feb. 1	" " 11,	10	"	=	1600	"	"
190,	" " 11	" " 21,	10	"	=	1900	"	"
340,	" " 21	" " 28,	7	"	=	2380	"	"
						11630		

Total daily balance = $11630 for 1 day.

Which, at 5% interest = $1.62.

3. What is the balance due on March 1st of the following account:—

THE NATIONAL SAVING INSTITUTION

In account with PORTER A. FLORENCE.

			Dr. Amts.		Cr. Amts.		Days.	Daily Balance.
1867.								
Jan.	2	To Cash	300	00				
"	17	By "			100	00		
"	27	To "	250	00				
"	"	By "			150	00		
Feb.	6	" "			350	00		
"	7	To "	250	00				

GEORGE M. GRANT *In acct. with* BROWNSON & Co., *to July 1st, 1867.*

Days.		Dr.		Cr.		Daily Balance.				Days.	Total Daily Balance.			
1867. Jan.	7			1000	00			1000	00	10			10000	00
"	17			250	00			1250	00	7			8750	00
"	24	1500	00			250	00			7	1750	00		
"	31			500	00			250	00	6			1500	00
Feb.	6	1000	00			750	00			10	7500	00		
"	16			850	00			100	00	24			2400	00
Mar.	12	1250	00			1150	00			30	34500	00		
Apr.	11			1000	00	150	00			65	19750	00		
June	15			3000	00			2850	00	16			45600	00
		3750	00	6600	00						53500	00	68250	00
Bal. Int. to July 1st,				2	46								53500	00
													6)14750	00
		3750	00	6602	46					Credit Bal. of Int.			2.458	33
Bal. of a/c,		*2852*	*46*											
		6602	46	6602	46									
Bal. of a/c,				$2852	46									

CINCINNATI, July 1st, 1866.

BROWNSON & Co.

PARTIAL PAYMENTS.

95. Partial Payments are payments made at different times of part of a Note, Bond, or other obligation, and should be indorsed upon the back of it.

96. When a partial payment is made *before the debt is due*, it cannot be apportioned part to the debt and part to the interest; but interest is allowed on the payment as well as on the principal to the time the debt becomes due.

97. Interest is not allowed to form part of the principal, so as to carry interest.

98. The following rule for computing interest when partial payments have been made has been adopted by the Supreme Court of the United States, and by New York, Massachusetts, and most of the other States of the Union, and is called

THE UNITED STATES RULE.

I. The rule for casting interest when partial payments have been made, is to apply the payment, in the first place, to the discharge of the interest due.

II. If the payment exceeds the interest, the surplus goes towards discharging the principal, and the subsequent interest is to be computed on the balance of principal remaining due.

III. If the payment be less than the interest, the surplus of interest must not be taken to augment the principal; but interest continues on the former principal until the period when the payments, taken together, exceed the interest due, and then the surplus is to be applied towards discharging the principal, and interest is to be computed on the balance as aforesaid.

Decision of Chancellor Kent, Johnson's Chancery Rep., vol. i. p. 17.

Or,

99. *Apply whatever payments may be made to the discharge of the interest then due, and the surplus, if any, to the discharge of the principal.*

NOTE.—The principal remains unaltered when the payment is less than the interest at the time due.

100. It will be perceived that, by the above rule, if a person owing the debt makes a payment less than the interest, he loses the use of it until the time when the sum of the payments exceeds the interest.

For instance, the interest on $1000 is $5 per month. If $5 per month is paid, at the end of the year $1000 would still be due, while the interest on the payments, $1.65, would be lost.

101. The Connecticut rule differs from the United States rule only in this respect, that if a payment greater than the interest at the time due be made before the principal has been on interest one year, the person making it is allowed interest on it to the end of the year. If settlement be made within one year, interest is allowed on the payments from the time they are made to the time of settlement.

EXAMPLES.

1. A bond was given for $1500, dated July 1st, 1863, payable 1 year after date, with interest. The following indorsements appear on the bond:—

July 1st, 1864, Received Fifty Dollars.
Jan. 1st, 1866, " One Thousand Dollars.

How much was due at the time of settlement, July 1st, 1866?

Original sum named in the bond,		$1500.00
Interest from July 1st, 1863, to July 1st, 1864,	$90.	
First payment, a sum less than interest,	50.	
	40.	
Interest from July 1st, 1864, to Jan. 1st, 1866,	135.	
	175.	
Second payment, a sum greater than interest,	1000.	825.00
Balance for new principal,		675.00
Interest from Jan. 1st, 1866, to July 1st, 1866,		20.25
Amount of principal and interest due July 1st, 1866,		$695.25

2. $3500. NEW YORK, Aug. 17, 1862.

For value received, I promise to pay to Henry L. Barnes, or order, on demand, Three Thousand Five Hundred Dollars, with interest. ROBT. H. WILSON.

Indorsements. March 17th, 1863, One Hundred Dollars. July 17th, 1863, Fifty Dollars. Nov. 17th, 1863, Three Hundred Dollars Feb. 17th, 1864, Fifteen Hundred Dollars.

How much remains due August 17th, 1864?

102. As it is customary among merchants to settle their accounts yearly, or oftener, the following rule is much used by them, and is called

THE MERCHANTS' RULE.

I. *First find the interest on the principal from the time it becomes due to the time of settlement, and add it to the principal.*

II. *Find the interest on each payment from the time it was made to the time of settlement, and add the sum of the interest thus found to the sum of the payments.*

III. *Deduct the sum of the payments and interest thereon from the amount of principal and interest, and the difference will be the balance due.*

NOTE.—This is substantially the same as the First Method for finding interest on Accounts Current. (See Art. 92.)

EXAMPLES.

1. $600. PHILADELPHIA, June 12, 1865.

For value received, on demand, I promise to pay to the order of Andrew W. Dawson, Six Hundred Dollars, with interest, without defalcation.

CHAS. C. RUNYON.

Indorsements.

August 12th, 1865, Received One Hundred Dollars.
November 12th, 1865, " Two Hundred and Fifty Dollars.
January 12th, 1866, " One Hundred and Twenty Dollars.

How much was due February 12th, 1866?

Principal,		$600.00
Int. from June 12th, 1865, to Feb. 12th, 1866, 8 mos.,		24.00
Amount of note to Feb. 12th, 1866, ...		624.00
First payment, Aug. 12th, 1865,	$100.00	
Interest 6 months,	3.00	
Second payment, Nov. 12th, 1865,	250.00	
Interest 3 months,	3.75	
Third payment, Jan. 12th, 1866,	120.00	
Interest 1 month,	.60	
Amount of payments and interest,	477.35	477.35
Balance due February 12th, 1866,		$146.65

2. $350. CLEVELAND, May 9, 1865.

Six months after date, I promise to pay to the order of James Brown & Co., Three Hundred and Fifty Dollars, value received. EDWARD S. LONG.

Indorsements.

July 12th, 1866, Received Seventy-Five Dollars.
Oct. 27th, 1866, " Two Hundred Dollars.

How much was due Jan. 3d. 1867?

TABLE

Showing in how many YEARS *a given principal will double itself.*

RATE.	AT SIMPLE INTEREST.	AT COMPOUND INTEREST.		
		Compounded Yearly.	Compounded Half-Yearly.	Compounded Quarterly.
1	100.	69.666	69.487	69.400
1½	66.66	46.556	46.382	46.298
2	50.00	35.004	34.830	34.743
2½	40.00	28.071	27.899	27.812
3	33.33	23.450	23.278	23.191
3½	28.57	20.150	19.977	19.890
4	25.00	17.673	17.502	17.415
4½	22.22	15.748	15.576	15.490
5	20.00	14.207	14.036	13.946
5½	18.18	12.946	12.775	12.686
6	16.67	11.896	11.725	11.639
6½	15.38	11.007	10.836	10.750
7	14.29	10.245	10.075	9.989
7½	13.33	9.585	9.914	9.328
8	12.50	9.006	8.837	8.751
8½	11.76	8.497	8.346	8.241
9	11.11	8.043	7.874	7.788
9½	10.52	7.638	7.468	7.383
10	10.00	7.273	7. +	7. +

AVERAGE OF PAYMENTS.

103. The average of several numbers is that number each would be if their sum was divided equally. Thus, the average number of yards in four pieces of cloth, one containing 24 yards, one 36 yards, one 38 yards, and one 42 yards, is 35 yards. The total number of yards equals 140, which, divided by the number of pieces, equals 35,—the average number of yards in each piece.

104. Average or Equation of Payments is the method of finding the time when the payment of several sums, due at different times, may be made at once, without loss of interest to either party.

105. Accounts are settled both by the methods given in Interest Accounts and by averaging. When several bills of goods are sold on credit, and become due on different dates, instead of settling each bill separately as it becomes due, it is customary to average the time, and settle the amount of all the bills at the averaged time. This saves the labor of computing interest on the several bills.

106. When all the amounts are alike, the average time is found by adding the different terms of credit together and dividing their sum by the *number* of the amounts. This, however, is seldom the case, and other rules have been found necessary.

107. To find the average time when all the terms of credit begin at the same time.

RULE.—*Multiply each amount by its term of credit, and divide the sum of the several products by the sum of the debts; the quotient will be the average time of credit.*

EXAMPLES.

1. A merchant purchases goods, January 6th, amounting to \$900: \$300 payable in 6 months, \$300 in 8 months, \$300 in 10 months. When may the whole be paid without loss to either party?

\$300	for 6	months	= 1800	for	1 month,		
300	" 8	"	= 2400	"	"		
300	"10	"	= 3000	"	"		
900			)7200	"	"		Ans. 8 months.

\$900 at the different terms of credit equals \$7200 for 1 month, or as many months as \$900 is contained times in \$7200, which is 8 times. Therefore, if the merchant gives his note payable 8 months after January 6th, it will be equivalent to giving three notes payable according to the terms of credit first proposed.

NOTE.—If the result contains a fraction less than a day, reject it; if it is more, add one to the number of days. Also, when the cents are less than 50, disregard them; when more, call them \$1.

108. The accuracy of the above rule has been questioned. The author of this book has in his possession fourteen different Arithmetics, some of them excellent ones, in which the rule is stated to be erroneous. The following example is generally used to illustrate its inaccuracy:—

"If a man owes me \$200, \$100 payable now and \$100 payable in 2 years, what is the equated time? Ans. 1 year."

It is said that this is incorrect, because I lose the interest on \$100 for 1 year, which is \$6; but for the other hundred I gain only the true discount, \$5.66+, making a difference of nearly 34 cents.

Or, for the first payment I should receive \$100 and interest for 1 year, which is \$106; and for the \$100 paid 1 year before it is due, I should receive the present worth of \$100, which is \$94.33$\frac{51}{53}$, making a total of \$200.33$\frac{51}{53}$, or 34 cents more than I receive by the usual method.

The fallacy is in supposing that \$5.66 is all that I gain for the \$6 which I lose; for if I receive the discount 1 year before it is due, it is clear that I gain the interest on it for 1 year; and the interest on true discount is always equal to the difference between true discount and interest. Interest on $5.66 for 1 year = 34 cents; $5.66 + .34 = $6.00.

Again, if I am not paid the $100 due now until 2 years have elapsed, I ought to receive as interest $12; if I receive $200 at the end of the first year, I gain the interest on $200 for 1 year, which is $12, the same as before. Interest on $200 for 1 year is the same as interest on $100 for 2 years.

109. The following has been given as the true rule for the Equation of Payments:—

"*Find the present worth of each debt, then find the time at which the sum of the present worths will amount to the sum of the debts; this gives the true time.*"

EXAMPLE CALCULATED BY THE "TRUE RULE."

Interest at 4 per cent.

Amount.	Time.	Present Worth.
1080	2 years	1000
6960	4 "	6000
8040		7000
7000		
1040 disc't.		

Interest on $7000 for 1 year, $280.

280) 1040 (3 yrs. 8 4/7 mos.

For $7000 to gain $1040 will require 3 yrs. 8 mos. 17 1/7 days.

SAME EXAMPLE.

Interest at 40 per cent.

Amount.	Time.	Present Worth.
1080.	2 years	600.
6960.	4 "	2676.92
8040.		3276.92
3276.92		
4763.08 disc't.		

Interest on $3276.92 for 1 year = 1310.77.

1310.77) 4763.08 (3 yrs. 7 mos. 18 days.

Difference in results, *29 days.*

As the rate of interest ought not to affect the result, the accuracy of this "true" rule is questionable. Even if it were correct, the amount of labor required to find the average time by this method is sufficient to prevent it from coming into general use.

The present worth is not in exact proportion to the time and amount due. The true discount of $500 for 1 year is not the same as the discount of $100 for 5 years.

MISCELLANEOUS EXAMPLES.

1. If A lends B $300 for 4 months, how long ought B to lend A $600, to equal the favor? Ans. 2 months.

2. If I owe $400, payable in 6 months, and pay $100 immediately, how long may I keep the balance as an equivalent? Ans. 8 months.

3. A man bought goods at different times to the amount of $10,000, which are due per average July 1st. He wishes to give 4 notes in payment, due 1 month apart. When ought they to mature, to equal the average?
Ans. May 15th, June 15th, July 15th, Aug. 15th.

110. To find the average time when the credits begin at different times.

Rule I.—*Find the date when each debt becomes due.* (See Time Tables.)

Find the time intervening between the earliest of these dates and the date of each succeeding amount.

Multiply the amount first due by 0.

Multiply each succeeding amount by the time intervening between the earliest date and the time the amount becomes due.

Divide the sum of the products by the sum of the debts; the quotient will be the average time required.

Add this average time to the day of maturity of the amount first falling due, for the day of payment.

Taking the time from the date of maturity of the amount first due, and the terms of credit as extending to the dates when actually due, makes the process similar to that of the preceding rule.

NOTE.—When a purchase is made for cash, it is due on the day of the purchase.

When the term of credit is the same for each amount, labor may be saved by averaging the dates of the purchase and adding the term of credit to the average date so found. When all the debts have the same term of credit except one or two amounts which have no credit, add interest to those amounts for the general term of credit, and then average as before. For finding the time, see INTEREST; also TIME TABLE.

EXAMPLES.

1. Required the time when the amount of the debts as below stated becomes due per average.

Date of Purchase.	Amount.	Time Credit.	When due.	Time from.
Jan. 6,	$300	6 mos.	July 6.	July 6 to Aug. 7,
Apr. 10,	200	6 "	Oct. 10.	32 days.
May 7,	400	3 "	Aug. 7.	July 6 to Oct. 10,
				96 days.

Statement arranged.

Due.	Amount.		Time (in days).	Product.
July 6,	300		0	00000
Aug. 7,	400	×	32	12800
Oct. 10,	200	×	96	19200
	900			)32000($35\frac{5}{9}$

Ans. 36 days from July 6th is August 11th.

111. ABBREVIATED METHOD.

The cents and dollars may be disregarded, in averaging, without any important change in the result.

EXAMPLE.

Due.	Amount.	Time.		Amount, omitting dolls. and cents.		Product.
Jan. 5,	$372.50	0	×	$37	=	000
" 15,	264.25	10	×	26	=	260
" 25,	227.50	20	×	23	=	460
" 30,	329.10	25	×	33	=	825
				119		)1545($12\frac{117}{119}$.

USUAL METHOD.

372.50 × 0	=	000000
264.25 × 10	=	264250
227.50 × 20	=	455000
329.10 × 25	=	822750
1193.35		)1542000(12$\frac{109980}{119335}$.

Ans. *Jan. 18th*, by both methods, the difference being only about $\frac{8}{119}$ of a day.

112. By Interest.—*Find the interest on each amount for the time obtained as before; then*

Find how long it will take for the whole debt to gain that amount of interest; the result will be the average time.

Note.—The equated time will be the same, whatever may be the rate of interest: we can, therefore, take that rate which is most convenient. Interest tables can also be profitably used.

EXAMPLE UNDER RULE I.

Due.	Amount.	Days.	Int. at 6%.
July 6,	300	0	000
Aug. 7,	400	32	2.133
Oct. 10,	200	96	3.200
	$900		$5.333

Interest on $900 for 1 day = .150.

For $900 to gain 5.333 requires ($5.333 ÷ 150) 35$\frac{83}{150}$ days.

36 days from July 6th = Aug. 11, Ans. as before.

2. Calculate the above at the rate of 12 per cent.

3. When shall a note to settle the following account be made payable?

Henry Field

To James L. Edwards *Dr.*

1867.				
Mar.	3	To Mdse @ 3 mos., as per bill rendered,	250	00
Apr.	4	" " 30 days, " " "	100	00
"	15	" " 60 " " " "	300	00
May	10	" " 3 mos. " " "	420	00
			1070	00

Due.	Amount.	Time.	Int. at 12 per cent.
May 4,	100	0	000
June 3,	250	30	2.500
June 14,	300	41	4.100
Aug. 10,	420	57	7.980

For $1070 at 12% to gain 14.580 will require 45 days; 45 days from May 4th is June 18th.

By taking $\frac{1}{3}$ of the number of days as a multiplier, interest at 12% for 1 day on $1070 = .356$\frac{2}{3}$.

113. ABBREVIATED METHOD, BY INTEREST.

Labor is saved by the use of the following rule in finding the time when due.

RULE.—*Count the time from the* FIRST *day of the first month given.*

Set opposite each month the number of months intervening between it and the first month.

This number added to the term of credit, with the day of the month opposite to which it is set, will give the time for which to calculate interest.

Then calculate interest for the months and days thus found, at 12 per cent., in the same manner as in the previous rule.

EXAMPLE.

Date of Sale.	Time of Credit.	Amount.
Jan. 6,	3 mos.	$300
Feb. 12,	4 "	400
Mar. 18,	3 "	250

STATEMENT.

Amount	No. of Months from 1st mo.	Total Time, mos. days.	Int. at 12 per cent.
$300	0	3 6	.600 = Int. 6 days. 9.000 = " 3 mos.
400	1	5 12	1.600 = " 12 days. 20.000 = " 5 mos.
250	2	5 18	1.500 = " 18 days. 12.500 = " 5 mos.
$950		Total Int.	45.200

Interest on amount of debt, \$950, for 1 mo. @ 12% = \$9.50.

```
9.50)4520(4 mos.
     3800
     ----
      720
        30 days in a month.
     ------
950)21600(22 70/95 days.
```

Average time, 4 mos. 23 days, which, counted from Jan. 1st, gives May 23d, Ans.

BY USUAL METHOD.

Amount.	When due.	Days.	Product.
\$300	Apr. 6	0	000
400	June 12	67	26800
250	" 18	73	18250
950			

```
950)45050(4 mos.
     3800
     ----
      705
       30
     -----
950)21150(22 25/95 days.
```

The abbreviated method is used to a considerable extent in New York, Philadelphia, and Boston, on account of the labor saved in counting time and in reckoning interest. Some have claimed that results may be obtained by this method with greater facility than by the use of Equation Tables.

In some instances, the result will not exactly agree with that obtained by the use of days for the time between the dates when due, from the fact that some months contain more days than others; but in ordinary cases the difference will be but a trifle, while the labor of averaging is very much diminished. The correct time may be obtained by adding to the total time one day for every month intervening between the first day and the day of maturity which contains 31 days.

2. Bought goods as follows:—

Jan. 8, 1867,	\$250 @ 3 mos. credit.	
Feb. 13, "	360 " 4 " "	
Mar. 6, "	125 " 60 days "	

What is the average date of payment?

AVERAGE OF ACCOUNTS,

OR COMPOUND EQUATION

114. In the settlement of accounts it is frequently desirable to know when the balance of an account may be paid, so that no interest need be calculated and yet have neither party suffer loss. For instance, a commission merchant sells, at a credit of 6 months, goods for a consignor amounting to $2000, the charges on which are $500, due at the time of sale. Instead of remitting $1500, the balance of account, as soon as the cash for the goods is received, the commission merchant retains it until the interest on $1500 is equal to the interest on $500 for 6 months; and as $1500 is three times as large as $500, he retains the balance ⅓ of 6 months, which is 2 months. This, added to the 6 months' credit, gives 8 months from the day of sale to the time when the balance of account should be paid.

115. To find the equated time for the settlement of an account when there are both debit and credit amounts.

RULE I.—1. *Find the time when due for each side of the account separately.*

2. *Multiply the* SMALLER *side of the account by the time between the two dates thus found, and divide the product by the balance of the account. The quotient will be the time to be counted from the date of the larger side.*

If the LARGER *side of the account falls due* LATEST, *count* FORWARD *from the* LATER *date.*

If the LARGER *side of the account falls due* EARLIEST, *count* BACK *from the* EARLIER *date.*

EXAMPLES.

1. When shall a draft for the settlement of the following account be made payable?

DR. **James B. Chauncey.** CR.

1866. July	16	To Cash,	600	00	1866. Aug.	15	By Mdse.,	1800	00

$600 \times 30 = 18000$ $18000 \div 1200 = 15$

15 days counted forward from the later date, on which the larger amount falls due, gives August 30th.

The interest on $600 for 30 days equals that on $18000 for 1 day: as many days are required, therefore, as 1200 is contained times in 18000, which are 15. Then, as Mr. Chauncey has retained $600 for 30 days, to get an equivalent, we retain the balance of account, $1200, after it has become due, for fifteen days, which brings us to August 30th.

2. Find the time when the balance of the following account becomes due:—

DR. **James B. Chauncey.** CR.

1866. Jan.	16	To Mdse.,	1800	00	1866. Feb.	15	By Cash,	600	00

From January 16th to February 15th = 30 days.

1800 — 600 = 1200, Bal. of account. Smaller side, $600 $\times$ 30 = 18000
18000 $\div$ 1200 = 15

15 days counted back from January 16th, the earlier date, gives January 1st.

In the above account, as the larger sum is due first, it is evident the balance, $1200, should be paid long enough before January 16th to produce interest equal to the interest on $600 for the time between January 16th and February 15th, viz., 15 days before January 16th; or, $30 + 15 = 45$ days before February 15th. When the balance becomes due in time past, interest is added to obtain the amount to be paid at the time of settlement.

3. The following account appears on my Ledger:—

DR. **Samuel T. Hanson.** CR.

1859. Jan.	11	To Mdse. at 6 months,	171	24	1859. Jan.	11	By Cash,	100	00

When should the balance be paid, or draw interest?

From January 11th to July 14th, counting 3 days of grace, the time when the debit amount is due, is 184 days.

$100 \times 184 = 18400 \qquad 171.24 - 100 = 71.24$, Bal. of account.

$18400 \div 71.24 = 258+$

Then 258 days counted forward from July 14th, the later date, is March 29th. Ans. March 29, 1860.

4. Find the average of the following account:—

Dr. Charles D. Carlton. **Cr.**

1867.					1867.				
Mar.	31	To Charges,	31	31	Mar.	3	By Mdse. @ 8 mos.,	323	00
					"	4	" " " 6 "	263	00
					"	24	" " " 6 "	241	00

Credits due October 3d.

Ans. Oct. 10/13.

116. Rule II.—*Multiply each sum by the number of days intervening between the date of its maturity and the earliest day on which any sum on either side of the account becomes due.*

Then divide the difference between the sum of the products on the debit and the sum of the products on the credit side, by the balance of the account.

The quotient will be the time to be counted FORWARD *from the date on which the first amount becomes due, when the balance of the account and the difference of the sums of the products are* BOTH ON THE SAME SIDE *of the account, but* BACKWARD *from the same date if they are on* OPPOSITE SIDES *of the account.*

EXAMPLE I.

BY PRODUCTS.

Due.	Amt.	Days.	Product.	Due.	Amt.	Days.	Product.
May 22,	300	0		May 27,	200	5	1000
June 1,	150	10	1500	June 6,	100	15	1500
July 11,	200	50	10000	July 10,	120	40	4800
	650		11500		420		7300
	420		7300				
	230		) 4200($18\frac{6}{23}$				

18 days counted forward from May 22d gives June 9th.—Ans.

The discount on the debit side of the account equals the interest of $650 for the time which is equivalent to $11500 for 1 day, and, starting at the same date, the discount on the credit side will equal the interest on $420 for the time equivalent to $7300 for 1 day. The balance of the account can remain unpaid as long after May 22d as the time required for it to equal $4200 for 1 day, which is 18 days.

EXAMPLE II.

BY INTEREST.

Due.	Am't.	Days.	Int. 12 per cent.	Due.	Am't.	Days.	Int. 12 per cent.
May 15,	2500	0		May 21,	400	6	.800
" 24,	1300	9	3.900	" 30,	1200	15	6.000
June 14,	400	21	2.800	June 2,	800	18	4.800
	4200		6.700		2400		11.600
	2400						6.700
	1800						4.900

For $1800 to gain $4.90 will require $8\frac{1}{6}$ days.
Eight days counted backwards from May 15th is May 7th.

If the above account were settled May 15th, $11.60 should be charged as interest, and $6.70 allowed as discount. Instead of adding $4.90 to the balance of the account, time is counted back to a date from which the interest on the balance of the account will equal the balance of interest.

EXAMPLE III.

BY ABBREVIATED INTEREST METHOD.

CREDIT SIDE OF THE ACCOUNT.

Date. 1866.	Time of Credit.	Am't.	No. mos. from earliest mo.	Total Time. mos. days.	Int. at 12 per cent.
July 12,	3 mos.	$100	1	4 12	$4.000 int. 4 mos. 400 " 12 ds.
Aug. 15,	Cash	250	2	2 15	5.000 " 2 mos. 1.250 " 15 ds.
Oct. 10,	3 mos.	350	4	7 10	24.500 " 7 mos. 1.050 " 9 ds. .117 " 1 day.
		$700			

Total credit interest, $36.317

DEBIT SIDE OF THE ACCOUNT.

Date.	Time of Credit.	Am't.	No. mos. from earliest mo.	Total Time. mos.	days.	Int. at 12 per cent.
1866. June 15,	3 mos.	$200	0	3	15	6.000 int. 3 mos. 1.000 " 15 ds.
Aug. 9,	3 "	400	2	5	9	20.000 " 5 mos. 1.200 " 9 ds.
Sept. 18,	1 "	300	3	4	18	12.000 " 4 mos. 1.800 " 18 ds.
		900	Total debit int.			42.000
		700	" credit "			36.317
Bal. of account,		$200	Bal. of interest,			$5.683

Interest on $200 for 1 month = $2.

5.683 ÷ 2 = 2 months 25 days.

2 months 25 days forward from June 15th is Aug. 25th, Ans.

For additional practice, average the examples already given by each of the different methods.

Average the following Account Sales:—

Account Sales of Merchandise for joint account of NEWHALL, HART & Co., H. FOSTER & Co., *and Ourselves.*

1866. April	9	Sold Leonard Barker & Co., @ 6 mos.:—		
		Ⓐ 15 hhds. Cuba Sugar, 25,422 lbs., @ 16c.	$4067	52
		Ⓐ 32 half-chests Oolong Tea, 1805 lbs., tare 480 = 1325, @ 1.10	1457	50
			$5525	02
		—— CHARGES. ——		
		Fire Ins. on $6000 @ 1½%, $90.00		
		Cooperage, Weighing, Labor, &c., 17.37		
		Com. and Guar. on $5525 @ 5%, 276.25	383	62
		Net proceeds due per average,	$5141	40

PAUL & THOMPSON.

E. E. NEW YORK, April 9th, 1866.

NOTE 1.—Take the sales as the credit side, and the charges as the debit side.

2. Accounts Sales are averaged to know when the proceeds may be paid without charging interest to either party.

Average the following accounts:—

DR. Parker Burton. CR.

1866.					1866.				
May	22	To Mdse. at 3 mos.,	500	00	May	25	By Cash,	300	00
"	29	" " " "	250	00	June	9	" Sundries,	400	00
June	10	" " " 30 days,	150	00	July	2	" Cash,	100	00

Ans. Balance $100, due per average,

DR. R. P. Lossing & Co. CR.

1866.					1866.				
Mar.	10	To Mdse. (net)	250	75	Mar.	20	By Cash,	250	75
"	15	" " @ 3 mos.,	187	50	"	2	" Draft @ 30 days,	120	00
Apr.	14	" " 4 "	262	25	Apr.	26	" Cash,	150	00
May	24	" " 3 "	465	60	May	24	" Sundries,	50	00

The following table will be found useful when averaging accounts.

To find the time between two dates:—Look on the left for the month containing the earlier date, and on the same line, to the right, for the month containing the later date: the number of days under the name of the month, or the number of months at the top of the column, will give the required time, if both dates are on the same day of the month. If the day of the month of the later date is different from that of the earlier date, add or subtract, as the case may be.

To find the day which is a given number of days after a certain date:—Find the number of days in the table, opposite the month, containing the given date which is next larger than the given number of days; subtract the given number of days, and count back from the same day of the month above the number taken, as the day of the month of the given date.

For example, to find the day which is 144 days after June 28th, look opposite June for the number next greater than 144, which is 153 in Nov. 144 from 153 = 9; and 9 days back from Nov. 28th brings us to Nov. 19th, the required date.

TIME TABLE.

Showing the time, in months and in days, from any day in one month to the same day in any other month, and also what month is a given number of days from another month.

No. days.	No. of mo.	From	1 mo.	2 mos.	3 mos.	4 mos.	5 mos.	6 mos.	7 mos.	8 mos.	9 mos.	10 mos.	11 mos.	12 mos.
31	1	January to	Feb. 31 days.	March, 59 days.	April, 90 days.	May, 120 ds.	June, 151 ds.	July, 181 ds.	August, 212 ds.	Sept., 243 ds.	Oct., 273 ds.	Nov., 304 ds.	Dec., 334 ds.	Jan., 365 ds.
28	2	February "	March, 28 days.	April, 59 days.	May, 89 days.	June, 120 ds.	July, 150 ds.	August, 181 ds.	Sept., 212 ds.	Oct., 242 ds.	Nov., 273 ds.	Dec., 303 ds.	Jan., 334 ds.	Feb., 365 ds.
31	3	March "	April, 31 days.	May, 61 days.	June, 92 days.	July, 122 ds.	August, 153 ds.	Sept. 184 ds.	Oct., 214 ds.	Nov., 245 ds.	Dec., 275 ds.	Jan., 306 ds.	Feb., 337 ds.	March, 365 ds.
30	4	April "	May, 30 days.	June, 61 days.	July, 91 days.	August, 122 ds.	Sept., 153 ds.	Oct., 183 ds.	Nov., 214 ds.	Dec., 244 ds.	Jan., 275 ds.	Feb., 306 ds.	March, 334 ds.	April, 365 ds.
31	5	May "	June, 31 days.	July, 61 days.	August, 92 days.	Sept., 123 ds.	Oct., 153 ds.	Nov., 184 ds.	Dec., 214 ds.	Jan., 245 ds.	Feb., 276 ds.	March, 304 ds.	April, 335 ds.	May, 365 ds.
30	6	June "	July, 30 days.	August, 61 days.	Sept., 92 days.	Oct., 122 ds.	Nov., 153 ds.	Dec., 183 ds.	Jan., 214 ds.	Feb., 245 ds.	March, 273 ds.	April, 304 ds.	May, 334 ds.	June, 365 ds.
31	7	July "	August, 31 days.	Sept., 62 days.	Oct., 92 days.	Nov., 123 ds.	Dec., 153 ds.	Jan., 184 ds.	Feb., 215 ds.	March, 243 ds.	April, 274 ds.	May, 304 ds.	June, 335 ds.	July, 365 ds.
31	8	August "	Sept., 31 days.	Oct., 61 days.	Nov., 92 days.	Dec., 122 ds.	Jan., 153 ds.	Feb., 184 ds.	March, 212 ds.	April, 243 ds.	May, 273 ds.	June, 304 ds.	July, 334 ds.	August, 365 ds.
30	9	Septemb'r "	Oct., 30 days.	Nov., 61 days.	Dec., 91 days.	Jan., 122 ds.	Feb., 153 ds.	March, 181 ds.	April, 212 ds.	May, 242 ds.	June, 273 ds.	July, 303 ds.	August, 334 ds.	Sept., 365 ds.
31	10	October "	Nov., 31 days.	Dec., 61 days.	Jan., 92 days.	Feb., 123 ds.	March, 151 ds.	April, 182 ds.	May, 212 ds.	June, 243 ds.	July, 273 ds.	August, 304 ds.	Sept., 335 ds.	Oct., 365 ds.
30	11	November "	Dec., 30 days.	Jan., 61 days.	Feb., 92 days.	March, 120 ds.	April, 151 ds.	May, 181 ds.	June, 212 ds.	July, 242 ds.	August, 273 ds.	Sept., 304 ds.	Oct., 334 ds.	Nov., 365 ds.
31	12	December "	Jan., 31 days.	Feb., 62 days.	March, 90 days.	April, 121 ds.	May, 151 ds.	June, 182 ds.	July, 212 ds.	August, 243 ds.	Sept., 274 ds.	Oct., 304 ds.	Nov., 335 ds.	Dec., 365 ds.

MONEY, WEIGHTS, AND MEASURES.

MONEY.

117. **Money** is value, or its representative, used as a medium of exchange and as a standard of measure.

118. The word money is derived from the Latin *monetas*, which some derive from *monere*, to "admonish," to "inform,"—the stamp on a coin informing the holder of its value. The Latin word *pecunia*, "money," is supposed to be derived from *pecus*, "a sheep," because in early times sheep, or stamped skins, were used in place of money.

119. In different countries, and in different conditions of society, various articles have been made to serve as money. Homer tells us the armor of Diomede cost nine oxen, while that of Glaucus cost one hundred; and the oldest Greek coins were stamped with an ox,—intimating the previous employment of cattle as money. The laws of the ancient Germans imposed penalties for offences, to be paid in cattle; while slaves and cattle—or "living money," as it was then called—were in common use among the Anglo-Saxons. The Carthaginians and Spartans employed for this purpose skins and pieces of leather marked with a stamp. In Hindostan, small shells called *cowries* are used in the smaller payments; they also circulate widely in Africa. In Abyssinia, rock-salt, in Iceland, dried fish, and among the North American Indians, the *belt of wampum*, is used as money. In 1776, according to Adam Smith, the workmen of a certain Scottish village carried nails as money to the baker's and to the ale-house.

120. Various metals have been used: the Spartans adopted iron; the ancient Romans, copper; the Russians, at one time, platinum; but gold and silver have been preferred by modern nations, as best adapted for the purposes of money, for the following reasons:—

I. Their value is comparatively uniform, and less subject to variations, and they may be kept or used without much deterioration.

II. Their nature is such that they can easily be identified.

III. They are capable of division or combination without loss of value.

IV. They possess great value in small compass, and are capable of being easily transported from place to place.

Gold and silver, in their purity, are soft, easily bent or injured, and exposed to rapid wear: they are therefore moderately hardened by the admixture of an alloy. For gold coin both copper and silver are employed as an alloy; and the color of the coin inclines to yellow or red, as the silver or copper may predominate.

121. Money is either *real* or *imaginary*. Real money includes all coins,—such as dollars, sovereigns, and the like; imaginary, or nominal money, is that which does not exist in specie,—such as mills, pounds, &c.

122. The Moneys of Account are those in which accounts are kept, and include imaginary as well as real money; but the relations of the denominations are not susceptible to fluctuations, like currency.

123. *Paper money* is a substitute for metallic currency.

124. Aside from the amount in actual existence, *the rapidity and value of exchanges* affect the abundance or scarcity of money. Any thing which dispenses with its use diminishes the amount of circulating medium necessary for a community, and in effect is the same as adding so much to the currency. The accounts of merchants, notes, bills of exchange, and credits generally, are of this nature.

125. When two kinds of money are in circulation, the one of least value will displace the other.

126. The term **Bullion** is applied to uncoined gold or silver, and includes gold dust, amalgamations, and ingots, or bars.

127. **Coin,** or **Specie,** is metal of known weight and fineness, stamped for the purpose of being used as money.

128. The smallest coin is believed to be the Turkish *para*, weighing from 1½ to 2½ grains, containing a small portion of silver, and its value is one-thirtieth of our cent. The smallest copper coin of Europe is the *centime* of Genoa, weighing fourteen grains, and worth one-twelfth of our cent. The ten-copeck piece of Russia is equal in weight to 4⅛ copper cents; a copper piece of 1795 weighs 890 grains; about as heavy as 5⅓ copper cents.

129. **Currency** is money in common circulation, whether coin or paper.

130. **Billon** (from the French, signifying base coin) is the name of a mixture having a small proportion of silver combined with some base metal.

131. **Tokens** are coins whose intrinsic value is below that assigned to them by law, and are not a legal tender above certain small amounts. Coins in *billon*—the nickel cent, and the one, two, three, and five cent pieces of 1866—are tokens. (See VALUE OF U. S. COINS.)

RELATIVE VALUES OF GOLD AND SILVER.

132. In the United States, as 15.988 to 1.
" England, " 14.287 " 1.
" France, " 15.50 " 1.
" Spain, " 16.00 " 1.
" China, " 14.25 " 1.

133. In America and Great Britain, gold is the standard of value. Silver is the standard of value in France, Belgium, Holland, Austria, and the Zollverein States, Russia, and the East Indies. Payments made in China are either in silver dollars or silver ingots.

134. In Great Britain,

A pound of standard gold $\frac{11}{12}$ fine is coined into £46 14*s.* 6*d.* = £3 17*s.* 10½*d.* per ounce, which is the mint price for standard gold, and is equivalent to $18.94 per ounce.

A pound of silver ($\frac{37}{40}$ fine) is coined into 66 shillings = 5*s.* 6*d.* per ounce. The mint price is 5*s.* per ounce, $\frac{37}{40}$ fine.

A pound of copper is coined into 24 pence.

A pound of bronze of 1860, 95 parts of copper, 4 of tin, and 1 of zinc, is coined into 48 penny pieces, or 80 half-pennies, or 160 farthings.

135. In France,

A kilogramme of gold is coined into 155 napoleons, or 3100 francs.

A kilogramme of silver is coined into 200 francs.

136. The standard of the various moneys in the north of Europe and Germany is the Cologne mark weight, Hamburg standard of fine silver; that is, 3608 grains Troy.

In Sweden, Norway, Denmark, and Mecklenburg, it is coined, when alloyed with copper, into 9¼ silver-species, dalers or thalers.

In Russia, into 13 silver roubles.

In Prussia and Hanover, into 14 thalers.

In the Southern States of the Zollverein, into 24½ gulden.

In Austria, into 20 gulden.

In Hamburg and Lubeck, into 35 marks current.

The acts of Congress of 1834 and 1843, fixing the value of certain foreign coins, and declaring the same as legal tender, were repealed by act of February 21, 1853.

It will be seen in the following table that the half-dollar, and smaller silver coins issued since 1853 are worth less, in proportion, than the silver coins issued before that time.

The smaller coins are designed chiefly for the purpose of making change, and are not a legal tender above certain small sums. (See Legal Tender.)

TABLE

Showing the weight and fineness of the Coins of the United States, as given by acts of Congress.

GOLD.

$\frac{11}{12}$ or .913$\frac{2}{3}$ FINE.	Standard Weight.	Pure Gold.	Coml. Val.
Eagle, coined before 1834	270 grains	247.5 grains	$10.62
$\frac{1}{2}$ " " " "	135 "	123.75 "	5.31
$\frac{1}{4}$ " " " "	67.5 "	61.87 "	2.65
.900 FINE.			
Eagle coined since 1834	258. "	232.2 "	10.00
$\frac{1}{2}$ " " " "	129. "	116.1 "	5.00
$\frac{1}{4}$ " " " "	64.5 "	58.05 "	2.50
1 Dollar piece,	25.8 "	23.22 "	1.00
1 Double Eagle,	516. "	464.4 "	20.00
3 Dollar piece,	7.74 grains	69.66 "	3.00

SILVER.

	Standard Weight.	Pure Silver.	Coml. Val.
Dollar before 1837, and shares in proportion, 892.4 fine,	416. grs.	371.25 grs.	$1.05
Dollar since 1837, 900 fine,	412.5 "	371.25 "	1.05
$\frac{1}{2}$ " '37 to June, '53, " "	206.25 grs.	185.625 grs.	.52$\frac{1}{2}$
$\frac{1}{4}$ " " " " "	103.125 "	92.8125 "	.26
Dime " " " "	41.25 "	37.125 "	.10$\frac{1}{2}$
$\frac{1}{2}$ " " " " "	20.625 "	18.5625 "	.05
3 Cent piece, March, 1851, to March, 1853, $\frac{3}{4}$ fine,	12.375 "	10.8 "	.03
$\frac{1}{2}$ Dollar since June, 1853,	192. "	172.8 "	.50

(And smaller coins in proportion.)

Old Cent, 178 grains copper.

Cent of 1866, 48 grs. 95% copper, 3% zinc, and 2% tin.
2 " piece " 96 " 95 " 5% nickel.
3 " " " 32 " 75 " 25% "
5 " " " 5 grams, or 77$\frac{16}{100}$ grs., 75% copper, 25% nickel.

A STATEMENT OF FOREIGN GOLD AND SILVER COINS.

(PREPARED BY THE DIRECTOR OF THE UNITED STATES MINT.)

EXPLANATORY REMARKS.—The first column of the Tables of Foreign Coins embraces the names of the countries where the coins are issued; the second contains the names of the coin, only the principal denominations being given. The other sizes are proportional; and, when this is not the case, the deviation is stated.

The third column expresses the weight of a single piece in fractions of the troy ounce, carried to the thousandth, and, in a few cases, to the ten-thousandth, of an ounce. The method is preferable to expressing the weight in grains for commercial purposes, and corresponds better with the terms of the mint. It may be readily transferred to weight in grains by the following rule:—*Remove the decimal point; from one-half deduct four per cent. of that half, and the remainder will be grains.*

The fourth column expresses the fineness in thousands, *i.e.* the number of parts of pure gold or silver in 1000 parts of the coin.

The fifth and sixth columns of the first table express the valuation of gold. In the fifth is shown the value as compared with the legal content, or amount of fine gold in our coin. In the sixth is shown the value as paid at the mint after the uniform deduction of one-half of one per cent. The former is the value for any other purposes than recoinage, and especially for the purpose of comparison; the latter is the value in exchange for our coins at the mint.

For the silver there is no fixed legal valuation, the law providing for changing the price according to the condition of demand and supply. The present price of standard silver is 122½ cents per ounce, at which rate the values in the fifth column of the second table are calculated. In a few cases, where the coins could not be procured, the data are *assumed* from the legal rates, and so stated.

The silver purchased for coinage will be paid for in silver coins of the United States, of less denomination than the dollar; fine silver, 136⅛ cents per ounce; American plate, usual manufacture, 120 to 122 cents per ounce; genuine British plate, 125.8 cents per ounce.

FOREIGN GOLD COINS.

COUNTRY.	DENOMINATION.	Weight.	Fineness.	Value.	Value after Deduction of ½ per ct.
		Oz. Dec.	Thous.		Price paid at Mint.
Australia	Pound of 1852	0.281	916.5	$5.32.37	$5.29.71
"	Sovereign of 1855–60	0.256.5	916	4.85.58	4.83.16
Austria	Ducat	0.112	986	2.28.28	2.27.04
"	Souverain	0.363	900	6.75.35	6.71.98
"	New Union crown (assumed)	0.357	900	6.64.19	6.60.87
Belgium	Twenty-five francs	0.254	899	4.72.03	4.69.67
Bolivia	Doubloon	0.867	870	15.59.25	15.51.46
Brazil	Twenty milreis	0.575	917.5	10.90.57	10.85.12
Central America	Two escudos	0.209	853.5	3.68.75	3.66.91
Chili	Old doubloon	0.867	870	15.59.26	15.51.47
"	Ten pesos	0.492	900	9.15.35	9.10.78
Denmark	Ten thaler	0.427	895	7.90.01	7.86.06
Ecuador	Four escudos	0.433	844	7.55.46	7.51.69
England	Pound or sovereign, new	0.256.7	916.5	4.86.34	4.83.91
"	Pound or sovereign, average	0.256.2	916	4.84.92	4.82.50
France	Twenty francs, new	0.207.5	899.5	3.85.83	3.83.91
"	Twenty francs, average	0.207	899	3.84.69	3.82.77
Germany, North	Ten thaler	0.427	895	7.90.01	7.86.06
" "	Ten thaler, Prussian	0.427	903	7.97.07	7.93.09
" "	Krone (crown)	0.357	900	6.64.20	6.60.83
Germany, South	Ducat	0.112	986	2.28.28	2.27.14
Greece	Twenty drachms	0.185	900	3.44.19	3.42.47
Hindostan	Mohur	0.374	916	7.08.18	7.04.64
Italy	Twenty lire	0.207	898	3.84.26	3.82.34
Japan	Old cobang	0.362	568	4.44.0	4.41.8
"	New cobang	0.289	572	3.57.6	3.55.8
Mexico	Doubloon, average	0.867.5	866	15.52.98	15.45.22
"	Doubloon, new	0.867.5	870.5	15.61.05	15.53.25
Naples	Six ducati, new	0.245	996	5.04.43	5.01.91
Netherlands	Ten guilders	0.215	899	3.99.56	3.97.57
New Granada	Old doubloon, Bogota	0.868	870	15.61.06	15.53.26
" "	Old doubloon, Popayan	0.867	858	15.37.75	15.30.07
" "	Ten pesos, new	0.525	891.5	9.67.51	9.62.68
Peru	Old doubloon	0.867	868	15.55.67	15.47.90
"	Twenty soles	1.035	898	19.21.8	19.12.2
Portugal	Gold crown	0.308	912	5.80.66	5.77.76
Prussia	New Union crown (assumed)	0.357	900	6.64.19	6.60.87
Rome	Two-and-a-half scudi, new	0.140	900	2.60.47	2.59.17
Russia	Five roubles	0.210	916	3.97.64	3.95.66
Spain	One hundred reals	0.268	896	4.96.39	4.93.91
"	Eighty reals	0.215	869.5	3.86.44	3.84.51
Sweden	Ducat	0.111	975	2.23.72	2.22.61
Tunis	Twenty-five piastres	0.161	900	2.99.54	2.98.05
Turkey	One hundred piastres	0.231	915	4.36.93	4.34.75
Tuscany	Sequin	0.112	999	2.31.29	2.30.14

FOREIGN SILVER COINS.

COUNTRY.	DENOMINATION.	Weight.	Fineness.	Value.
		Oz. Dec.	Thous.	
Austria	Old rix dollar	0.902	833	$1.02.27
"	Old scudo	0.836	902	1.02.64
"	Florin before 1858	0.451	833	51.14
"	New florin	0.397	900	48.63
"	New Union dollar	0.596	900	73.01
"	Maria Theresa dollar, 1780	0.895	838	1.02.12
Belgium	Five francs	0.803	897	98.04
Bolivia	New dollar	0.643	903.5	79.07
"	Half dollar	0.432	667	39.22
Brazil	Double milreis	0.820	918.5	1.02.53
Canada	Twenty cents	0.150	925	18.87
Central America	Dollar	0.866	850	1.00.19
Chili	Old dollar	0.864	908	1.06.79
"	New dollar	0.801	900.5	98.17
Denmark	Two rigsdaler	0.927	877	1.10.65
England	Shilling, new	0.182.5	924.5	22.96
"	Shilling, average	0.178	925	22.41
France	Five franc, average	0.800	900	98.00
Germany, North	Thaler, before 1857	0.712	750	72.67
" "	New thaler	0.595	900	72.89
Germany, South	Florin, before 1857	0.340	900	41.65
" "	New florin (assumed)	0.340	900	41.65
Greece	Five drachms	0.719	900	88.08
Hindostan	Rupee	0.374	916	46.62
Japan	Itzebu	0.279	991	37.63
"	New Itzebu	0.279	890	33.80
Mexico	Dollar, new	0.867.5	903	1.06.62
"	Dollar, average	0.866	901	1.06.20
Naples	Scudo	0.844	830	95.34
Netherlands	Two-and-a-half guild	0.804	944	1.03.31
Norway	Specie daler	0.927	877	1.10.65
New Granada	Dollar of 1857	0.803	896	97.92
Peru	Old dollar	0.866	901	1.06.20
"	Dollar of 1858	0.766	909	94.77
"	Half-dollar, 1835–38	0.433	650	38.31
Prussia	Thaler before 1857	0.712	750	72.68
"	New thaler	0.595	900	72.89
Rome	Scudo	0.864	900	1.05.84
Russia	Rouble	0.667	875	79.44
Sardinia	Five lire	0.800	900	98.00
Spain	New pistareen	0.166	899	20.31
Sweden	Rix dollar	1.092	750	1.11.48
Switzerland	Two francs	0.323	899	39.52
Tunis	Five piastres	0.511	898.5	62.49
Turkey	Twenty piastres	0.770	830	86.98
Tuscany	Florin	0.220	925	27.00

GREAT BRITAIN.

MONEY.

4 Farthings = 1 Penny, *d.*
12 pence = 1 Shilling, *s.*
20 shillings = 1 Pound, £.

137. The *Gold coins* are the sovereign, which represents the pound, and the half-sovereign. The guinea, of 21 shillings, and its subdivisions, have not been coined since 1816. The standard for gold is 11 parts fine gold and 1 part alloy. The sovereign weighs $123\frac{171}{623}$ grains, and contains $113\frac{1}{623}$ or 113.001 grains pure gold.

The *Silver coins* are crowns of 5*s.*, half-crowns, florins of 2*s.*, shillings, the 6*d.*, the 4*d.* or groats, and 3*d.* pieces. The *shilling* weighs $87\frac{3}{11}$ grains, and contains $80\frac{8}{11}$ grains pure silver.

The *Copper coins* are the penny, half-penny, and farthing, coined at the rate of 24 pence per pound avoirdupois.

138. *Bank-of-England Notes* are a legal tender for any sum over £5; silver is not a legal tender over 40*s.*; copper, for not more than 12*d.* in pennies or half-pennies; or 6*d.*, in farthings.

139. £ is a contraction of *libræ*, *s.* of *solidi*, *d.* of *denarii*, and *q.* of *quadrantes;* farthing is another word for *four-thing.*

In accounts, a straight line is written between shillings and pence when both are mentioned: thus, 2/6 for 2*s.* 6*d.*

The word sterling is supposed to be derived from the first coiners of English silver, who came into England from Germany in the reign of Richard I., and were called *Easterlings.* It is used to distinguish the currency of Great Britain from that of the Colonies, and from some continental money bearing the same denominations.

140. Intrinsic par value of £1 = \$4.866; U. S. Custom-House value, £1 = \$4.84. Freight bills are paid at the rate of \$4.80 per £1. In British America, £1 = \$4.

The English mint price of gold is £3 17*s.* 10½*d.* for standard gold, or $\frac{11}{12}$ fine. The mint price of silver is 5*s.* per ounce for standard silver, or $\frac{37}{40}$ fine.

141. The average yearly loss on the wear of gold is estimated at 1 in 950, and of silver 1 in 200.

WEIGHTS AND MEASURES.

142. Before 1826, the chief of the measures of capacity agreeing with those of the United States, were the wine gallon of 231 cubic inches, the beer gallon of 282 cubic inches, and the Winchester bushel of 2150.42 cubic inches.

143. By act of Parliament, which came into operation January 1, 1826, certain weights and measures, under the name of Imperial Weights and Measures, were declared to be the only lawful ones in the United Kingdom.

144. By this act, the imperial gallon, both Liquid and Dry Measure, contains 277.274 cubic inches, or 10 lbs. avoirdupois distilled water, the temperature 32°, barometer 30 inches. The imperial bushel contains 2218.192 cubic inches, or 8 imperial gallons; 8 bus. = 1 quarter; 10 qrs. = 1 last.

100 Imperial Bushels = 103.15 Winchester bushels.
100 Winchester " = 96.94 Imperial "

5 Imperial Gallons nearly equal 6 Wine Gallons.
59 " " 60 Ale "

144 lbs. Avoirdupois = 175 lbs. Troy.
192 oz. " = 175 oz. "

145. The standard avoirdupois pound of the United States and the imperial pound avoirdupois are alike.

The Troy pound = 22.815689 cubic inches distilled water

The linear, superficial, and cubic measures are the same in England as in the United States. (See COMPARATIVE TABLES.)

FRANCE.

146. The **Decimal** or **Metric System** of moneys, weights, and measures is now established in France, and has been adopted, to a greater or less extent, in Belgium, Spain, Portugal, Holland, Switzerland, Sweden, Austria, Turkey, Brazil, and several other countries.

147. MM. Delambre and Mechain estimated the length of the meridian from the Equator to the Pole by the measurement of an arc between Dunkirk and Barcelona, and the *ten-millionth* part of this meridian, or one-fourth of the circumference of the earth, was taken as the unit of *length*, and is termed a **Metre.**

148. The square of 10 metres is the unit of *surface measure*, and is called an **Are** (pronounced *air*).

149. The cube of the *tenth part of a metre* is the unit of capacity for either Liquid or Dry Measure, and is called a **Litre** (pronounced *le'-tur*).

150. A kil'olitre, the cube of a metre, is the unit of Solid Measure, and is known as the **Stere.**

151. A **Gramme** is the weight of a quantity of water, at 32° Fahr. (the temperature of melting ice), contained in a cube of the *one-hundredth part of a metre.*

152. The names of the *multiples* of these integers are derived from the Greek, and those of the *divisions* from the Latin language.

Deca	signifies	10	times.	Deci,	the	10th	part.
Hecto	"	100	"	Centi,	"	100th	"
Kilo	"	1000	"	Mille,	"	1000th	"
Myria	"	10000	"				

MONEY.

10 Centimes = 1 Decime.
10 Decimes, or 100 Centimes = 1 FRANC.

153. The French coin is based upon the unit of weight,—the *gramme.*

154. Silver is the legal standard of value in France. The franc in silver is valued at 9.384 pence sterling. The value of the franc in gold is 9.516 pence sterling, giving fr.25.22 for £1 sterling. The United States Custom-House valuation of the franc is 18.6 cts.; United States Mint price, 19.6 cts.

155. The mint standard for both gold and silver is $\frac{9}{10}$ pure and $\frac{1}{10}$ alloy. The gold coins are the napoleon, of 20 francs, and the 100, 50, 10, and 5 franc pieces.

A kilogramme of standard gold is coined into 155 twenty-franc pieces.

The silver coins are the silver napoleon, of 5 francs, and the 2, 1, ½, and ¼ franc pieces.

The copper or bronze pieces are 10, 5, 2, and 1 centimes, weighing, respectively, 10, 5, 2, and 1 grammes.

156. Accounts were formerly kept in livres tournoise, with its subdivisions of the sou and denier. 12 deniers = 1 sou or sol, 20 sous = 1 livre tournoise, 24 livres = 1 louis-d'or, 3 livres = 1 ecu or crown, 81 livres = 80 francs.

WEIGHTS.

Gramme = 15.432349 grains Troy.

The kilogramme (1000 grammes) is the weight most frequently used in commerce, and is equal to 2.679227 lbs. (2 lbs. 8 oz. 3 dwt.) Troy; or, 2.204621 lbs. (2 lbs. 3 oz. 4.652 dr.) avoirdupois. A kilogramme is generally taken as $2\frac{1}{5}$ lbs.

373¼ grammes = 1 lb. Troy. $453\frac{3}{5}$ grammes = 1 lb. avoirdupois.

1 cwt. = 50.80234 kilogrammes.

100 myriogrammes = 1 ton, $20\frac{1}{6}$ lbs.

1 quintal métrique = 100 kilogrammes.

NOTE.—At the U. S. Post-Office, 15 grammes are taken as ½ oz.

MEASURES OF LENGTH.

1 METRE = 39.371 English inches.
1 decimetre = 3.9371 " "
1 kilometre = 0.62138 miles.
1 Eng. mile = 1.609036 kilometres.

Old Measure.—1 aune = 1¼ yds. 1 brace = ⅝ yds.

MEASURES OF SURFACE.

1 ARE = a square decametre = 119.6046 sq. yds.
1 centiare = 10.76441 sq. ft.
1 " = 1.196046 sq. yds.
1 hectare = 2 acres, 1 rood, 35 perches.
1 acre, Eng. = .40466 hectares.
100 sq. ft. = 9.28987 sq. metres.

MEASURES OF CAPACITY.

1 LITRE = 61.02803 cubic inches.
1 " = 2.1135 wine pints, or 1.7608 imperial pints, or 908 qts. dry measure.
1 hectolitre = 3.53171 cubic ft. = 22.01 imperial gals., or 26.419 wine gals., or 2.839 Winchester bus.

MEASURES OF SOLIDITY.

1 STERE or kilolitre = 35.31714 cubic feet = .2759 cord.
1 " = 1.308042 " yds.
100 cubic inches = 16.38592 " centimetres.

157. The terms of the Metric System are now generally used by scientific men. Congress, by act of July 27, 1866, made it lawful in contracts and in legal proceedings to employ the weights and measures of the Metric System; and Great Britain, in 1864, passed an act authorizing its use.

SYNOPSIS OF

FOREIGN MONEYS OF ACCOUNT.

Money at		Dolls. Cts.
Amsterdam, 5 cents = 1 stiver, 20 stivers = 1 guilder or florin.	1 florin	= .40
Berlin, 30 silver groschen = 1 thaler.	1 thaler	= .69
Bremen, 5 schwaren = 1 grote, 72 grotes = 1 rix-daler, 5 rix-dalers = 1 louis-d'or.	1 s. daler	= .79$\frac{7}{8}$
Calcutta, 12 pies = 1 anna, 16 annas = 1 rupee.	1 rupee	= .44$\frac{1}{2}$
Christiania, 120 skilling = 1 specie-daler. 1 banco rix-dollar = .39$\frac{3}{4}$.	1 s. daler	= 1.06
Constantinople, 40 paras = 1 piastre, 100 piastres = 1 medjidie.	1 medjidie	= 3.35
Copenhagen, 96 skilling = 1 rigsbank daler. 1 banco rix-dollar = .55.	1 s. daler	= 1.05
Frankfort, 60 kreutzer = 1 Zollverein florin or guilder.	1 florin	= .40
Genoa, 100 centesimi = 1 lira Italiana.	1 lira	= .18$\frac{6}{10}$
Hamburg, 12 pfenning = 1 schilling, 16 schilling = 1 mark.	1 m. banco	= .35$\frac{1}{2}$
Lisbon, 1000 reis = 1 milreis.	1 milreis	= 1.12
London, 240 pence = 12 shillings = 1 pound.	1 pound	= 4.86
Madrid, 34 maravedis = 1 real, 20 reals = 1 duro.	1 duro	= 1.00
Naples, 10 grani = 1 carlino, 10 carlini = 1 ducat.	1 ducat	= .80
New York, 100 cents = 1 dollar.		
Palermo, 20 grani = 1 taro, 30 tari = 1 onza.	1 onza	= 2.40
Paris, 100 centimes = 1 franc.	1 franc	= .19$\frac{6}{10}$
Pekin, 1 tael = 10 mace = 100 candareens = 1000 cash.	1 tael	= 1.48
Rio de Janeiro, 1000 reis = 1 milreis.	1 milreis	= .83$\frac{1}{2}$
Rome, 10 bajocchi = 1 paolo, 10 paoli = 1 scudo Romano.	1 s. Romano	= .99$\frac{1}{2}$
St. Petersburg, 100 copeck = 1 silver rouble.	1 s. rouble	= .75
Stockholm, 12 runstyken = 1 skilling, 48 skillingar = 1 daler in banco.	1 daler	= 1.06
Venice, 100 centesimi = 1 lira Austriaca, 3 lire Austriache = 1 florin Austriaco.	1 lira	= .16
Vienna, 100 kreutzer = 1 gulden or florin.	1 florin	= .48$\frac{1}{2}$

COMPARATIVE TABLES OF WEIGHTS AND MEASURES.

1 Imperial Gallon = 277.274 cubic inches = 1.2 Wine Gallons.

Wine Measure,	1 quart = $57\frac{3}{4}$	"	1 gall. = 231	cubic inches.
Dry "	1 " = $67\frac{1}{5}$	"	1 " = 268	"
Beer "	1 " = $70\frac{1}{2}$	"	1 " = 282	"

Troy Weight, Apothecaries' Weight, } 1 pound = 5760 grains.
Avoirdupois " 1 " = 7000 "
175 lbs. Troy = 144 lbs. Avoirdupois.

Dry Measure, 1 Bushel of U. S. (Winchester bu.) = 2150.42 cub. in.
" 1 Imperial Bushel of Great Britain = 2218.192 "
" 1 Bushel U. S. heaped measure = 2747.7167 "

FOREIGN WEIGHTS AND MEASURES

FREQUENTLY MET WITH IN REPORTS OF MARKETS.

Ahm, in Rotterdam (nearly)	40 gallons.
Almude, in Portugal	4.37 "
Almude, in Madeira	4 to 8 gallons.
Alquiere, in Madeira	$1\frac{5}{8}$ to 2 pecks.
" in Bahia	1 bushel.
" in Maranham	$1\frac{1}{4}$ "
" in Rio Janeiro	1 to $1\frac{1}{4}$ bushels.
" in Pernambuco	1 to $1\frac{1}{4}$ "
Anna of rice, in Ceylon	260.4 lbs.
Arroba, in Portugal	32 "
" in Spain	25 "
" of wine, in Spain (large)	4.246 gallons.
" " " (small)	3.34 "
Arroba, in Malaga	$4\frac{1}{5}$ "
Arsheen, in Russia	28 inches.
Bahar, in Batavia (large)	$4\frac{1}{2}$ piculs.
" " (small)	3 "
Bale of cinnamon, in Ceylon (net)	$104\frac{5}{8}$ lbs.
Barilla, in Naples	11 gallons.
Cantar, in the Levant	118.8 lbs.
" of oil, in Leghorn	88 "
" of brandy "	120 "
" in Malta	$174\frac{1}{2}$ "
" (grosso) in Naples	$196\frac{1}{2}$ "
" (piccolo) "	106 "
" (grosso) in Sicily	$192\frac{1}{2}$ "
" (sottile) "	175 "
Carro, in Naples	52.2 bushels.
" of wine, in Naples	264 gallons.

Catta of tea, in China	1⅓ lbs.
Cayang of rice, in Batavia	3581 lbs.
Chetwert, in Russia	5.95 bushels.
Fanega, in Spain	1.6 "
Hectolitre, in France . . 2.84 bus. or	26.42 gallons
Kilogramme, in France and Netherlands	2⅕ lbs.
Last of grain, in Amsterdam	85¼ "
" " in Bremen	80⅔ "
" of salt, in Cadiz	75⅘ bushels.
" or moyo of salt, in Portugal	70 "
" of grain, in Dantzic (nearly)	93 "
" " in Flushing	92½ "
" " in Hamburg	89.7 "
" - " in Lubeck	91 "
" " in Rotterdam	85 3/16 "
" in Sweden	75 "
" Utrecht	59+ "
Lispound, in Hamburg	14 lbs.
Mark, in Holland	9 ounces.
Maund (factory), in Calcutta	74⅝ lbs.
" (bazaar), 10% heavier	82.4 "
Mina of grain, in Genoa	3.43 bushels.
Moyo, of Lisbon	23+ "
" in Oporto	30 "
Oke, in Smyrna	2.83 lbs.
Orna (or eimer) of wine, in Trieste	14.94 gallons.
" of oil "	17 "
Palmo, in Naples	10⅓ inches.
Picul, in Batavia and Madras	136 lbs.
" in China and Japan	133⅓ "
Pipe of wine, in Spain	160+ gallons.
Pood, in Russia	36 lbs. 1 oz. 10 drs
Quintal, in Portugal	89.05 lbs.
" in Smyrna	127.2 "
" (of 4 arrobas), in Spain	100 "
" in Turkey	124½ "
" of cotton (45 okes), in Turkey	127.3 "
Rottolo, in Portugal	12¼ "
Rottolo, in Genoa	24 "
" in Leghorn	3 "
Salma of grain, in Sicily	9.77 bushels.
" (general) "	7.85 "
" of wine "	23.06 gallons.
Scheffel, in Germany	1½ to 3 bushels.
Ship pound, in Denmark	352 lbs.
" " in Hamburg	299½ "
Staro (or stajo), in Trieste	2.34 + bushels.
Tale, in China	1⅓ ounces.
Vara, in Rio Janeiro . . (nearly)	1¼ yards.
" in Spain	9⅕ "

EXCHANGE.

158. The term Exchange, in commerce, signifies the giving or receiving of one currency for its value in another; or, the method of making payments by means of written orders without the transmission of money. See BILLS OF EXCHANGE.

159. **Exchange** is of two kinds, *Domestic* or *Inland*, and *Foreign.*

160. **Domestic Exchange** includes the exchanges made within the limits of one country.

161. **Foreign Exchange** relates to the transactions between different countries.

Foreign Exchange comprises *Nominal Exchange* and *Real Exchange.*

162. **Nominal Exchange** has reference to the comparative market value of the currencies of different countries.

163. **Real Exchange** is that which relates to the interchange of commodities without reference to the precious metals.

164. The **True** or **Intrinsic Par of Exchange** between two countries is the *exact equivalent of pure metal* in the coined piece which forms the unit of price of one country compared with the currency of the other. The alloy is reckoned of no value.

165. "Thus, according to the mint regulations of Great Britain and France, £1 sterling is equal to 25 fr. 20 cent., which is said to be the par between London and Paris. Exchange between the two countries is said to be at par when bills are negotiated at this rate; that is, when a bill for £100 drawn in London is worth 2520 francs in Paris, and conversely. When £1 in London buys a bill on Paris for more than 25 fr. 20 cent., the exchange is said to be in favor of London and against Paris; when £1 in London will not buy a bill on Paris for 25 fr. 20 cent., exchange is against London and in favor of Paris.

166. "Exchange is made to diverge from par by any discrepancy between the actual weight or fineness of the coins and the mint standard, and by the variations in the demand and supply of bills of exchange.

"The cost of conveying bullion or coin forms the limit within which the rise and fall of real exchange is confined; for if a merchant can send a bill for less than the expense of sending gold, he will send a bill, but if sending a bill would cost more than the expense and risk of sending gold, then he will send gold."

167. The **Commercial Par of Exchange** is the market value of the currency of one country when sold for the currency of another.

168. The **Course** or **Rate of Exchange** is the current prices of exchanges, or the *variable* price of the money of one country which is paid for a *fixed* amount of that of another country.

DOMESTIC EXCHANGE.

169. The calculations connected with Domestic Exchange require only the ordinary applications of Percentage.

EXAMPLES.

1. What is the cost of a bill for $240 on New York, purchased at $1\frac{1}{4}\%$ premium? Ans. $243.

2. What is the cost of a draft on New Orleans for $1800, at $1\frac{3}{4}\%$ premium?

3. Sold $375 uncurrent money at $2\frac{1}{4}\%$ discount. How much did I receive? How much did I lose?

4. Exchanged $600 in bank notes for gold at 5% premium. How much did I receive?

5. Bought goods, $1250, and sold them at a profit of 25%; purchased a draft on St. Louis, with the proceeds, at a discount of $\frac{3}{4}\%$. What was the amount of the draft?

6. Shipped goods to Havana, and received a draft for $2500, which gave me a profit of 20%; sold the draft at $4\frac{1}{2}\%$ premium. How much did I gain by both transactions?

7. A commission merchant sold goods, the net proceeds of which were \$2750. How large a draft can he buy to remit to his consignor, if he pays $\frac{1}{2}$% premium for the draft? How large a draft if he purchases at $\frac{1}{2}$% discount?

FOREIGN EXCHANGE.

170. In Foreign Exchange it is usual to reckon the money of one country as fixed, and the other as variable. The country whose money is calculated at a fixed price is said to receive the variable price, while the other country is said to give the variable price. Thus, if I buy a bill of exchange on Paris, I receive so many francs per dollar,—the dollar is the fixed price, and the francs the variable price. If I buy a bill on Hamburg, I pay so many cents per marc banco; the marc banco is called the fixed price, and the cents the variable price. In quotations of exchange rates, it is usual to give only the variable prices.

171. Nearly all the bills of exchange drawn in this country are drawn and negotiated on one of the following places: viz., London, Paris, Bremen, Hamburg, Cologne, Leipsic, Frankfort, and Amsterdam.

QUOTATION OF FOREIGN BILLS OF EXCHANGE,

By Drexel & Co., Bankers, *Philada., June 1, 1866.*

Exchange.			*Explanation.*
On London,	60 days,	109 @ 109$\frac{5}{8}$	Premium (on old par of 4.44$\frac{4}{9}$), from 9 to 9$\frac{5}{8}$ per cent. on bills at 60 days' sight.
" "	3 "	109$\frac{3}{4}$ @ 110$\frac{1}{2}$	Premium from 9$\frac{3}{4}$ to 10$\frac{1}{2}$ per cent. on bills at 3 days' sight.
" Paris,	60 "	5.11	At 5 francs, 11 centimes per dollar.
" "	3 "	5.08	" 5 " 8 " " "
" Bremen,	60 "	.80	" 80 cents per rix-dollar.
" Hamburg,	60 "	.37	" 37 " " marc banco.
" Cologne,	60 "	.73$\frac{1}{2}$	" 73$\frac{1}{2}$ " " thaler.
" Leipsic,	60 "	.74	" 74 " " "
" Frankfort,	60 "	.42	" 42 " " guilder or florin.
" Amsterdam,	60 "	.42 @ .42$\frac{3}{4}$	From 42 to 42$\frac{3}{4}$ cts. per guilder.

See, also, London Course of Exchange.

172. Bills of exchange are drawn in the money of the country in which they are made payable. (See Forms of Bills of Exchange.)

Exchange on England.

173. By the usage of bankers for ages, the pound sterling has been valued by the old Spanish Carolus pillar dollar, now entirely out of circulation in Europe and America; of these, 4.44\frac{4}{9}$ were equivalent to the pound sterling.

This rate originally represented the true par of exchange between the two countries. In 1834 the eagle was reduced in weight to 258 grains (see TABLES OF COINS OF U. S.), and now contains 232.2 grains pure gold.

The English sovereign is the coined piece of which the pound sterling is the money of account, and contains 113.001 grains pure gold.

Standard weight of sovereign, grains	123.274
Alloy, $\frac{1}{12}$ part	10.273
Fine gold in the sovereign . . .	113.001

By the proportion—

232.2 grains : 113.001 grains : : $10,

we find that the equivalent of the pound sterling is $4.8665; and, allowing for the wear of coin, we have $4.84, the value established by Congress in 1842, and the rate at which duties are estimated in the Custom-Houses.

It has been found convenient to retain the *old* value as the basis of exchange, and to express the present exchangeable value by a *premium* on this basis. It requires the addition of 9% to make the Custom-House value, and the addition of about 9½% to equal the intrinsic value, of a pound sterling in our currency.

Old par value of £1.	= $4.444	Old par value,	$4.4444
9% premium,	= .399	9½% premium,	.4222
Custom-House value,	$4.8443	Intrinsic value,	$4.8666

Exchange quotations refer to the old par. When, therefore, exchange is quoted at about 9½% premium, there is in fact no real premium, but the true par has been attained. When nothing is said to the contrary, the quotations are for bills at *usance*, or 60 days' sight and 3 days of grace, which, at 6% interest, involves a loss of more than 1% besides the time of transportation. On the other hand, 1% is about the cost, including freight, insurance, &c., of shipping gold; and as one of these items balances the other, the real par of exchange on England is 9½%, at which rate it is as well, or better, to remit good 60-day bills as specie.

PRO FORMA ACCOUNT OF A SHIPMENT OF MEXICAN DOLLARS FROM NEW YORK TO LONDON.

10000 dollars purchased in New York at 1¾ prem. . .	10175.00
Packing Charges, Shipping, &c.	7.50
Insurance at ½% on 10175.00, and Policy $1 . .	51.87
Total cost in New York	$10234.37

	£	s.	d.	£	s.	d.
Value in London, 10000 dollars weighing 8660 ounces, and sold at 58⅛ pence per ounce . . .				2097	6	11
Charges in London, Freight, ¼% . . .	5	4	9			
Primage, 5%		5	2			
Landing Charges, Postage, &c. . .		13	9			
Brokerage, ⅛%, Com. ½% = ⅝% =	13	2	2	19	5	11
Net Proceeds, Cash, in London				2078	1	0
Add Interest for 63 days, at 4%				14	10	11
				£2092	11	11

Par of £2092 11*s.* 11*d.* = $9300.43. This amount drawn at 60 days' sight, to produce the above $10234.37, would establish the rate of exchange on London at 110.04 per cent.

Gold is sometimes exported when exchange is quoted below the true par, by bankers who have branch-houses and therefore no commissions to cover, and who insure their own risks; by those who can save a guaranty commission on commercial bills, and by those who are compelled to procure specie.

Exports of Specie from New York for the week ending June 2, 1866, to Liverpool, Southampton, Havre, Bremen, and Hamburg.

May 30,	American Gold,	$2,715,700
" "	French "	6,208
" "	Spanish "	9,492
" 31,	American "	485,000
June 1,	" "	1,645,197
" "	Gold and Silver bars,	14,800
" "	Sovereigns,	62,920
" 2,	Gold and Silver bars,	82,500
		5,021,817
	Amount bro't forward,	$5,021,817
June 2,	Foreign Coin and American Gold,	1,179,468
" "	German Silver,	2.000
" "	Mexican "	40,828
" "	Silver Coin,	20,000
" "	American Gold,	606,834
" "	Foreign Coin,	50
	Total for the week,	$6,870,997

RULES FOR COMPUTING STERLING EXCHANGE,

USED BY BANKERS AND DEALERS IN EXCHANGE.

174. The par value of a pound sterling, \$4.44$\frac{4}{9}$, equals \$4$\frac{4}{9}$, or $\frac{40}{9}$ dollars; and as there are 40 sixpences in a pound, 1 sixpence is equal to $\frac{1}{9}$ of a dollar. To find the real value, a premium must be added.

175. To find the value of Sterling Money.

Rule I.—*Reduce the pounds and shillings to sixpences, by multiplying the pounds by 40 and the shillings by 2; to their sum add 1, if the pence equal or exceed 6; divide by 9, and to the quotient add the given premium, and 2 cents for every penny exceeding 6 in the given number of pence.*

EXAMPLE.

1. What is the value in U. S. Currency of £540 7*s.* 7*d.*, at a premium of 9½ %?

```
540 × 40 =    21600
  7 ×  2 =       14
7 = 6 + 1 =       1
              9)21615
               2401.6666
                      9½ %
              21615.0004
               1200.8333
              22.8158337 Premium.
             2401.6666
            2424.4824337
Value of 1d.,        2
           $2424.50
```

Rule II.—*Reduce the pounds and shillings to sixpences, and to their sum add ⅙ the number of pence; then divide by 9, and to the quotient add the given premium.*

EXAMPLE GIVEN UNDER RULE I.

```
  7 ÷  6 =      1.166
  7 ×  2 =     14
540 × 40 =  21600
          ───────────
          9)21615.166
            ─────────
             2401.685  Par value
                   9½  per cent.
            ─────────
            21.615165
             1.200842
            ─────────
            22.816007  Premium.
           2401.685
           ────────
    Ans.   2424.501
```

2. Reduce £1872 11*s*. 5*d*. to dollars at par. Ans. $8322.54.

3. Reduce £617 1*s*. 1*d*. to United States currency at 9% premium. Ans. $2989.40.

4. What is the value of £1500 at 8% premium?

5. What will be the cost of the following bill of exchange at 8¾% premium?

£150. NEW YORK, June 13, 1866.

Sixty days after sight of this FIRST of EXCHANGE (Second and Third of same tenor and date unpaid), pay to the order of R. J. Milligan One Hundred and Fifty Pounds, value received, and charge the same to account of

BROWN & BROS.

To BROWN, SHIPLEY & CO.,
Liverpool, England.

176. To reduce Federal money to Sterling.

RULE I.—*Divide the given amount by the value of £1 at the given premium.*

RULE II.—*Multiply the given amount by 9, and divide the product by 40; annex two ciphers to the quotient, and divide by 100 increased by the premium.*

EXAMPLES.

1. A commission merchant wishes to remit $7071.57 to

England. How large a bill of exchange can he purchase at 9% premium?

```
      7071.57                    1591.1033
            9                          100
  40)63644.13               109)159110.3300
    1591.1033                   1459.7277
                                       20
                                  14.5540
                                       12
Ans. £1459 14s. 6½d.               6.6480
```

2. What amount of exchange can I buy for $3567.60 at 8½% premium? £739 16s. 6d.

3. Purchased a bill of exchange, at 9⅝% premium, which cost $4275. How large was the bill?

4. How large a bill of exchange can I buy for $2850, if I pay 9¼% premium?

The cost of goods imported from England is often estimated by adding the proportion of charges to the value of the pound or shilling. For example:—

An invoice amounts to £2400, which, with	
Exchange at 9% premium =	$11626.66
Duties, freight, and other charges, amount to	600.34
Making the total cost	$12227.00

Then, if £2400 cost $12227, one pound cost 12227 ÷ 2400 = $5.09½ nearly, and 1 shilling costs 25½ cts., 1 penny 2⅛ cts. Cloth at 16*d.* per yd. would cost 33 cents.

TABLE

Showing the value of £1 sterling from 4 to 12½ per cent. premium on the old par of $4.44⅘.

Old par	$4.444	7¾ per cent.	$4.789	9⅝ per cent.	$4.872
4 per cent.	4.622	8% (Eng. fr'ts)	4.800	9¾ "	4.878
4½ "	4.644	8¼ per cent.	4.811	9⅞ "	4.883
5 "	4.667	8½ "	4.822	10 "	4.889
5½ "	4.689	8¾ "	4.833	10⅛ "	4.894
6 "	4.711	9 (Cust.-House)	4.844	10½ "	4.911
6½ "	4.733	9⅛ per cent.	4.850	11 "	4.933
7 "	4.756	9¼ "	4.856	11½ "	4.956
7¼ "	4.767	9⅜ "	4.861	12 "	4.978
7½ "	4.778	9½ "	4.867	12½ "	5.000

STERLING TABLE.

Calculated at the Par Value of $4.444 to £1 Sterling.

£	$ cts. m.	£	$ cts. m.	£	$ cts. m.	Shill'gs.	$ cts. m.
1	4.44.4	41	182.22.2	81	360.00.0	1	0.22.2
2	8.88.9	42	186.66.7	82	364.44.4	2	0.44.4
3	13.33.3	43	191.11.1	83	368.88.9	3	0.66.7
4	17.77.8	44	195.55.6	84	373.33.3	4	0.88.9
5	22.22.2	45	200.00.0	85	377.77.8	5	1.11.1
6	26.66.7	46	204.44.4	86	382.22.2	6	1.33.3
7	31.11.1	47	208.88.9	87	386.66.7	7	1.55.6
8	35.55.6	48	213.33.3	88	391.11.1	8	1.77.8
9	40.00.0	49	217.77.8	89	395.55.6	9	2.00.0
10	44.44.4	**50**	222.22.2	**90**	400.00.0	**10**	2.22.2
11	48.88.9	51	226.66.7	91	404.44.4	11	2.44.4
12	53.33.3	52	231.11.1	92	408.88.9	12	2.66.7
13	57.77.8	53	235.55.6	93	413.33.3	13	2.88.9
14	62.22.2	54	240.00.0	94	417.77.8	14	3.11.1
15	66.66.7	55	244.44.4	95	422.22.2	15	3.33.3
16	71.11.1	56	248.88.9	96	426.66.7	16	3.55.6
17	75.55.6	57	253.33.3	97	431.11.1	17	3.77.8
18	80.00.0	58	257.77.8	98	435.55.6	18	4.00.0
19	84.44.5	59	262.22.2	99	440.00.0	19	4.22.2
20	88.88.9	**60**	266.66.7	**100**	444.44.4	**20**	4.44.4
21	93.33.3	61	271.11.1			Pence.	$ cts. m.
22	97.77.8	62	275.55.6	200	888.88.9	1	0.01.9
23	102.22.2	63	280.00.0	300	1333.33.3	2	0.03.7
24	106.66.7	64	284.44.4	400	1777.77.8	3	0.05.6
25	111.11.1	65	288.88.9	500	2222.22.2	4	0.07.4
26	115.55.6	66	293.33.3	600	2666.66.7	5	0.09.3
27	120.00.0	67	297.77.8	700	3111.11.1		
28	124.44.4	68	302.22.2	800	3555.55.6	6	0.11.1
29	128.88.9	69	306.66.7	900	4000.00.0	7	0.13.0
30	133.33.3	**70**	311.11.1	**1000**	4444.44.4	8	0.14.8
						9	0.16.7
31	137.77.8	71	315.55.6	1100	4888.88.9	10	0.18.5
32	142.22.2	72	320.00.0	1200	5333.33.3		
33	146.66.7	73	324.44.4	1300	5777.77.8	11	0.20.4
34	151.11.1	74	328.88.9	1400	6222.22.2	**12**	0.22.2
35	155.55.6	75	333.33.3	1500	6666.66.7		
36	160.00.0	76	337.77.8	1600	7111.11.1		
37	164.44.4	77	342.22.2	1700	7555.55.6	¼	0.00.5
38	168.88.9	78	346.66.7	1800	8000.00.0	½	0.00.9
39	173.33.3	79	351.11.1	1900	8444.44.4		
40	177.77.8	**80**	355.55.6	**2000**	8888.88.9	¾	0.01.4

(See, also, IMPORTERS' ADVANCE TABLE.)

To find the value of any given amount not mentioned in the table, take the sum of those numbers that will equal the given amount.

London Course of Exchange.

177. London has been called the great clearing-house of the world. Nearly all the foreign trade of the United States is settled through England and France.

LONDON RECEIVES FROM, OR GIVES TO,

Variable, according to the exchanges,

Amsterdam	12 florins and 3 stivers	for	£1 sterling.	
Bremen	$609\frac{1}{4}$ rix-dollars	"	£100 sterling.	
Berlin	6 dollars, 25 silver groschen	"	£1	"
Christiania	4 specie-daler, 30 skilling	"	"	"
Constantinople	140 piastres	"	"	"
Copenhagen	9 rigsbank daler, 10 skilling	"	"	"
Frankfort	121 Zollverein florins	"	£10	"
Genoa	25 lire, 35 centesimi	"	£1	"
Hamburg	13 marks, 12 schillings	"	"	"
Milan	25 lire, 40 cents	"	"	"
Leghorn	25 " 50 "	"	"	"
Paris	25 francs, 21 centimes	"	"	"
Rome	46 Paoli	"	"	"
Stockholm	12 dalers in banco, 1 skilling	"	"	"
Vienna	13 florins, 70 kreuzers	"	"	"

Calcutta	23 pence sterling	for	1 Comp. rupee.
Gibraltar	$48\frac{1}{2}$ " "	"	1 duro, or hard dollar, or Spanish dollar.
Lisbon	$53\frac{1}{4}$ " "	"	1 milreis.
Madrid	$50\frac{1}{4}$ " "	"	1 hard dollar.
Naples	$39\frac{5}{8}$ " "	"	1 ducat.
New York	$49\frac{1}{2}$ " "	"	1 U. S. dollar.
Palermo	$119\frac{1}{2}$ " "	"	1 onza.
Pekin	$78\frac{1}{4}$ " "	"	a thousand cash.
Rio Janeiro	30 " "	"	1 milreis.
St. Petersburg	$38\frac{1}{4}$ " "	"	1 silver rouble.
Venice	47 " "	"	6 lire Austriache.

(See, also, SYNOPSIS OF MONEYS OF ACCOUNT.)

Exchange on France.

100 Centimes make 1 Franc.

1. What is the cost of a bill of exchange on Paris for fr.10277.76—exchange at fr.4.89 per dollar?

Ans. \$2101.76.

2. What must be paid for a bill on Paris for fr.3875.50, at fr.5.19 per dollar?

3. What is the difference between the Custom-House value of 18.6 cts. per franc, and exchange at fr.5.19 per dollar, on a bill for 58000 francs?

4. Estimating fr.5.21 to be the par value of \$1, what is the premium on gold when exchange for currency is quoted at fr.345 per dollar?

PRO FORMA ACCOUNT OF A SHIPMENT OF MEXICAN DOLLARS FROM NEW YORK TO PARIS.

10000 dollars purchased at $1\frac{3}{4}$ premium,				10175.00
Packing Charges, Shipping, &c.,				7.50
Marine Insurance, at $\frac{1}{2}\%$ on \$10175.00,			50.87	
Policy,			1.	51.87
Total cost in New York,				\$10234.37
Value in Paris 10000 dollars sold at fr.5.34				fr.53400.00
Charges in Havre:—				
Import Duty and Permits,		fr.6.40		
Cartage, Cooperage, &c.,		10.10		
Freight, $\frac{1}{4}\%$ on \$10000,	25.00			
Primage, 10%,	2.50			
At fr.5.25,	\$27.50 =	144.37	160.87	
Charges in Paris:—				
Freight,	fr.72.25			
Viewing and Delivering,	3.25			
Brokerage $\frac{1}{8}\%$, Com. $\frac{1}{2}\%$ = $\frac{5}{8}\%$,	333.75		409.25	570.12
Net proceeds, cash, in Paris,				fr.52829.88
Add Interest for 63 days, at 4%,				369.80
Total,				fr.53199.68

This amount drawn at 60 days' sight, to realize the above \$10234.37, will require the rate of exchange to be fr.5.20 per dollar. Without commission in Paris, the rate would be fr.$5.22\frac{1}{3}$, or $\frac{1}{2}\%$ lower.

PROFIT AND LOSS.

178. The difference between the cost of an article and the amount received for it is the gain or loss.

179. The cost of goods consists of the price paid to the person from whom they were purchased, or the expense of producing them, and all charges, such as commissions, freight, packing, duties, exchange, insurance, drayage, &c., necessary to place the goods in a condition ready for use or sale.

TOTAL GAINS AND LOSSES.

180. The total gains or losses on goods may be easily ascertained, when all are sold, by taking the difference between the cost and selling price; but when part remains unsold—

RULE I.—*Add the value of the merchandise unsold to the amount received for sales, and take the difference between the sum thus obtained and the cost of the merchandise; the difference will be the gain or loss.* Or,

RULE II.—*Find the difference between the amount of sales and the cost of the merchandise;* then—

When there is an excess of COST over SALES—

If the value of the goods remaining unsold is more than this excess, the difference is a gain.

If the value of the goods is less, the difference is a loss.

When the SALES exceed the COST—

Add the value of the goods unsold to the difference between the SALES *and the* COST; *the result will be the gain.*

181. In estimating the value of goods remaining unsold, when an "account of stock" is taken, it is customary to use the invoice or purchase price; but if the market value of the goods has depreciated, either from the nature of the goods or the state of the market, or if there has been a decided advance in prices, an allowance must be made accordingly. A safe rule is, if they are salable goods, to estimate them at what it would cost to replace them.

GAINS AND LOSSES ON PARTICULAR GOODS.

182. CASE I.—To find the gain or loss, when the cost and rate per cent. are given.

RULE.—*Multiply the cost by the rate per cent., and divide by 100.*

NOTE.—The selling price is found by adding the gain to the cost, or deducting the loss.

EXAMPLES.

1. Bought broadcloth for $250, and sold it at 15% advance. How much did I gain?

$250 \times 15 = 3750$ $37.50, Ans.

2. How much do I gain per barrel, if I sell flour which cost $11 per bbl. at a profit of 25%? Ans. $2.75.

3. Bought a cargo of wheat for $11500, and sold it at a profit of 16½%. How much did I gain?

4. A merchant purchased a quantity of lumber for $2200. He paid for freight and drayage $75; commission for selling, $125. He gained 27% on the entire cost. How much was it sold for, and how much did he make?

5. Bought 100 barrels of sugar for $1500.75, which I sold at an advance of 12½%. How much did I gain, and how much did I receive?

6. What difference will it make in the cost per yard to the American merchant who buys his goods in England for $4 per yard, and pays a duty of 30% on them, if the price in England is reduced to $3 per yard?

EXAMPLES.

1. What is the selling price of the following goods at 25% above the given price?

5 gross steel pens, gr. $\frac{1}{.60}$, $\frac{2}{\$1.00}$, $\frac{2}{\$1.20}$. (See ABBREVIATIONS.)
20 diamond satin bonnets, @ 30c.
50 doz. tassels, @ $1.50 per doz.
1 case, 12 pairs men's calf sewed boots, @ $4.
3 " 60 " misses' lasting gaitor boots, @ $1.40.
8 ps. mousseline de laine, 240 yds., @ 60c.
12 doz. bl'k Italian cravats, @ doz. $\frac{3}{\$12}$, $\frac{2}{\$15}$, $\frac{7}{\$16}$.

183. Case II.—To find the rate per cent., when the gain or loss, or cost and selling price, are given.

Rule.—*Multiply the gain or loss by 100, and divide the product by the cost.*

EXAMPLES.

1. Sold a house for $7995, which cost me $6500. What per cent. did I gain?

$7995 - 6500 = 1495 \qquad 1495 \times 100 = 149500$
$149500 \div 6500 = 23.$ Ans. 23%.

2. Bought a cargo of flour for $18000, and sold it for $20000. What per cent. did I gain?

3. If by a decline of prices I was obliged to sell a lot of coffee for $2200 which cost me $2500, what per cent. did I lose?

4. A merchant bought a quantity of silks at $2.50 per yard, and sold them at $2.87½. What per cent. did he make?

184. Case III.—To ascertain the cost, when the selling price and rate per cent. gained or lost are given.

Rule.—*Multiply the selling price by 100, and divide the product by 100 increased by the gain per cent. or diminished by the loss per cent.*

EXAMPLES.

1. An invoice of goods purchased in England was sold for $3600, realizing a gain of 20%. What was the cost?

$100 + 20 = 120 \qquad 360000 \div 120 = 3000.$
Ans. $3000.

2. A merchant sold sugar for $1260, by which he lost 10%. What was the cost?

$100 - 10 = 90 \qquad 126000 \div 90 = 1400.$
Ans. $1400.

185. Case IV.—To find the cost, when the gain or loss and the rate per cent. are given.

Rule.—*Multiply the gain or loss by 100, and divide the product by the rate per cent.*

EXAMPLES.

1. I gained $2250 by selling goods at a profit of 15%. What did they cost?

225000 ÷ 15 = 15000. Ans. $15000.

2. How large sales must I make, at a profit of 12½ per cent., to clear $3000? Ans. $27000.

3. Sold flour at an advance of 20%, and gained $136. What did it cost?

186. Case V.—To find the rate, when the cost and gain or loss are given.

Rule.—*Multiply the gain or loss by 100, and divide by the cost.*

EXAMPLES.

1. Bought goods for $1875, and sold them so as to gain $468.75. What was the rate per cent.?

46875 ÷ 1875 = 25. Ans. 25%.

2. Sold teas which cost me 45 cts. per pound, and gained 9 cts. per pound. What was the rate of gain?

3. A merchant sold corn which cost him $325, and gained $48.75. What was the gain per cent.?

4. If the United States wine gallon contains 231 cubic inches, and the beer gallon 282 cubic inches, what per cent. is the latter larger than the former?

5. What per cent. do I gain if I sell cloth which cost $2.50 for $3.75 per yard?

187. To find what the gain or loss per cent. would be if sold at another price, the selling price and rate per cent. of gain or loss being given.

Rule.—*Multiply the proposed selling price by 100, increased by the given rate per cent. gained, or diminished by the given per cent. of loss, and divide the product by the actual selling price, and take the difference between the quotient and 100.*

EXAMPLES.

1. If by selling cloth at \$5 per yard I gain 25%, what per cent. will I gain if I sell it at \$6 per yard?

$100 + 25 = 125 \qquad 125 \times 6 = 750$

$750 \div 5 = 150 \qquad 150 - 100 = 50.$ Ans. 50%.

2. Sold flour for \$10, and lost 20%. What per cent. would I have lost if I had sold it for \$8? Ans. 36%.

PREMIUM AND DISCOUNT.

188. Premium is the percentage by which an amount is increased. **Discount,** the percentage by which an amount is diminished.

189. In purchasing one currency with another of different value, the discount on that of the highest value is not the same as the premium on that of the lowest at the same rate.

\$100 in currency, at a discount of 5%, is worth \$95 in gold. \$95 in gold, at a premium of 5%, is worth $95 + 4.75 = 99.75$.

190. Merchants are usually allowed a discount of 5% on invoices and bills purchased at 6 months' credit, for cash payment within 30 days. The 5% is allowed on the amount of the bill or invoice; but often, when part is paid, the discount is calculated on the cash payment, instead of on the proportion of the bill settled, which causes a loss to the purchaser. If an invoice costs \$2500, and \$1900 is paid, it will cancel \$2000, thus saving to the purchaser \$100; but if the 5% is calculated on \$1900, the amount paid, the payment will cancel only \$1995, making a difference of \$5 between the two methods.

191. To find what amount is settled when part only is paid, a discount on sales being allowed for prompt payment.

RULE.—*Annex two ciphers to the cash payment, and divide by 100 less the rate per cent. of discount.*

$100 - 5 = 95 \quad 190000 \div 95 = 2000.$ Ans. \$2000.

By Analysis.—If 5% discount is allowed, \$95 will pay a bill of \$100, and \$1900 will pay as many hundreds as 95 is contained times in it, = 2000, the answer.

By Proportion.—95 : 100 : : 1900 : 2000.

The difference between 5% on the amount of invoice and 5% on the amount of cash paid equals 25 cents for every \$100 of the invoice; at 6%, the difference equals 36 cts.; at 3%, 9 cts.

TABLE

Showing the Comparative Value of Gold and Currency.

When \$1 in Gold is sold for Currency at	The Discount on Currency is	The Amount in Gold which can be bought for \$100 in Currency.
1.05 or 5 per cent. Prem.	4.77 per cent.	\$95.23 or \$95$\frac{25}{105}$ accurately.
1.10 " 10 " "	9.10 "	90.90 " 90$\frac{10}{11}$ "
1.15 " 15 " "	13.04 "	86.96 " 86$\frac{20}{23}$ "
1.20 " 20 " "	16.67 "	83.33 " 83$\frac{1}{3}$ "
1.25 " 25 " "	20.00 "	80.00 " 80 "
1.30 " 30 " "	23.08 "	76.92 " 76$\frac{12}{13}$ "
1.40 " 40 " "	28.58 "	71.42 " 71$\frac{3}{7}$ "
1.50 " 50 " "	33.33 "	66.66 " 66$\frac{2}{3}$ "
1.60 " 60 " "	37.50 "	62.50 " 62$\frac{1}{2}$ "
1.70 " 70 " "	41.18 "	58.82 " 58$\frac{14}{17}$ "
1.80 " 80 " "	44.45 "	55.55 " 55$\frac{5}{9}$ "
1.90 " 90 " "	47.37 "	52.63 " 52$\frac{12}{19}$ "
2.00 " 100 " "	50.00 "	50.00 " 50 "
2.50 " 150 " "	60.00 "	40.00 " 40 "
5.00 " 400 " "	80.00 "	20.00 " 20 "
7.50 " 650 " "	86.67 "	13.33 " 13$\frac{1}{3}$ "
10.00 " 900 " "	90.00 "	10.00 " 10 "
50.00 " 4900 " "	98.00 "	2.00 " 2 "
100.00 " 9900 " "	99.00 "	1.00 " 1 "

The accuracy of the above figures can be tested by simply adding to those in the last column that per cent. of each which is designated in the column containing the rate of premium.

The above Table may also be used for finding what rate taken off the selling price is equivalent to a certain rate added to the cost or purchase price. For instance, 20%, as shown in the discount column, deducted, is equivalent to 25% added to the remainder, as shown in the premium column.

To find how much gold can be bought for a given amount of currency. *Multiply the amount of currency by 100, and divide the product by 100 increased by the rate of premium on gold.*

DISCOUNTING BILLS AND INVOICES.

192. In discounting Bills and Invoices, losses sometimes occur when they are not suspected. If an article is sold at a profit of 40%, and 10% be deducted from the selling price, the gain is not 30%, but 26%, because the discount is calculated on the first cost and also on the profit, whereas the profit is calculated on the first cost only. So, also, if 40% be added, and then 30% deducted, the apparent profit is 10%, but the *real loss* is 2%.

Cost,	$200	Cost,	$1.00
40 per cent.,	80	40 per cent.,	.40
Advanced price,	280	Advanced price,	1.40
Less 10 per cent.,	28	Less 30 per cent.,	.42
Cash price,	252	Cash price,	.98
26 per cent. profit.		2 per cent. loss.	
10 per cent. of $200 (cost)	= $20	30 per cent. of $1.00 (cost)	= .30
10 per cent. of $80 (profit)	= 8	30 per cent of .40 (profit)	= .12
	$28		.42
= 14 per ct. of cost.		or 42 per ct. of cost.	

Ex. 10.—What is the difference between discounting a bill of $1200 at 40%, and then taking a discount off the remainder of 5% for cash payment, and discounting the whole bill at 45%?

Ex. 11.—If a merchant buys a book at a discount of 20% on the retail price, and sells it at the retail price, what per cent. on the purchase-price does he gain? What per cent. does he gain if he buys at 33⅓% discount and sells it at the retail price?

193. To find the selling price from which a certain per cent. may be deducted and the goods sold at cost, or a given per cent. above or below cost.

RULE.—To sell at cost.

Multiply the cost by 100, and divide the product by 100 diminished by the rate per cent. to be deducted.

To sell at a given rate per cent. above or below cost.

Multiply 100 increased by the per cent. to be gained or diminished by the per cent. to be lost, by the cost, and divide the product by 100 diminished by the rate to be deducted from the selling price.

EXAMPLES.

1. Bought goods for $100: for how much shall I sell them that I may deduct 20% and yet obtain what they cost?

$100 \times 100 = 10000$
$10000 \div 80 = 125.$ Ans. $125.

2. For what must I sell goods worth $100, so that I may deduct 45% and yet gain 30%?

$100 + 30 = 130$ $100 \times 130 = 13000$
$13000 \div 55 = 236.31.$ Ans. $236.31.

NOTE.—236.31 = 136.31% advance on 100. When a long list is to be made out at a uniform rate of profit, labor may be saved by adding the total advance at once.

3. If I buy cloth for $1.90 per yard, at what price must I mark it, that I may deduct 5% for my cash customers from the marked price, and yet gain 20%? Ans. $2.40.

4. A bookseller wishes to increase the price of a book which he now sells for $2, so that he can deduct 20% and yet receive the present price. What must be the advanced price?

5. A dry-goods merchant sells cloths for $168, by which he gains 20%. What must be the advanced price so that he can deduct 5% and still make the same profit?

6. What must be the price from which 20% may be deducted and leave 40 cts.?

7. Bought cassimeres for $1.20 per yard: at what price must they be sold that 5% may be deducted for cash payment and leave a profit of 25%?

8. Find the selling price of French plate glass that cost $60 per light, from which 45% may be deducted and 30% gained on cost.

What is the selling price of the goods in the following invoice, so that 25% may be gained on the prices given, and yet allow a discount of 5% for cash payment?

PHILADELPHIA, April 20, 1867.

Mr. CHAS. P. GREGORY

Bo't of J. J. BAILEY & Co.

1 doz. long shawls,	@ $6 75	81	00
2 pieces sheeting, 30.35 yds.,	" .15		
6 doz. linen hdkfs.,	" .30		
3 pieces twilled muslin, 84 yds.,	" .20		
1 piece mousseline de laine, 32 yds.,	" .24		

PHILADELPHIA, March 12, 1867.

J. HARRIS BROWN

Bo't of MYERS & CLAGHORN.

240 yds. ingrain carpet, @ $1.20,	288	00
Less 5%,	14	40
	$273	60
Rec'd payment, MYERS & CLAGHORN, per J. B. JONES.		
Freight and other expenses to Madison,	21	89
	$295	49

At what must I sell the carpeting per yard, to gain 20% and allow a discount of 10% from selling price?

SOLUTION.—5% of $1.20 = 6¢. 1.20 — 6 = 1.14, net cash price per yard in Philadelphia. Charges, 21.89 = 8% of total cost in Philadelphia. 8% of 1.14 = 9+. 1.14 + 9 = $1.23, advanced cost per yard.

Proof.—240 yds. @ $1.23 = $295.20, which, allowing for fractions, is the cost of the invoice.

20% of $1.23 = 25¢, nearly; adding this to the cost, we have $1.48 as the amount to be received. Then, to obtain the selling price, 100 — 10 = 90 148 ÷ 90 = 1.64+. Ans. $1.64 per yd.

Proof.—10% of 1.64 = 16+ 1.64 — 16 = 1.48.

Invoice of Merchandise, marked as in the margin, and forwarded by J. POWERS & Co., *Philadelphia, per Penna. R.R., to Messrs.* BROWN & GREGG, *Chicago, as per their order and at their risk.*

		$	cts.
B. & G.	25 Boxes Valencia Raisins, Gross weight, 710 lbs. Tare, 4½ lbs. per box, 112½ " 597½ @ 15 cts.	89	62½
B. & G.	5 Bags Canary Seed, 1184 lbs. — 15 lbs. tare = 1169 net, 19$\frac{29}{60}$ bushels @ 4.85,	94	49
B. & G.	10 Bbls. Currants, 266, 254, 236, 264, 244, 243, 260, 260, 260, 243, Total, 2530 Tare, 26 lbs. per bbl. 260 2270 @ 18c.	408	60
B. & G.	10 Boxes Castile Soap, 406 lbs. Tare, 8 lbs. per box, 80 326 lbs. @ 14c.	45	64
B. & G.	5 Cases ¼ Sardines, 500 boxes @ 35c.	175	00
		813	35
	Cartage, 3.00 Ins. on $900 @ ½ per cent. 4.50	7	50
		820	85
	Rec'd Payment, J. POWERS & Co.		

Charges in Chicago :—

Freight on 4050 lbs. @ $1.10 per h'd.	44.55
Cartage,	3.00
	47.55

Total charges equal 7%, nearly, of first cost of goods.

What must be the selling prices in the above invoice, that I may gain 30%?

SOLUTION.

Total invoice price,		$813.35
Charges in Philada.	$7.50	
Chicago,	47.55	55.05
Total cost,		$868.40

55.05 = 7%, nearly, of $813.35.

	Invoice Price.				Selling Price.
Raisins,	15c.	+ 7%	= 16c.,	increased 30%	= .21
Canary Seed,	4.85	+ "	= 5.19	" "	= 6.75
Currants,	.18	+ "	= .19	" "	= .25
Castile Soap,	.14	+ "	= .15	" "	= .20
Sardines,	.35	+ "	= .37	" "	= .48

The above is given simply as an exercise in calculation. Goods are not generally sold at a uniform rate of profit.

IMPORTERS' ADVANCE TABLE,

Showing the value of Sterling Money from 1 penny to £5, at par, and at an advance from 7½ to 50 per cent.

Invoice price.	ADVANCE PER CENT.										
	Par.	7½	10	12½	15	20	25	30	33⅓	40	50
s. d.	$ cts.	$ cts.	$ cts.	$ cts.	$ cts.	$ cts.	$ cts.	$ cts.	$ cts.	$ cts.	$ cts.
1d.	.0185	.0199	.0204	.0208	.021	.0222	.0231	.0241	.0261	.0259	.0278
6	.11	.12	.13	.13	.13	.13	.14	.14	.15	.15½	.16¾
7	.13	.14	.14	.15	.15	.16	.16	.17	.17	.18¼	.19½
8	.14¾	.16	.16	.17	.17	.18	.19	.19	.20	.20¾	.22½
9	.16¾	.18	.18	.19	.19	.20	.21	.22	.22	.23¼	.25
10	.18½	.20	.20	.21	.21	.22	.23	.24	.25	.26	.27¾
11	.20¼	.22	.22	.23	.23	.24	.25	.27	.27	.28½	.30½
1s.0	.22¼	.24	.24	.25	.26	.27	.28	.29	.30	.31	.33¼
1 1	.24	.26	.26	.27	.28	.29	.30	.31	.32	.33¾	.36
1 2	.26	.28	.29	.29	.30	.31	.32	.34	.35	.36¼	.39
1 3	.27¾	.30	.31	.31	.32	.33	.35	.36	.37	.39	.41¾
1 4	.29½	.32	.33	.33	.34	.36	.37	.39	.40	.41½	.44½
1 5	.31½	.34	.35	.35	.36	.38	.39	.41	.42	.44	.47¼
1 6	.33¼	.36	.37	.38	.38	.40	.42	.43	.44	.46¾	.50
1 7	.35¼	.38	.39	.40	.40	.42	.44	.46	.47	.49¼	.52¾
1 8	.37	.40	.41	.42	.43	.44	.46	.48	.49	.51¾	.55½
1 9	.39	.42	.43	.44	.45	.47	.49	.51	.52	.54½	.58¼
1 10	.40¾	.44	.45	.46	.47	.49	.51	.53	.54	.57	.61
1 11	.42½	.46	.47	.48	.49	.51	.53	.55	.57	.59½	.64
2 0	.44½	.48	.49	.50	.51	.53	.56	.58	.59	.62¼	.66¾
3	.66¾	.72	.73	.75	.77	.80	.83	.87	.89	.93¼	1.00
4	.89	.96	.98	1.00	1.02	1.07	1.11	1.16	1.19	1.24½	1.33¼
5	1.11	1.19	1.22	1.25	1.28	1.33	1.39	1.44	1.48	1.50	1.66¾
6	1.33¼	1.43	1.47	1.50	1.53	1.60	1.66	1.73	1.78	1.86¾	2.00
7	1.55½	1.67	1.71	1.75	1.79	1.87	1.94	2.02	2.07	2.17¾	2.33¼
8	1.77¾	1.91	1.96	2.00	2.04	2.13	2.22	2.31	2.37	2.49	2.66¾
9	2.00	2.15	2.20	2.25	2.30	2.40	2.50	2.60	2.67	2.80	3.00
10	2.22¼	2.39	2.44	2.50	2.56	2.67	2.78	2.89	2.96	3.11	3.33¼
£1	4.44½	4.78	4.89	5.00	5.11	5.33	5.56	5.78	5.93	6.22¼	6.66¾
2	8.89	9.56	9.78	10.00	10.22	10.67	11.11	11.56	11.85	12.44½	13.33½
3	13.33⅓	14.33	14.67	15.00	15.33	16.00	16.66	17.33	17.78	18.66	20.00
4	17.77¾	19.11	19.56	20.00	20.44	21.33	22.22	23.11	23.70	24.89	26.66¾
5	22.22¼	23.89	24.44	25.00	25.56	26.67	27.78	28.89	28.63	31.11	33.33¼

EXPLANATION.—Find the value of an article invoiced at 2 shillings, when the charges on the invoice are 33⅓ per cent. on the cost of the goods:—Look under 33⅓, and opposite 2 shillings, and we have 59,—the advance cost of the article. When the invoice price is not in the table, take the sum of such numbers as will equal the required cost. When the rate of advance is not given, add the required rate to the value in the par column.

Invoice of Queensware shipped by GEORGE HAMMERSLY, *Liverpool, Eng., per "Emily Augusta," and consigned to* MESSRS. FIELD & COGLEY, *Philadelphia, for their account and at their risk.*

			£.	s.	d.	£.	s.	d.
◇ F. & C. 15	36 Teapots, $\frac{18}{18}$ $\frac{18}{24}$, "Niagara" F. Gold Band	27/–	2	7	3			
	18 Sugars, 24 "Niagara" F. Gold Band .	"	1		3			
	18 Creams, 24 " "	6		9				
	20 Bowls, 30 " "	8/–		5	4			
	14 doz. Teas unhd. " "	5/–	3	10				
	27 " Plates, $\frac{4}{5}$ @ 2/–, $\frac{20}{7}$ @ 3/–, $\frac{3}{8}$ @ 3/6, "Niagara" F. Gold Band		3	18	6			
	5 " Dishes, $\frac{2}{10}$ @ 9/–, $\frac{2}{12}$ @ 15/–, $\frac{1}{14}$ @ 21/–, "Niagara" F. G'd Band		3	9				
	5 " Bakers', $\frac{2\frac{1}{2}}{7}$ @ 6/–, $\frac{2\frac{1}{2}}{8}$ @ 9/–, "Niagara" F. Gold Band . . .		1	17	6			
	6 Cover dishes, 92, "Niagara" F. Gd. Bd.	2/3		13	6			
	4 Sauce Tureens Comp., " "	2/6		10				
	10 Pickles, " "	6		5		18	5	4
	25 per cent. discount, ...					4	11	4
						13	14	
	Crate and Straw						13	6
	Shipping Charges						9	10
						14	17	4

	$	c.
Ft. In. 65 11 Freight 13/-	$3	12
£14. 17*s*. 4*d*. at par = ...	66	08
Exchange, 10¼ per cent.	6	76
Insurance, 1¼ per cent. on $5	1	12
Duties and Entry	18	70
Interest from Shipment, ...		54
	$96	32

What is the value of a shilling in the above invoice at the advanced cost price?

Find the percentage of the particular charges and of the general charges of the following invoice; and, also, find the percentage to be added to allow a discount of 5% from the selling price and retain a profit of 25%.

BIRMINGHAM, ENG., April 30, 1867.

Invoice of Hardware purchased by order and for account and risk of H. L. HARRISON & BRO., *Philadelphia, and forwarded to* MESSRS. ALFRED FIELD & CO., *Liverpool, for shipment.*

		£.	s.	d.			
H. L. H. 170 F.	13/6						
	½ doz. Jap'd Oval Trays, 10883, 21 in. . . .		6	9			
	11/- 8/-						
	½ " " " " ea. 10882, 10778, 20 in.		9	6			
	7/3 8/6 10/- 11/6						
	2 " Oval Trays, 7128, ea. 18, 20, 22, 24, in ¼ dozs.		14	6	4	10	9
	Extra pap'g 2 parcels ½*d.*, and 1 @ 8*d.* . .						9
	Case, &c., 5/6; Freight to Liverpool, 4/- . .					9	6
					6	1	0
	171						
	9/9						
	12 doz. Painted Scale Beams, No. B, 12 in. . .	5	17				
	65 per cent. discount . .	3	16	1	2	0	11
	8/- 9/- 10/6 14/-						
	10 gro. Tin'd Kettle-Ears, ea. A, B, 0, 1,						
	16/- 20/- 23/6						
	2, 3, 4, ...	50	10				
	77½ per cent. discount . .	39	2	9	11	7	3
	Cash, &c., 7/6; Freight to Liverpool, 12/3 .					19	9
					14	7	11
	169						
	4/- 2/- } cwt. qr. lb.						
	4 doz. Brt. Ov. Bake Pans, ea. 1.3 } 5 1 5						
	3 " " " " 4.5 } @ 7*d.* ℔ lb.	17	5	11			
	40 per cent. discount . .	6	18	4	10	7	7
	Cash, &c., 6/-; Freight to Liverpool, 6/6 . .					12	6
					11	0	1
	Amount of Case, 170				6	1	10
	" " Cask, 171				14	7	11
	" " " 169				11	0	1
					31	9	0
	Commission, 4 per cent. . .				1	5	2
	Dock and Town Dues, 1/3; Cartage, Porterage, &c., 4/6; Shipping, 3/-		8	9			
	Bills of Lading, 1/6; Canal Ins. ⅛ per cent., 3/2; Consul's fee, 11/-		15	8	2	4	5
	E. E.				35	8	7
	pro ALFRED FIELD & CO.						
	W. MINCHER.						

Charges on arrival in Philadelphia:—

Duties on case 170, $29, @ 40%,	11.60	
" " cases 171, 169, $123, @ 35%,	43.05	54.65
Brokerage,		2.00
Fees, &c., 2.75, Triplicate Invoice, 1.25,		4.00
Cartage,		3.00
Bonded Warehouse Fees,		7.00
Freight from Liverpool,		18.35
		89.00

In reckoning the cost of goods, the amount of all the charges is found, and then the invoice price of each article is increased in the proportion that the charges bear to the purchase price of the goods. The profits are to be added after finding the total cost.

In foreign invoices, when the prices are in pounds, shillings, or francs, it is frequently found convenient to increase the true value of the pound or franc in the proportion that the charges bear to the purchase price, and then obtain the total cost of each article by taking the currency at this increased valuation. For instance, if the charges were equal to 20% of the first cost of the goods, the shilling would be estimated at an advance of 20% on 22.2c.,—the par value of a shilling,—or at the valuation of 26.6c. Then, 300 yards extra ticking, @ 2 shillings per yard, would be marked as costing $53\frac{1}{5}$c. per yard.

A franc, in an invoice on which the charges are equal to 66% of the invoice, would be reckoned at 66% advance on the exchange value of a franc. Or, the total cost of the invoice in United States currency may be divided by the number of shillings or francs in the total purchase price of the goods.

In the invoice on the next page, the cost is calculated in this manner, no account being taken of the particular discounts or charges, although for strict accuracy this should be done. The entire cost of each item is reckoned at $41\frac{5}{6}$c. per franc. Thus, 4 gross combs, @ 36 fr. per gross, cost $36 \times 41\frac{5}{6} = \$15.06$ per gross.

PARIS, October 16, 1865.

Invoice of One Package Merchandise purchased by J. GLAENZER & VESSEPUY, JR., *of Paris, for account and risk of* MESSRS. E. CLINTON & CO., *of Philadelphia, and shipped at Havre by* SHERBETTE, KANE & CO. *on board the Steamer Bosphorus, bound for New York, and consigned to themselves.*

Marks	Description	fr.	c.	fr.	c.
E. C. & Co. ※134	1 CASE.				
	※ 6. 13 kilo. Beau Blanc Bristles, @ fr.11.50 . .	149	50		
	7. 12 " " " " " 12.50 . .	150	00		
		299	50		
	3 per cent. discount . .	8	95	290	55
	※ 3233. 4 gro. Buffalo Tuck Combs, @ fr.36 net . .	144			
	3234. 3 " " " " " 42 " . .	126			
	3235. 2 " " " " " 48 " . .	96			
	3331. 36 doz. Hair Brushes, " 6 " . .	216		582	00
	2899. 5 gro. Tooth Brushes, 4 R, @ fr.51 . . .	255			
	2900. 5 " " " 5 R, @ fr.63 . . .	315			
		570			
	4 per cent. discount . .	22	80	547	20
	※ 2911. 4 gro. Tooth Brushes, @ fr. 21	84			
	2913. 3 " " " " 33	99			
	" bis 3 " " " " 33	99			
	2919. 3 " " " " 45	135			
	" bis 1 " " " "	45			
		462			
	2 per cent. discount . .	9	20	452	80
				1872	55
	Commission 3 per cent. on fr. 290.55 = 8.70 " 5 " " 1582. = 79.10			87	80
	Packing 20. Boxes 15. Visa 13.40 Postage 5.25			53	65
	Freight from Paris to Havre			10	80
				2024	80
	15 days' interest, @ 6 per cent. . . .			5	05
				2029	85

Charges and Duties paid in New York for account of invoice consigned to E. CLINTON & Co., *Nov. 15/65.*

25 kilos. = lbs. 55, @ fr.15 per lb.,	8	25		
Francs, 290.55 = $54.00				
366. = 68.00 @ 35%,	23	80		
1216. = 226.00 " 40%,	90	40	122	45
1872.55				
Entry Bond, @ $0.50				
Oath, Transfer Order, &c., 1.25				
Postage, .15				
Cartage, .75				
Bond for Triplicate Invoice, .65				
Premium on Gold, @ 47$\frac{3}{8}$%, 58.00				
Contingent Exp. 50¢, Com. 3.50, 4.00	65	30		
Insurance, fr.2024.80, @ 40¢ pr. fr. = $810, @ 2$\frac{1}{4}$%,	18	22		
Freight from Havre to New York, per "Scotland," £1 9*s.* 11*d.* @ 139$\frac{1}{2}$,	9	67		
	215	64		
Freight and Drayage from New York to Philadelphia,	2	00	217	64
Francs 2029.86, @ 5.20,	390	36		
Gold Premium @ 47$\frac{3}{8}$%,	184	93	575	29
			792	93

1872.55 fr. cost $792.93.
Cost of 1 franc, 41$\frac{5}{8}$¢.

NOTE.—25 kilogrammes B. B. Bristles pay a specific duty.

194. The length of credit has much to do with the accumulation of profits. The difference between long credits and short credits is shown in their effects in the following example:—

If a young man commences business with a capital of $1000, and is able to turn it over every *three* months at 10% profit, in five years it will

Amount to	**$6727.50**	If every 3 mos. at 8%,	**$4660.96**
If every 4 mos. at 10%,	4177.25	" 4 " "	3172.17
" 6 " "	2593.74	" 6 " "	2158.93
" 7½ " "	2143.59	" 7½ " "	1850.93
" 10 " "	1771.56	" 10 " "	1586.87
" 12 " "	1610.51	" 12 " "	1469.33
" 2½ yrs. "	1210.00	" 2½ yrs. "	1166.40

195. One of the practical questions to be determined when reducing prices, is, Can enough more goods be sold at the reduced price to compensate for the reduced profits?

QUICK SALES AND SMALL PROFITS.

A man commenced business on a borrowed capital of $4000, and paid interest monthly at the rate of 6% per annum,—that is, $20 per month. His expenses were $180 per month additional. He invariably paid cash, thereby saving 5% discount on the invoice price. He sold his entire stock every month at an advance of 5% on the invoice price, and immediately reinvested the proceeds. What profit did he make by the end of the year? Ans. $4879.18.

ECONOMY THE SOURCE OF WEALTH.

AT COMPOUND INTEREST, IN TEN YEARS,

2¾ cts. a day,	or	$10 a year,	will	become	$130.
11	"	40	"	"	520.
27½	"	100	"	"	1300.
50	"	182.50	"	"	2305.
100	"	365	"	"	4814.

MARKING GOODS.

196. It is customary in many mercantile houses to use a private mark, which is placed on the goods to denote their cost and selling price. A word or phrase containing ten different letters is taken, the letters of which are written instead of figures. For instance, the word "Cumberland" is selected; then the letters represent the figures as follows:—

C	u	m	b	e	r	l	a	n	d
1	2	3	4	5	6	7	8	9	0

If it is required to mark 1.50, it is done thus, *ced;* 75 would be *le;* 37, *ml,* &c.

Blacksmith, Importance, Republican, Perth Amboy, Fair Spoken, Now be sharp, Noisy Table, and Cash Profit, are among the words and phrases which can be used in this manner.

197. It sometimes happens that the selling price contains three figures, while the buying price contains but two. To prevent this difference from being noticed, the letter denoting the cipher is prefixed to the buying price. For instance, if the buying price was 87, it would be marked *dal;* and the selling price, 1.25, *cue;* thus giving each price three letters.

198. An extra letter, called a "Repeater," is used to prevent the repetition of a figure. Instead of writing *cdd* for 100, which would show at once that the two right-hand figures were alike, and thus aid in giving a clue to the key-word, some additional letter would be selected for a repeater,—*y,* for instance,—and then the price would be written *cdy;* 225 would be written *uye.*

199. Instead of letters, arbitrary characters are frequently used, something like the following:—

┘	Z	┬	┐	◺	□	×	‡	⊥	⊓
1	2	3	4	5	6	7	8	9	0

Fractions may be designated by additional letters or characters. Thus, *f* may represent ½, *w* ⅔, &c.; or ½ may be written ◠, ¼ +, &c.

200. The marks on packages, barrels, &c. are often some arbitrary mark, or letter selected at random, or the initials of the purchaser placed there for the purpose of showing that the goods belong to some particular lot, and are put on for the sake of distinction merely.

What is the profit, and what the selling price, of the following?—

			Gain.	Selling Price.
First cost,	$1.10,	Freight, 10%,	20%,	
"	.50,	" 20%,	10%,	
"	1.00,		30%,	
"	4.80,		15%,	
"	2.50,	" 10%,	20%,	
"	1.75,		5%,	
"	3.00,	Charges, 7½%,	25%,	

Mark the selling price of the above, using the word "Cumberland" instead of figures.

Annual Production of the Gold and Silver Mines of the World before 1865. (Value in Francs.)

	Silver.	Gold.
United States and British America	92,888,000	227,333,000
Mexico	103,444,000	14,500,000
New Granada	1,333,000	17,222.000
Peru	28,889,000	4,133,000
Bolivia	13,333,000	2,067,000
Brazil	....	10,333,000
Chili	18,889,000	4,133,000
Other American Countries	5,556,000	3,617,000
	264,332,000	283,338,000
Europe and Australia	47,784,000	418,456,000
Africa, India, China, Japan, &c	111,111,000	275,555.000
	423,227,000	977,349,000

What is the value of the above in United States currency, estimating the franc at 5.18 per dollar, and specie at a premium of 30%?

DIVIDENDS AND INVESTMENTS.

201. Stocks is a general term applied to the bonds of the Government or State, and to the bonds and shares of incorporate companies. They are usually bought and sold, through the medium of brokers, at the Stock Exchange.

202. Bonds are obligations or deeds securing the payment of a certain sum of money on or before a future day appointed.

When issued by governments or corporations, they are made in denominations of convenient size, bearing interest usually payable semi-annually. They frequently have *coupons* or *interest-tickets* attached, bearing date, amount, signature, &c., which are due at the expiration of each successive half-year; these are cut off as they are paid, and held as receipts. For temporary loans, Treasury Notes have also been issued by the United States Government, payable with interest, some with and some without coupons. Exchequer Bills have been issued in England in the same manner.

203. A **Joint Stock Company** is an association of men having a capital that is divided into shares of equal value, which are transferable and may be bought and sold like any other property.

204. Certificates of Stock are issued to each stockholder, indicating the number of shares to which he is entitled. The first or original value of the shares is called their *nominal* or *par value*. When they sell for more than their par value, they are said to be *above par*, or at a *premium;* when for less, *below par*, or at a *discount*.

205. An **Instalment** is a certain portion of the capital paid at a particular time.

206. An **Assessment** is an amount for which the stockholders are called upon to make up deficiencies or losses.

207. The **Gross Earnings** consist of the entire receipts of a company.

208. The **Net Earnings** are what remains after the expenses are deducted.

209. The **Dividend** is the sum divided among the stockholders from the gains of the business.

210. Sometimes, in addition to the cash dividend, which is payable at a stated time, the company declare a *Scrip dividend*, for which certificates are issued payable on the contingency that the affairs of the company continue prosperous. This Scrip bears interest, or not, as the company may determine. (See FORM OF CERTIFICATE OF SCRIP.)

211. A **Mortgage** is a conveyance of property as a pledge for the security of a debt, and becomes void when the debt is paid.

212. **Ground-Rents** is a term applied to leases of building lots, the rent of which is considered equivalent to the interest on the valuation of the land. The payment is generally secured by a claim on the building erected on the land occupied. By a recent law in Pennsylvania, no new ground-rent can be made irredeemable, but may be extinguished upon payment of a sum the interest of which is equal to the rent annually paid.

213. **Building Lots** are sometimes sold at so much per foot. The price is obtained by dividing the interest per annum on the valuation of the whole lot by the number of feet on the front; the quotient is the price per foot. Thus, a lot valued at $3000, with a front of 20 feet, is said to be worth $9 per foot; the interest on $3000, which is $180 per annum, being divided by 20, the number of feet on the front, gives $9 as the price.

214. The value of an investment depends upon its **security,** its **productiveness,** its **permanency,** its **facility of transfer,** and the **readiness** with which the income derived from it may be collected.

National Debt of the United States.

The following is a statement of the Public Debt of the United States on the 1st of March, 1866:—

Debt bearing Coin Interest.

6 per cent. Bonds, Dec. 31, 1867, and July 1, 1868	$18,323,591.80	
5 per cent. Bonds, Jan. 1, 1874	20,000,000.00	
5 per cent. Bonds, Jan. 1, 1871	7,022,000.00	
6 per cent. Bonds, Dec. 31, 1880, and June 30, 1881, called 6's of '81	282,693,100.00	
6 per cent. 5-20 Bonds, May 1, 1867, or May 1, 1882, int. May and Nov.	514,780,500.00	
6 per cent. 5-20 Bonds, Nov. 1, 1869, or Nov. 1, 1884, int. May and Nov.	100,000,000.00	
6 per cent. 5-20 Bonds, Nov. 1, 1870, or Nov. 1, 1885	61,263,000.00	
5 per cent. 10-40 Bonds, March 1, 1874, or March 1, 1904	172,769,100.00	
6 per cent. Bonds, Oregon War., July 1, 1881	1,016,000.00	$1,177,867,291.80

Debt bearing Currency Interest.

6 per cent. Bonds, Union Pacific R.R. Co., Nov. 1, 1895	$1,632,000.00	
6 per cent. Bonds, Central Pacific R.R. Co., Jan. 16, 1895	2,362,000.00	
4, 5, 6 per cent. Temporary Loan, ten days' notice after thirty days	118,577,939.50	
Certificates of Indebtedness 1 year from date	62,264,000.00	
1 and 2 year 5 per cent. notes, 1 and 2 years from date	8,536,900.00	
3-year Compound Interest Notes, 3 years from date,	174,012,141.00	
3-year 7-30 Treasury Notes, 3 years from date	818,044,000.00	$1,185,428,980.50

Matured Debt not presented for Payment.

Texas Indemnity Bonds	$618,000.00	
3-year 7-30 Treasury Notes	167,350.00	
Bonds	81,268.00	
Treasury Notes	118,161.64	
Temporary Loan, coin	1,200.00	$985,979.64

Debt bearing no Interest.

United States Notes	$423,435,373.00	
Fractional Currency	27,523,734.[illegible]2	
Gold Certificates of Deposit	12,627,600.00	$463,586,707.52
Total Debt		$2,827,868,959.46

The Public Debt of the United States on the 1st of March, 1867:—

Debt bearing Coin Interest.

5 per cent. Bonds	$198,091,350.00	
6 per cent. Bonds, '67 and '68	15,679,591.80	
6 per cent. Bonds, 1881	283,745,250.00	
6 per cent. 5-20 Bonds	954,839,000.00	
Navy Pension Fund	12,500,000.00	$1,464,855,191.80

Debt bearing Currency Interest.

6 per cent. Bonds	$12,922,000.00	
3 year Compound Interest Notes	141,308,830.00	
3 year 7-30 Notes	632,798,050.00	$787,028,880.00
Matured Debt not presented for payment		14,576,689.07
United States Notes	$376,235,626.00	
Fractional Currency	29,514,722.32	
Gold Certificates of Deposit	18,376,180.00	424,126,528.32
Total Debt		$2,690,587,289.19

Amount in the Treasury.

Coin	$107,271,031.12	
Currency	52,552,368.27	159,823,399.39
Amount of Debt, less cash, in Treasury		$2,530,763,889.80

The foregoing is a correct statement of the public debt, as appears from the books and Treasurer's returns in the Department on the 1st of March, 1867. (Signed) Hugh McCulloch,
Secretary of the Treasury.

Reduction of debt in one year $137,281,670.00

Amount in Treasury

	March 1, 1866.	March 1, 1867.
Coin	$55,736,192	$107,271,031
Currency	60,282,767	52.552,368
Total	$116,018,959	$159,823,399

Debt, less amount in Treasury March 1, 1866	$2,711,850,000
Debt, less amount in Treasury March 1, 1867	2,530,763,890
Actual reduction of debt in one year	$181,086,110

At this rate of reduction, the entire debt could be paid in fifteen years.

Receipts and Expenditures of the United States for the year ending June 30th, 1866.

RECEIPTS.		EXPENDITURES.	
From Customs	$179,046,630.64	Civil, Foreign and Mis.	$41,049,965.96
From Public Lands	665,031.03	Pensions and Indians	16,253,300.44
From Direct Tax	1,974,754.12	War	284,449,701.82
From Internal Revenue	309,226,812.81	Navy	43,519,632.21
From Miscellaneous	65,125,966.46	Interest	133,074,737.27
Total	$556,039,195.06	Total	$518,347,337.70

Total receipts	$556,039,195.06
Total expenditures	518,347,337.70
Excess of receipts	$37,691,857.36

UNITED STATES BONDS.

215. The term "**Five-Twenties**" is applied to the 6% gold-bearing bonds of the United States, to which twenty years' half-yearly coupons are attached, but which may be paid off in gold by the Government, on due notice to the holders, at any time after *five years*.

216. The **5-20's** which were issued MAY 1, 1862, called "Old 5-20's," because they were the first issued, are redeemable after May 1, 1867, payable May 1, 1882. They bear interest at 6% payable on May 1st and November 1st.

217. The **5-20's of 1864** were issued November 1, 1864. Interest payable May 1st and November 1st.

218. The **5-20's of 1865,** NOVEMBER ISSUE, bear date November 1, 1865. Interest payable May 1st and November 1st.

219. The **5-20's of 1865,** JULY ISSUE, are issued in exchange for 7-30's, and bear date July 1, 1865. Interest on them is payable January 1st and July 1st.

220. The term "**Ten-Forties**" is applied to the 5% gold-bearing bonds of the United States, to which half-yearly coupons are attached for 40 years, but which may be paid off in gold, on notice to the holders, at any time after 10 years. Interest on them is payable, on the $500 and $1000 coupon bonds, and on all the registered bonds, March 1st and September 1st; and on the $100 and $50 coupon bonds yearly, on March 1st.

221. The "**Seven-Thirties**" represent a *Currency* Loan having 3 years to run, then convertible at the option of the holder into a gold-interest 6% stock having 20 years to run, but with the right reserved to the Government of paying off the loan in gold at any time after five years. The term "Seven-Thirties" is derived from the rate of interest which these three years' convertible notes bear, to wit: 2 cents per day on each $100, or for 365 days, seven dollars and thirty cents on each $100.

222. The **First Series 7-30 Treasury Notes** are dated August 15, 1864, and interest on them is payable in currency August 15th and February 15th.

223. **Second Series 7-30 Notes,** the same as first, except that they bear date June 15, 1865, and interest is payable June 15th and December 15th. They are convertible June 15, 1868, either into 5-20 bonds or money, at the option of the holder.

224. The **Third Series 7-30 Notes,** same as the first two, except that the Government reserves the right to pay the interest at any time at 6% in gold instead of $7\frac{3}{10}$ in currency, convertible 3 years from their date, viz., July 15, 1865, into 5-20's. Interest payable July 15th and January 15th.

225. The **6 per cents. of 1881,** sometimes called the long or unconditional 6% gold-bearing loan, cannot be redeemed by the Government at all, except by purchase, until after the year 1881, making this the most desirable of all the United States loans as a permanent investment. Interest on them is payable January 1st and July 1st.

226. The terms "Greenbacks" and "Legal-Tenders" are convertible. All the Greenbacks are legal tender.

All gold-bearing bonds are either coupon or registered.

All the coupon bonds are issued in denominations of $50, $100, $500, and $1000. Registered bonds the same, with $5000 and $10,000 additional.

The 7-30 Notes are issued in sums of $50, $100, $500, $1000, and $5000, all with coupons attached.

Any coupon bonds will be exchanged by the Government for registered of the same issue.

UNITED STATES TREASURY DEPARTMENT REGULATIONS.

227. INSTRUCTIONS TO CORRESPONDENTS.—"Letters relating to the redemption of public securities, the conversion of $7\frac{3}{10}$ Treasury Notes, or the exchange of coupon bonds for registered certificates, should be addressed to the Secretary of the Treasury. Letters relating to the transfer of registered stock, or payment of interest on the same, should be addressed to the Register of the Treasury. The transfer-books are closed for thirty days previous to the day for payment of dividends, and stockholders desiring the place of payment changed, must give notice to the Register one month at least before the day of payment. When bonds are sent for transfer, state where interest is to be made payable, and always inclose stock of different loans in separate letters. When specifying the different loans, or referring to the interest, name the amount of stock, and describe the loan by the date of the act of Congress authorizing it. Powers of attorney for the assignment of United States stock, and assignments, must be properly filled before transmission to the Register, as no blanks can be filled in his office. Powers of attorney to draw interest should be addressed to the First Auditor of the Treasury."

228. The **National Debt of Great Britain** is of two kinds, funded and unfunded. When a certain portion of the public revenue is appropriated for the payment of the interest on the debt, it is called funded, and it is called unfunded when no such division is made. *Exchequer Bills* (see FORMS), which are somewhat similar to United States interest-bearing Treasury Notes, are a part of the unfunded debt. England has effected loans at different rates, 5, 4, $3\frac{1}{2}$, 3 per cent., &c.; and one of the conditions of such loans is, that while the stipulated interest is regularly paid, the Government cannot be called upon to return the principal.

229. Consols are a 3% English stock, which had its origin in the act of Parliament *consolidating* several separate Government stocks, called in the act *Consolidated Annuities*, and commonly quoted, for brevity, "Consols."

The stock, from its amount, and the immense number of its holders, is more sensitive to financial influence than any other. Its dividends are payable semi-annually,—January 5th and July 5th.

230. The other kinds of stock, bearing 3%, are the *Reduced Annuities*, which formerly bore a higher rate of interest, and the New Three per cent. Annuities.

NATIONAL DEBTS.

	Debt.	Population.	Average Amount per capita.
Great Britain,	$3,999,010,695	30,000,000	133.33
United States,	2,827,868,959	35,000,000	87.70
France,	2,000,000,000	36,500,000	54.79
Austria,	1,580,000,000	75,000,000	21.06
Russia,	1,395,000,000	68,932,000	20.23
Italy,	770,000,000	21,770,000	35.37
Spain,	745,000,000	16,000,000	46.56
Netherlands,	425,000,000	3,619,000	117.43
Turkey,	255,000,000	16,440,000	15.51
Prussia,	215,000,000	18,000,000	11.94
Portugal,	165,000,000	4,000,000	41.25
Hamburg,	23,000,000	222,000	103.60
Greece,	20,000,000	1,000,000	20.00

1. What is the annual interest on the debt of England, at the average rate of 3½ per cent., and what is the proportion for each inhabitant to pay?

2. What is the annual interest on the debt of the United States, as per Statement March 1st, 1867, and how much is each person's share? How much must be raised by the Government annually to pay the interest and cancel the debt in 30 years?

THE STOCK EXCHANGE

231. The Stock Exchange is an association organized for the purpose of buying and selling stock. It is governed by stringent regulations, to prevent improper persons from being admitted, and to insure fidelity in the performance of engagements. The members are elected by ballot; if a certain number of black balls appear against a candidate, he is rejected. In Philadelphia, five are sufficient to prevent his becoming a member.

The admission fee varies: to the New York Stock Exchange it is $3000; to the Philadelphia and the Boston Stock Exchange it is $2000. In London the admission fee is 20 guineas, besides a yearly subscription of 10 guineas. The fee to become a member of the New York Open Board is $2000; to the Gold Board it is $2500. There are no dues to be paid in addition, but members are fined for non-attendance.

Rules are enacted by which the proceedings of the Exchange are governed, disputes settled, and by which the prices and terms in buying and selling stocks are regulated. The charges in our large cities for buying and selling United States bonds are ⅛ per cent., or 12½ cents for a bond of $100; for other bonds, ¼ per cent., or 25 cents per $100; for shares of companies, ¼ per cent., or 25 cents per share when the par value of the shares is $50 or more; when the par value is between $5 and $50, ⅛ per cent., or 12½ cents per share; when $5 or less, 6¼ cents per share. In London, the commission on the sale or purchase of stock in the English or foreign funds is ⅛, or 2*s.* 6*d.* per cent.; on exchequer bills, 1*s.* per cent.; on railway shares, when over £50 in value, ½ per cent. upon the value.

Stock is bought and sold during the sessions, or "boards," as they are termed, at which time a clerk calls the names of the different stocks in the market, and the members offer to sell or to buy at a price which they mention.

A charge against a member is instantly investigated, and, if he is found guilty of misconduct, or fails to fulfil his engagements, he is expelled.

The Stock Exchange has a language peculiar to itself. A stock "broker" is one who receives and executes orders for persons who are not members of the exchange. A stock "jobber" deals in stocks for his own account. A "stag," or "outsider," conducts his transactions outside the Exchange.

A "bull" is one who operates for a rise in prices,—so called from the nature of a bull to toss with his horns. He is usually one who has agreed to purchase stock, without any intention of holding or paying for it, but with a view to sell out again before "settling-day" arrives. A "bear" is one who endeavors to depress prices,—so called from the nature of a bear to tear down with his claws. He, generally, has agreed to deliver more stock than he possesses, and is consequently obliged to buy in order to settle his account. A "lame duck" is a member unable to fulfil his contracts, and is therefore expelled.

"Opening-day" is the first day the books of a corporation are opened after a dividend has been declared.

The term "selling short" is applied to sales of stock which the seller does not own, and over which he has no control. Securities sold in this manner are generally deliverable at a specified time, not exceeding 60 days. If the contract is for a longer period than three days, the seller receives interest.

"Seller's option" gives the person selling the privilege of making delivery at any time intervening before the expiration of that mentioned in the contract, by his giving one day's notice. "Buyer's option" gives the purchaser a claim for delivery at any time before the maturity of the contract, by a similar notice. The contract must be settled at least by maturity, unless extended by mutual agreement. The transactions are adjusted by delivery of property, or the payment in cash of the difference in prices. A postponement of settling-day is termed a "contango." By a law in Pennsylvania, contracts for the sale of stock to be executed or performed at any future period exceeding five judicial days next ensuing the date of such contracts, are prohibited under heavy penalties.

The "cornering" process, or "getting up a corner," is the act of a combination of operators, and is always the result of short sales. All the floating shares of a company are bought for future delivery, and when the stock has been rendered scarce in this manner, the shares thus bought are suddenly called for, to the loss of the short sellers, who are obliged to buy at an advanced rate, or pay the buyer the difference in price.

The following extract was taken from the *United States Gazette*:—

REPORTED BY JAY COOKE & CO., BANKERS.

SALES.		EXPLANATION.
26000 U. S. 5-20 bonds,	103⅝	5-20 bonds at $3.62½ premium.
100 Reading R.R., 2 ds.,	51⅜	Railroad stock sold at 2 days' credit.
100 " " 5 w.n.,		" " to be delivered before five days, without notice.
1000 Camden & Amboy 6's, 1889,	108½	6 per cent. bonds, due in 1889, at 8½ per cent. premium.
100 Reading R.R., b. 30,	67¾	To be delivered before 30 days.
100 N. Y. Central, b. 15 and int.,	103	" " before 15 days, with int.
15500 U. S. 6's, 1881, lots,	109½	U. S. 6 per cent. bonds, due in 1881, sold in lots, aggregating $15,500.
100 U. S. Treasury 7-30 F. & A.,	111¼	7-30 bonds, interest payable in February and August. A. & O. means Apr. & Oct.
100 Catawissa pref. s., w.n.,	26	Catawissa preferred stock, without notice.
2000 Penna. R.R., 2d M., 6's,	100¼	Second mortgage, bearing 6 per cent. int.
100 Penna. 6's, int. off,	104	Penna. 6 per cent. bonds, the interest last due having been paid.
100 " 5's,	99½	Penna. 6 per cent. bonds, bearing 5 per cent. interest.
400 " R.R. ex. div.,	75	Penna. R.R. shares without dividend.
500 Phila. & Erie R.R., b.o.,	32	500 shares at $32, at buyer's option when to take the stock.
300 " " " s.o.,	31	300 shares at $31, at seller's option when to deliver the stock.

The value of a given number of shares is found by multiplying the number of shares by the price per share.

NOTE.—In finding the cost of bonds, the rate of brokerage may be added to the price, as the brokerage and price are both calculated on the same amount.

EXAMPLE 1.—What must I pay for 100 shares of Chicago & Rock Island R.R. stock, purchased at $112.50 per share, brokerage at ¼% and revenue stamp included?

100 shares @ $112.50,	$11250.
¼% on $10000, par value of 100 shares,	25.
Revenue stamp, 1c. on every $100 of sales,	1.13
	$11276.13

Ex. 2.—What will I receive if I sell 300 shares Cleveland & Pittsburg R.R. stock, @ $72.00, after paying for revenue stamp and brokerage @ ¼% per share?

$72 × 300 = $21600

300 shares at ¼% per share (par value, $50) =	$75.00
Revenue stamp,	2.16
	$77.16

$21600 — 77.16 = $21522.84, Ans.

To find the dividend on any given number of shares of stock.

RULE.—*Multiply the par value of the stock by the rate of dividend, and divide the product by 100.*

EXAMPLES.

1. If I own 100 shares of Penna. Railroad stock, the par value of which is $50, how much will I receive when a dividend of 5% is declared?

50 × 5 = 2.50, dividend on 1 share.
100 × 2.50 = 250, " " 100 shares. Ans. $250.

2. How much will a stockholder of the New York Central Railroad Co. receive of a 4% dividend, who owns 500 shares, the par value being $100 per share?

232. To find the rate of dividend.

RULE.—*Multiply the dividend by 100, and divide by the par value of the stock.*

EXAMPLES.

1. The receipts of a mining company in one year are $170,000, clear of all expenses. The company has a capital of $500,000, divided into shares of $10 each. Reserving $50,000 as a contingent fund, what rate of dividend can it declare for the year? what per month? and how much can be paid on each share of stock?

170000 — 50000 = 120000, amount to be divided.
120000 × 100 = 12000000   12000000 ÷ 500000 = 24.

Ans. 24% yearly, 2% monthly, 20c. per month on each share.

PROOF.—24% of 500000 = 120000, dividend to be declared.

2. A man subscribed for 300 shares of stock in a manufacturing company, the par value of which was placed at $50 per share; but, after paying three instalments, amounting to 75% per cent. of the par value, a dividend of 3% was declared. How much will he receive, and at what rate per cent. on the actual cost?

3% of 50 = 1.50, dividend on one share.
1.50 × 300 = $450, dividend on 300 shares.
75% of 50 = $37.50
1.50 × 100 = 150.00   150.00 ÷ 37.50 = 4
Ans. $450. Total dividend = 4% on actual cost.

233. To find what rate of income will be derived from a given investment.

RULE.—*Multiply the income by 100, and divide the product by the amount invested.*

EXAMPLES.

1. If I buy railroad stock at a premium of 6 per cent., and pay ¼ per cent. brokerage, what per cent. of income will I receive if its annual dividend is 7 per cent.?

7 × 100 = 700   700 ÷ 106¼ = $6\frac{10}{17}$ Ans. $6\frac{10}{17}$%.

2. What per cent. will I receive if I buy stock, which pays 4% dividend, at a discount of 20%?

100 — 20 = 80, amount invested.
4 × 100 = 400   400 ÷ 80 = 5   Ans. 5%.

3. If I pay 106 for United States 6% bonds, having 15 years to run, what per cent. will I receive if I keep them until they mature, and then obtain the principal?

6% per year for 15 years =	$90 interest.
Principal,	100
Total amount received,	190
Cost of bond,	106
Total income,	84

To find what rate is required for 106 to gain 84 in 15 years, see Art. 79.

106 at 1% = 1.06 × 15 = 15.90, interest at 1% for 15 years.

```
15.90)8400(5.283+        Ans. 5 283/1000 %.
      7950
      ----
       4500
       3180
       ----
       13200
       12720
       -----
         4800
         4770
         ----
```

NOTE.—The interest on the semi-annual payments of interest is also to be considered.

4. What rate per cent. will be gained if I purchase United States 5-20 bonds, at a premium of 8%, if they are paid at the end of 6 years? Ans. $4\frac{26}{81}$.

234. To find the price to be paid for stock to obtain a given rate upon the investment.

RULE.—*Annex two ciphers to the rate per cent. which the stock produces, and divide by the required rate; the quotient will be the price to be paid.*

EXAMPLES.

1. At what price must railroad stock be purchased, which pays 6% on the par value of $100, in order to obtain 7% income on the investment?

$600 \div 7 = 85.71\frac{3}{7}$ Ans. $85.71.

2. At what price must I purchase railroad stock of the par value of $50 per share, which pays a dividend of 6%, that I may obtain an income of 8% on the investment?

Ans. $37.50.

3. If I receive 9% on my investment in a company which pays a dividend of 6%, at what price did I purchase?

4. At what price must 5% stock be purchased in order to obtain 6% on the investment?

5. At what premium ought an 8% stock to sell, to equal 6% stock? Ans. $33\frac{1}{3}$.

6. At what rate must 6% stock be purchased to equal 8% stock? to equal 10% stock?

235. To find what rate must be obtained, that a given sum invested may bring a given income.

RULE.—*Multiply the given income by 100, and divide the product by the sum invested.*

EXAMPLE.

If I invest $5000, what rate per cent. must I receive to obtain an income of $325 per year?

$$32500 \div 5000 = 6\tfrac{1}{2}\%.$$

236. To find what sum must be invested, that a given income may be obtained.

RULE.—*Divide the required income by the rate of income per share, or per $100, for the number of shares or bonds required, and multiply the quotient by the given price.*

EXAMPLES.

1. What sum must be invested in United States 6% bonds, at 108, to realize an income of $1200 per annum?

$6 = income per $100,—$108 the price of $100 bonds.
1200 ÷ 6 = 200, the number of bonds of $100 each.
200 × 108 = 21600.

Ans. $21600.

2. What sum must be invested, at $65 per share, in railroad stock which pays a dividend of 10% on the par value of $50 per share, in order to obtain an income of $520?

10% of $50 = $5, income per share.
$520 ÷ $5 = 104, the number of shares.
104 × $65 = $6760. Ans. $6760.

3. If United States *Ten-Forties* are selling at 93, how much must I invest in them to obtain a yearly income of $1800, after paying 5% income tax?

237. To find the par value, when the premium or discount is given.

RULE.—*Divide the given value of the stock by 1 increased by the rate per cent. of premium, or diminished by the rate per cent. of discount.*

EXAMPLES.

1. Bought Mechanics' National Bank stock for 29, at which price I paid a premium of 16%. What is the par value? Ans. $25.

2. Sold Worcester & Nashua Railroad stock for $91.66⅔, and received 10% above the par value. What is the par value? Ans. $83.33⅓.

3. Bought Philadelphia & Erie Railroad stock for $47, which is 6% below par. What is the par value?

4. Bought Fulton Bank stock at 500% premium, for $180. What is the par value of the shares? Ans. $30.

238. To find at what price a bond, having several years to run, must be purchased, that the interest and final payment will be equivalent to a given rate per annum on the investment.

RULE.—I. *Find the Amount of the given bond.*

II. *Find the present worth of this amount at the proposed rate.*

NOTE.—No account is taken in this rule of interest on the annual payments of interest.

EXAMPLES.

1. What shall I pay for a bond of $100, having 5 years to run, with interest at 6%, in order to make it an 8% investment?

Amount of $100 for 5 years = $130.

By Art. 84, 130 ÷ 1.40 = 92.86. Ans. $92.86.

Interest on $92.86 at 8% for 5 yrs. = 37.14. 92.86 + 37.14 = 130.

2. At what price must I buy United States 5-20 Bonds, if they are paid in 4 years, in order to gain 7% on my investment?

3. Bought Kentucky State Bonds, bearing 5% interest, payable in 3 years, and received, when I obtained the principal, 6% on my investment. What did I pay?

MISCELLANEOUS.

1. What rate per cent. will the purchaser of Philadelphia Bank stock receive on his investment if the premium on the stock is 35% and the bank pays an annual dividend of 8%?

Ans. $5\frac{25}{27}$.

2. Which is the most profitable,—United States 10-40 Bonds purchased at 95, or the 5-20 Bonds purchased at 105?

3. Which is the better investment, a ground-rent bearing 6% interest, purchased at 98%, or railroad stock purchased at 10% premium, which pays an annual dividend of 7%? and how much?

4. What interest will a person receive who purchased United States 5-20 Bonds at 104, if he sells the gold received for interest at a premium of 30%?

STOCK TABLE,

Showing the rate of Interest received on Stocks purchased, from 25 per cent. discount to 25 per cent premium.

Purchase Price.	RATE RECEIVED ON STOCK BEARING INTEREST AT				
	5 per cent.	6 per cent.	7 per cent.	8 per cent.	10 per cent.
75.	6.666	8.00	9.333	10.666	13.333
80.	6.25	7.50	8.75	10.000	12.500
85.	5.882	7.143	8.235	9.411	11.764
90.	5.555	6.666	7.777	8.888	11.111
95.	5.263	6.316	7.263	8.421	10.526
97.50	5.128	6.156	7.179	8.205	10.256
100.	5.000	6.000	7.000	8.000	10.000
105.	4.761	5.714	6.666	7.619	9.523
110.	4.545	5.454	6.363	7.272	9.090
115.	4.347	5.130	6.086	6.956	8.695
120.	4.166	5.000	5.833	6.666	8.333
125.	4.000	4.800	5.600	6.400	8.000

UNITED STATES BONDS IN EUROPE.

The Five-Twenty Bonds issued in 1862, called the "Old" 5-20's, were the first known in Europe, and for that reason are in greatest demand, causing an advance over the issues of 1864 and 1865 of 1½ to 4½ per cent. The real value of the different issues is the same.

The quotations in London, Paris, Frankfort, Hamburg, and other places, are the prices of $100 bonds in American gold. Thus, "Frankfort, Feb. 9th, U. S. 5-20's 76¼," signifies that $76.25 in U. S. coin is the price of a bond for $100.

The interest which has accrued at the time of purchase forms a part of the value of the bond.

The principal causes of the difference in the quotations on the same day are the fluctuations in the rate of exchange and the difference in the basis of calculation.

It is necessary also to know whether the "old" or "new" issue is meant. The telegraphic report frequently omits the date of issue; in the Stock Exchange Circular, the prices of both are given.

To understand the subject fully requires a knowledge of exchange and stock calculations, and an acquaintance with the customs and manner of dealing among bankers.

Foreign Stock Quotations.

(PER ATLANTIC CABLE.)

LONDON, Mar. 1.	U. S. 5-20's,	73¼.
	Illinois Central R. R.,	76¼.
	Erie R. R.,	36½.
PARIS, "	U. S. 5-20's,	82⅞.
FRANKFORT, "	" "	76⅝.
LONDON, Mar. 23.	" "	74½.
FRANKFORT, "	" "	77½.

London Quotations.—The price quoted in London is at the nominal par of 4*s.* 6*d.* per dollar, or \$4.44$\frac{4}{9}$ per pound sterling. To this about 9½% must be added for the difference between the old par and the present value of our coins.

To obtain the currency value, the premium on gold must also be added.

EXAMPLES.

What is the value of \$1000 in U. S. 5-20 Bonds when quoted at 70 and the premium on gold is 35%?

1000	
70	
700.00	Nominal par value.
9½%	
630000	
35000	
66.5000	Exchange premium.
700	
766.50	Value in American gold.
35%	
383250	
229950	
268.2750	Premium on price in gold.
766.50	
1034.7750	\$103.48 in United States.

To a resident of the United States a purchase in London like this would require an addition of 1% commission, and interest equal to ½% more, which increases the price to \$105.03. The proceeds of a sale would be \$1.55 less than \$103.48 = \$101.93.

2. When gold is at a premium of 33%, what will be received from a sale of \$5000 U. S. 5-20's, at 72, allowing commission and interest at 1½%?

3. How much will a 5-20 Bond for \$5000, purchased in London, cost, in currency, when exchange is 109, and gold is at a premium of 30%, allowing commission at 1%?

Paris Quotations.—In Paris the price of exchange affects the quotations. On the Paris Bourse the bonds are estimated on the conventional basis of 5 francs to the dollar, while the actual value of a dollar in exchange transactions is 5.10 and 5.15, equal to a difference of $2 to $3 on $100.

London quotations, being based on the old par, require the addition of about 9½% and the difference between the Paris Bourse rates and actual exchange rates, to give the comparative value of both places.

EXAMPLE.—February 23, 1867. London, U. S. 5-20's 73¾; Paris, 83¼.

Premium on $73.75 @ 9½%,	=	$7.00
Difference between Bourse and exch. rates	=	2.50
To be added to London rate,		9.50

73.75 + 9.50 = 83.25 Paris rate, as above.

NOTE.—The difference between the Bourse rate and the exchange rate should be taken from the Paris quotations to obtain the real price in Paris.

In Frankfort, when American gold is not paid, the value is computed at the rate of 2½ guilders per dollar.

1. On March 1, 1867, the quotations per Atlantic Cable were: London, U.S. 5-20's 73¼; Frankfort, 76⅝. In New York, exchange on London the same day was 109.

Value of $73.25 in London, @ 9% prem.,	79.84
Price in Frankfort,	76.62
Difference between London and Frankfort,	3.22

With exchange on Frankfort at 41⅝, the difference is but a trifle.

2. On the same day, Illinois Central R. R. stock was quoted in London at 76¼, Erie Railroad at 36½. What are these prices equivalent to in U. S. currency, gold being at 140?

3. What is the value in United States currency of a bill of exchange on England, when quoted at 153, which includes the exchange premium and premium on gold?

VALUE OF LIFE INTERESTS, WIDOWS' DOWERS, ANNUITIES, &c.

Extract from Instructions issued by the Treasury Department, Washington, February 15, 1866.

"Where legacies are made payable at the expiration of a life or lives in being, the value of the legacy will be estimated by the Carlisle tables of life annuities, which are appended to these instructions.

"Where a legacy is made payable on a future contingency, the value of the legacy is to be estimated by a consideration of the time, certain or ascertainable by the annuity tables, when the legacy will become vested.

CARLISLE TABLES.

AGE.	Expectancy of life in years and hundredths.	Present value of annuity of $1.00 for the number of years and 100ths of years found in 2d column, at 6 per cent.	Present value of $1.00 to be received at the end of the number of years and 100ths of years as found in 2d column, interest at 6 per cent.	AGE.	Expectancy of life in years and 100ths.	Present value of annuity of $1.00 for the number of years and 100ths of years found in 2d column, at 6 per cent.	Present value of $1.00 to be received at the end of the number of years and 100ths of years as found in 2d column, interest at 6 per cent.
0	38.72	14.9202	.104788	41	26.97	13.2043	.207741
1	44.68	15.4325	.074065	42	26.34	13.0737	.215580
2	47.55	15.6225	.062645	43	25.71	12.9395	.223635
3	49.82	15.7521	.054874	44	25.09	12.8032	.231812
4	50.76	15.8008	.051953	45	24.46	12.6576	.240548
5	51.25	15.8252	.050490	46	23.82	12.5059	.249646
6	51.17	15.8213	.050722	47	23.17	12.3454	.259278
7	50.80	15.8029	.051830	48	22.51	12.1751	.269494
8	50.24	15.7742	.053551	49	21.81	11.9889	.280669
9	49.57	15.7385	.055689	50	21.11	11.7946	.292324
10	48.82	15.6972	.058168	51	20.39	11.5846	.304922
11	48.04	15.6523	.060860	52	19.68	11.3701	.317792
12	47.27	15.6055	.063670	53	18.97	11.1481	.331108
13	46.51	15.5573	.066559	54	18.28	10.9201	.344791
14	45.75	15.5072	.069566	55	17.58	10.6805	.359172
15	45.00	15.4558	.072650	56	16.89	10.4364	.373815
16	44.27	15.4028	.075832	57	16.21	10.1839	.388967
17	43.57	15.3501	.078996	58	15.55	9.9287	.404275
18	42.87	15.2956	.082267	59	14.92	9.6788	.419268
19	42.17	15.2384	.085695	60	14.34	9.4368	.433789
20	41.46	15.1778	.089331	61	13.82	9.2154	.447078
21	40.75	15.1151	.093095	62	13.31	8.9900	.460612
22	40.04	15.0500	.097002	63	12.81	8.7636	.474183
23	39.31	14.9972	.101248	64	12.30	8.5245	.488530
24	38.59	14.9068	.105592	65	11.79	8.2793	.503231
25	37.86	14.8307	.110157	66	11.27	8.0211	.518737
26	37.14	14.7521	.114876	67	10.75	7.7552	.534690
27	36.41	14.6685	.119892	68	10.23	7.4813	.551125
28	35.69	14.5829	.125024	69	9.70	7.1926	.568446
29	35.00	14.4982	.130105	70	9.18	6.9022	.585867
30	34.34	14.4123	.135258	71	8.65	6.5945	.604328
31	33.68	14.3240	.140560	72	8.16	6.3045	.621730
32	33.03	14.2343	.145938	73	7.72	6.0341	.637953
33	32.36	14.1366	.151789	74	7.33	5.7894	.652634
34	31.68	14.0344	.157932	75	7.01	5.5887	.664681
35	31.00	13.9291	.164255	76	6.69	5.3762	.677427
36	30.32	13.8174	.170957	77	6.40	5.1833	.688999
37	29.64	13.7021	.180796	78	6.12	4.9971	.700173
38	28.96	13.5833	.185000	79	5.80	4.7763	.713420
39	28.28	13.4579	.192530	80	5.51	4.5719	.725687
40	27.61	13.3289	.200208	81	5.21	4.3604	.738376

EXAMPLE.—If a person whose probability of life is 14.34 years inherits an estate having a rental value of $1000 per annum, the present worth of the annuity of $1000 for that term is 9.4368 × 1000 = $9436.80,—the valuation on which he is taxed.

THE CENTAL SYSTEM.

The Cental System has been adopted by the Boards of Trade in many of our larger cities; and after September 1st, 1867, all grain, seeds, &c. are to be bought and sold by the "cental," or hundred pounds, instead of by the bushel, as heretofore. The Philadelphia Board of Trade passed a resolution, to take effect March 1st, 1867, that all grain be sold by the cental, and that the proprietors of elevators and storehouses be requested to conform thereto, by making rates for storage and by issuing receipts in accordance with the contemplated change.

The advantage and convenience which will result from the adoption of this system must be apparent on a moment's reflection.

The Senate of Pennsylvania, also, has recently passed a bill in which it is decreed that various articles shall weigh so many pounds to the bushel. The weights decrease from articles weighing eighty pounds to a bushel down to those weighing only twenty. The effect will probably be that all articles mentioned in the bill will be bought and sold by weight instead of measure, and that the cental will thus be speedily brought into general use.

To find the price per cental when the price per bushel is given.

RULE.—*Multiply the price per bushel by 100, and divide by the number of pounds.*

EXAMPLE.—At $1.38 per bushel for wheat of the weight of 60 lbs. per bushel, what is the price per cental?

138 × 100 = 13800 13800 ÷ 60 = 230 Ans. $2.30.

To find the price per bushel when the price per cental is given.

RULE.—*Multiply the price per cental by the number of pounds in a bushel, and divide by 100.*

EXAMPLE.—At $2.50 per cental, what is the price of a bushel of wheat?

$250 \times 60 = 15000 \quad 15000 \div 100 = 150$ Ans. $1.50.

GAUGING.

Gauging is the process of finding the contents or capacity of casks and other vessels.

Ullage is the difference between the actual contents of a vessel and its capacity, or that part which is empty.

The usual manner of gauging is by the diagonal rod, which gives only approximate results, but sufficiently accurate for ordinary purposes.

FOR SMALL CYLINDRICAL VESSELS.

RULE.—*Multiply the square of the diameter, in inches, by 34, and that by the height, in inches, and point off four figures; the result will be the capacity, in wine gallons and decimals of a gallon.*

If beer gallons are required, multiply by 28 instead of 34.

EXAMPLE.

A can measures 15 inches in diameter, and is 2 ft. 2 in. in height. How many gallons will it contain?

$15 \times 15 = 225 \times 26$ in. (height) $= 5850$

$5850 \times 34 = 19.8900$ Ans. $19\frac{89}{100}$ gals.

To find the contents of ullage casks.

RULE.—When the cask is standing—

Find one-third the sum of the head, mean, and bung diameters, and square the result; multiply by the height of the fluid in inches, and that product by .0034 for wine gallons, and by .0028 for beer gallons.

To test the accuracy of *dry measures* which are in the form of a cylinder.

Divide 2738 by the square of the diameter, in inches; the quotient will be the depth for a bushel; one-half the quotient will be the depth for a half-bushel; one-quarter of the quotient, for a peck, &c.

To test the accuracy of measures for *fluids* which are in the form of a cylinder.

Square the diameter, in inches, for a divisor.

Divide 294 for wine gallons.
" 359 " beer "
" 342 " dry "

GRAIN MEASURE.

To find the quantity of grain in a bin or wagon.

RULE.—*Multiply the height, length, and breadth together, in inches, and divide by 2150.42; the quotient will be the number of bushels.*

To find the quantity of grain when heaped on the floor in the form of a cone.

RULE.—*Square the depth and square the slant height, in inches; take their difference and multiply by the depth, and this product by .0005; the result will be the contents, in bushels.*

To find the quantity of grain when heaped against a straight wall.

RULE.—*Square one-half the depth, and proceed as in the previous rule.*

Wheat	weighing	60	lbs. yields	nearly	48	lbs. flour.
Rye	"	54	" "	"	42	" meal.
Barley	"	48	" "	"	37½	" "
Oats	"	40	" "	"	22½	" "

STORAGE.

Storage is charged at a certain price per barrel, bale, box, etc., according to regulations adopted by the Chambers of Commerce or Boards of Trade of the different cities.

All goods stored are subject to one month's storage. In some places, if they remain any part of a month they are charged for a full month; in others, after the first month, if taken out within fifteen days, a half-month is charged; if after fifteen days, a whole month. The owners of the goods pay for putting the goods in store, stowing away, and the expenses of delivery.

When goods are received and delivered at the pleasure of the consignor, the dues for storage are usually determined by an average.

To compute storage.

RULE.—*Multiply the number of barrels, or other articles, first entered, by the number of days between the time of entrance and the time of the first delivery, or second entrance.* Then

Multiply each balance by the number of days it continues unchanged.

The sum of all the products will be the number of articles in store for one day. To find the number stored for one month, divide the sum of the products by 30.

EXAMPLE.—What is the cost of storage, at 1¢ per bushel per month, of wheat received and delivered as per following account, closed Oct. 2d, 1866?

Account of Storage of Wheat received and delivered for account of A. Y. Rodgers & Co., St. Louis.

Date.		Received.	Delivered.	Balances.	Days.	Products.
1866.						
July	2	200		200	9	1800
"	11		150	50	5	250
"	16	350		400	5	2000
"	21		300	100	20	2000
August	10	400		500	5	2500
"	15		450	50	5	250
"	20		50	0	0	0000
Septemb'r	5	200		200	5	1000
"	10	100		300	5	1500
"	15		200	100	17	1700
		1250	1150			30)13000
Bal. on hand Oct. 2,			100			$433\frac{1}{3}$
		1250	1250			

$433\frac{1}{3} \times 1¢ = \$4.33$, Ans.

PROPERTIES OF NUMBERS.

Any number may be divided by $1\frac{1}{4}$, 2, $2\frac{1}{2}$, $\frac{1}{3}$, or 5, without a remainder, when its right-hand figure may be thus divided.

The square root of a number is greater than any of its prime factors.

Any number may be divided by an aliquot part of a hundred when its *two right-hand figures* may be thus divided.

Any number may be divided by an aliquot part of a thousand when its three right-hand figures may be thus divided.

Any number divided by 3 or 9 will leave the same remainder as the sum of its digits divided by 3 or 9.

The difference between any number and the sum of its digits is a multiple of 9.

The difference between a number and the digits of the same number arranged in another order is always divisible by 9.

MISCELLANEOUS RULES.

To find two numbers when their *sum* and *difference* are given.

RULE.—*Add one-half their sum to one-half their difference, for the larger number, and take one-half their difference from one-half their sum, for the smaller.*

To find two numbers when their sum and product are given.

RULE.—*Take the square root of the difference between the square of the sum and four times their product; the result will be the difference between the numbers.*

To find two numbers when their difference and product are given.

RULE.—*To the square of their difference add four times the product, and the square root of the sum will be the sum of the numbers.*

To find two numbers when their sum and quotient are given.

RULE.—*Divide the sum by the quotient increased by 1; the result will be the smaller number.*

To find two numbers when their difference and quotient are given.

RULE.—*Divide the difference by the quotient less 1, for the smaller number.*

To find two numbers when their sum and the sum of their squares are given.

RULE.—*From the square of their sum take the sum of their squares, and half the remainder will be the product; then proceed by Rule above.*

To find two numbers when their sum and the difference of their squares are given.

RULE.—*Divide the difference of their squares by their sum; the quotient will be their difference.*

To find two numbers when their product and quotient are given.

RULE.—*Divide the product by the quotient, and the square root of the result will be the smaller number.*

To find two numbers when the square of their sum and the sum of their squares are given.

RULE.—*From the square of the sum take the sum of the squares; the remainder will be twice the product of the numbers. Subtract four times the product from the square of the sum, and the remainder will be the square of their difference. Extract the roots, and proceed as in Rule above.*

RULES IN MENSURATION.

To find the contents of an irregular body.

Immerse the body in a vessel full of water, and measure the quantity of water displaced.

To find the area of a rectangle.

Multiply the length by the breadth.

To find the area of a triangle.

Multiply the base by one-half the altitude. Or,

From half the sum of the three sides subtract each side separately; multiply together the half sum and the three remainders, and extract the square root of the product.

To find the circumference of a circle.

Multiply the diameter by 3.14156, or $3\frac{1}{7}$.

To find the diameter of a circle.

Divide the circumference by 3.14156; or multiply it by .318309.

To find the area of a circle.

Multiply half the diameter by half the circumference. Or,

Multiply the square of the diameter by .785398.

To find the side of a square equal to a given circle.

Multiply the diameter by .886227, or $\frac{1}{2}$ of $\sqrt{3.14156}$.

To find the diameter of a circle equal to a given square.

Multiply the side of the square by 1.12838.

To find the side of an inscribed square.

Multiply the diameter by .707106, or $\sqrt{5}$ *; or the circumference by .225079.*

To find the side of the largest inscribed equilateral triangle.

Multiply the diameter by .866025.

To find the circumference from an inscribed square.

Divide the side of the square by .225079.

To find the diameter of the three largest equal circles that can be inscribed in a given circle.

Divide the diameter of the given circle by 2.155.

To find the contents of a cube.

Multiply three sides together.

To find the surface of a cube.

Multiply the square of the length of one of its sides by 6.

To find the surface of a sphere.

Multiply the diameter by the circumference.

To find the solidity of a sphere.

Multiply the square of the diameter by 3.1416. Or,
Multiply the cube of the diameter by .5236.

To find the solidity of a cylinder.

Multiply the area of one end by the length.

A CUBIC FOOT OF

		Pounds.			Pounds.
Loose earth or sand	weighs	95	Clay and stones	weighs	160
Common soil	"	124	Cork	"	15
Strong "	"	127	Tallow	"	59
Clay	"	135	Bricks	"	125
Lead	"	708$\frac{3}{4}$	Marble	"	171
Brass	"	534$\frac{3}{4}$	Granite	"	165
Copper	"	555	Sea-water	"	64$\frac{3}{10}$
Wrought iron	"	486$\frac{3}{4}$	Oak wood	"	55
Anthracite coal	"	50 to 55	Red pine	"	42
Bituminous "	"	45 to 55	White pine	"	30
Charcoal (hard wood)	"	18$\frac{1}{2}$	Charcoal (pine wood)	weighs	18

BUSINESS FORMS

AND

INFORMATION.

BUSINESS MAXIMS.

Endeavor to be perfect in the calling in which you are engaged.

Think nothing insignificant which has a bearing upon your success.

There is more in the *use* of advantages than in the measure of them.

Make no investments without a full acquaintance with their nature and condition; and select such investments as have intrinsic value.

Of two investments, choose that which will best promote your regular business.

Become known,—and favorably known.

Never refuse a choice when you can get it.

Goods well bought are half sold.

Goods in store are better than bad debts.

Nothing valuable is lost by civility.

By prosecuting a useful business energetically, humanity is benefited.

Keep accurate accounts, and know the exact condition of your affairs.

Be economical: a gain usually requires expense; what is saved is clear.

Reality makes no allowances for wishes or bad plans.

PAYMENTS AND LEGAL TENDER.

The law gives the debtor who owes several debts to the same creditor, the right to apply a voluntary payment, *at the time of making it,* to whichever debt he prefers. If the debtor does not exercise the right, it passes to the creditor; and if neither party makes an application of it, the law will apply it according to its own view of the intrinsic justice and equity of the case.

Payment of debts cannot be enforced after the lapse of a certain number of years, which are specified in the several States in what are called the statutes of limitations.

STATUTE LIMITATIONS IN THE UNITED STATES.

NAMES OF STATES.	Open Acc't.	Notes.	Judgments.	NAMES OF STATES.	Open Acc'ts.	Notes.	Judgments.
	Yrs.	Yrs.	Yrs		Yrs.	Yrs.	Yrs.
Alabama,	3	6	20	Minnesota,	...	6	10
Arkansas,	3	5	10	Mississippi,	3	6	7
California,	1	4	5	Missouri,	5	10	20
Connecticut,	6	6	17	New Hampshire,	6	...	20
Delaware,	3	6	...	New Jersey,	6	16	16
Florida,	5	5	...	New York,	6	6	20
Georgia,	4	6	20	North Carolina,	3	3	...
Illinois,	5	5	20	Ohio,	6	15	...
Indiana,	6	20	20	Pennsylvania,	6	6	20
Iowa,	...	10	20	Rhode Island,	6	6	20
Kentucky,	1	5	15	South Carolina,	4	4	....
Louisiana,	3	5	...	Tennessee,	3	6	16
Maine,	6	6	20	Texas,	2	4	...
Maryland,	3	3	12	Vermont,	6	14	8
Massachusetts,	6	6	...	Virginia (store % 2y)	5	5	20
Michigan,	6	6	...	Wisconsin,	6	6	...

In some States, to renew the obligation and take the case out of the operation of the statute of limitations, it is necessary that a promise to pay, or acknowledgment of the debt, be made in writing; in others, a payment made, or an acknowledgment and promise to pay to the creditor, in the presence of witnesses, is sufficient.

The tender of payment of a debt, duly made, operates in bar of any claim for damages and interest, and also in bar of the costs of an action brought to recover the debt. A creditor who refuses a tender, sufficient in amount and duly made, cannot afterwards, for the purpose of oppression or extortion, avail himself of his refusal. The debtor, however, remains liable to pay whenever called upon.

A man to whom payment is made is not bound, under ordinary circumstances, to give a receipt or to make change.

A payment made to the proper person, in "*lawful money of the United States*," is indisputably good.

By an act of Congress, the payment of debts *with coin* is regulated as follows:—

All gold coins, at their respective values, for *any amount.*

The *half-dollar*, *quarter-dollar*, *dime*, and *half-dime*, at their respective values, for debts *under five dollars.*

Three-cent pieces, for debts of any amount *under thirty cents.*

The *one-cent pieces*, for debts of any amount *under ten cents.*

The Treasury notes, called "greenbacks," are also a legal tender.

Bank notes are a good tender, *unless expressly objected to*, if the bank is in good credit.

A payment made in *counterfeit coin or notes* is no payment, if the receiver gives notice to the payer within a reasonable time that the coin or notes are counterfeit.

The taking of a promissory note for a pre-existing debt, or a contemporaneous consideration, is treated *prima facie* as a conditional payment only; that is, as payment only if it is duly paid at maturity.

When the creditor voluntarily, having free choice, and not from necessity, accepts the promissory note or bill of a *third person* for a pre-existing debt, the debt is extinguished, though the security may prove to be worthless.

When money is *remitted by mail* to the creditor, the debt is discharged if the debtor can show that the letter containing the money was properly mailed, and that it was done in accordance with the express direction of the creditor, or a custom from which such authority might be implied. If this can be shown, and a loss occurs, it is the loss of the creditor; if otherwise, it is the loss of the debtor.

The receiver of a check, if he receives it in the town or city where it is payable, should present it for payment to the bank or bankers, at the *farthest, on the next succeeding day after it is received.* If payment is not thus demanded, and the bank or bankers should fail before the check is presented, the loss will be the loss of the holder.

A creditor is not bound to accept a check remitted to him, and he may commence a suit for debt even while the check remains in his hands.

Money paid voluntarily in a transaction, with full knowledge of the facts, cannot be recovered.

Interest is not due on a note except from maturity, unless it is so mentioned in the note.

One claim may be set off against another, when it exists at the commencement of a suit and in the claimant's own right.

When part of a claim is admitted, the debtor should tender the amount admitted; this will relieve him from costs, if the disputed portion is decided in his favor.

RECEIPTS.

A RECEIPT is an acknowledgment in writing that a sum of money, or other consideration of value, has been received. A receipt is evidence of a payment against the person who signs it, and is a voucher used by agents to prove the correctness of their accounts. It is also evidence in proving facts quite distinct from the payment stated in it.

A Simple Receipt is merely written evidence: it does not exclude verbal evidence of payment; and upon satisfactory proof that it was obtained by fraud, or given under error or a mistake as to facts, it may be inquired into and corrected at law or equity.

A man is not bound by law to give a receipt; although, by universal custom and courtesy of business, receipts are generally given when desired. When refused, the facts may be proved by witnesses.

A full and complete receipt states,—

That a payment has been received.

The date of the payment.

The amount or article received.

From whom; and if for another, on whose behalf payment is made.

To what debt or purpose it is to be applied.

By whom received; and if for another, on whose behalf it was received.

When the receipt is signed by the very person to whom the payment is ultimately to go, his signature is sufficient. Where the receipt is made out and signed by an agent, he may either write the receipt as if the principal himself were to sign it, then write his principal's name underneath, and his own name below his principal's, using the prefix "per" or "by," to signify the agency, in the following manner:—

Received, &c.

Edward M. Sawyer,
per John T. Warren.

Or, he may draw up the receipt for himself, and sign it in his own name, mentioning in the body of it, however, that he received the money "for" or "on account of" his principal.

The first form is more suitable for an agent who acts as a mere messenger to take the money and is not authorized to assume any responsibility or exercise any discretion in respect to the case. Clerks in stores are of this class.

The last form is suitable for an agent of more extended powers: of this class are lawyers, to whom collections are intrusted.

The most important of all the special clauses in the receipt is that which defines the debt or purpose to which the payment is to be applied.

Payments upon Account.—When, for want of time, or other circumstances, a payment is made in part, or with the intention to leave the application of it to future adjustment, it is common to state that the money was "received on account."

Payments upon a Specified Debt.—When a payment is made, and the debt intended to be paid is clearly distinguished, the receipt, as evidence of application, can only be set aside by proof of fraud or serious mistake.

Payments in full.—A receipt for a sum "in full" of a debt mentioned is evidence of something more than the mere payment of that sum. The law infers from it the adjustment of the amount due, after consideration of the rights of both parties, and payment of the sum specified as final satisfaction of those rights. Receipts "*in full of all ac-*

counts" do not affect claims which are not properly matters of account. Receipts "*in full of all demands*" prevent any further claim for any demand whatever, existing and known, or which ought to have been known, to the parties at the time, unless some serious or excusable mistake can be shown.

Payments to be accounted for.—As the law presumes that when money is paid it is paid in satisfaction of a debt, it is desirable, when money is received as a loan or deposit, or to be used or paid out for the benefit of the party paying it, to embody in the receipt an admission of the purpose for which it is received, somewhat as follows:—

Received, &c., One Hundred Dollars, to be repaid with interest; Received, &c., One Hundred Dollars, to be accounted for, or returned; Received, &c., One Hundred Dollars, to be expended in purchasing, &c.

Care should be taken in drawing a receipt when the transaction involves an agreement, because, in case of legal controversy, no explanation inconsistent with its language can be given.

If a person to whom a note is offered in payment consents to receive the note only upon the understanding that if it be not paid when due he shall return it to the debtor and renew his original claim, it is advisable to state the medium of payment, and that "*when paid*" it will be in full satisfaction for the debt.

A check made payable to the creditor's order is equivalent to a receipt for the amount, as the money cannot be obtained until the check has been properly indorsed.

It is not usual to take a receipt on paying a note, draft, or other instrument indorsed by the payee, because the instrument *itself*, with the indorsement, is returned, and thus becomes a receipt.

Partial payments indorsed on the instrument are concise admissions of payment, and need no other receipt. Partial payments of a bond should be indorsed on the bond.

A receipt for money paid to an estate is good when signed by but one executor; although it is well to have the signature of both.

It is advisable, when payments of importance are made, or disputes are apprehended, to take receipts. They should be kept where they are easy of access, and in a place of safety. When not in a receipt-book, they should be appropriately folded, labelled, and filed.

One of the advantages of the statutes of limitations is, that debtors are not obliged to take care forever of documents or vouchers which prove that a demand has been satisfied, and a limit is fixed beyond which there is no necessity for producing them.

When a bill which is receipted is retained by the person to whom it is presented, and payment is not made, the signature at the foot of the bill should be torn off or defaced. If payment is refused after a receipt has been delivered, evidence may be given to that effect.

Sealed or Special Receipts.—The Sealed or Special Receipt is, in general, conclusive and absolutely binding. Deeds signed and sealed, which include "the receipt of which is hereby acknowledged," are of this character.

FORMS OF RECEIPTS.

RECEIPT FOR PAYMENT ON ACCOUNT.

Received, Philadelphia, July 5, 1865, from S. H. Crittenden & Co., Two Hundred and Fifty Dollars on account.

$250. ———— *Ringwalt & Brown.*

RECEIPT IN SETTLEMENT OF ACCOUNT.

Philadelphia, Nov. 11, 1866.

Received from William H. Brown One Hundred and Twenty-Five $\frac{50}{100}$ Dollars, in settlement of account to date.

$125\frac{50}{100}$. *James, Kent, Santee & Co.*

RECEIPT IN FULL OF ALL DEMANDS.

St. Louis, Jan. 10th, 1867. Received of Henry D. Holmes One Thousand Dollars, in full of all demands.

$1000. *John Andrews.*

RECEIPT FOR A PARTICULAR BILL.

Rec'd, New York, July 2d, 1866, from James G. Atwater, One Hundred and Thirty-Five $\frac{62}{100}$ Dollars, in payment for a bill of Broadcloth of this date.

135\frac{62}{100}$. *A. T. Stewart & Co., per B. J. Yates.*

RECEIPT FOR A NOTE.

Baltimore, May 7th, 1867.

Rec'd from Messrs. Watson, Gray & Co. their Note of this date, at three months, our favor, for Twelve Hundred and Twenty-Five $\frac{75}{100}$ Dollars, which, when paid, will be in full for account rendered to 1st instant.

1225\frac{75}{100}$. *James H. Johnson.*

RECEIPT FOR RENT.

Rec'd, Rochester, March 6th, 1867, from Porter K. Smith, One Hundred and Twenty-Five Dollars, in full for one quarter's rent of House No. 10 St. Joseph St.; due on 1st inst.

$125. *George H. Matthews, Trustee.*

RECEIPT FOR INTEREST DUE ON A BOND.

Received, Boston, September 18th, 1866, of Gilbert Lawrence, One Hundred and Eighty Dollars, in full for six months' interest due this day, on his Bond to me, bearing date Sept. 18th, 1864, for Six Thousand Dollars.

$180. *John W. Thornton.*

RECEIPT FOR SERVICES.

Rec'd, Lowell, June 13th, 1866, from Joseph T. Chester & Co., Ninety-Six Dollars, in full for services to date.

$96. *Henry T. Chase.*

INDORSEMENT OF A PARTIAL PAYMENT ON A NOTE.

Rec'd, Phila., March 6th, 1867, on account of the within Note, Six Hundred Dollars.

$600. *Walter H. DeHaven.*

RECEIPT FOR PAYMENT BY THE HAND OF A THIRD PARTY.

Rec'd, Memphis, Dec. 30th, 1864, from Leonard W. Bailey & Co., by the hand of Samuel Trumpler, Four Hundred Dollars, in full for proceeds of sales of Iron, Invoice bearing date of Nov. 10th, 1864.

$400. *George S. Powell.*

RECEIPT FOR BORROWED MONEY.

(Or Borrowed-Money Due Bill.)

$300. *Syracuse, Mar. 17th, 1865.*

Borrowed and received, from William S. Balch, Three Hundred Dollars, which I promise to pay on demand, with interest.

Daniel S. Browning.

SHIPPING RECEIPT.

Albany, Sept. 10th, 1864.	*Albany, Sept. 10th, 1864.*
Shipped on board *bound for* *packages* *Marks*	*Received from Charles Sansom & Co., in good order, on board the "Isaac Newton," bound for New York, the packages marked and entered as below:—* Marks. M. T. *10 sacks Garden Seeds.* C. H. *100 bbls. Oswego Flour.* *Robert L. Brown, Ag't.*

When a large number of hands are employed, or when payments to a large number of persons are to be made, it is usual to have forms of receipts printed, leaving the date and amount to be filled according to circumstances; or a large book ruled in the manner shown below. Some take a receipt at every payment; while others take receipts only quarterly, yearly, or at other stated intervals, or when business relations are dissolved, and then in full to date of receipt.

The following is a convenient form when a large number of persons are paid:—

We, the undersigned, do hereby severally acknowledge that we have received from Matthew Baldwin & Co. the sums set opposite our respective names, in full for services to date.

No.	Date.		Amount.			Stamp.	Signatures.
	1865.						
1	July	20	Forty-Five Dollars.	45	00	☐	*Joseph L. Barrett.*
2	"	"	Thirty-Seven $\frac{50}{100}$ Dolls.	37	50	☐	*Thomas P. Jones.*
3	"	"	Twelve "	12	00		*Samuel G. Brown.*
				$94	50		

FORM FOR DIVIDEND LIST OF JOINT STOCK COMPANIES.

We, the subscribers, severally acknowledge that we have received from the Treasurer of the Saratoga Fire Insurance Co., of New York, the sums set opposite our respective names, in full for Dividend on all Stock of said Company held by us.

NAMES.	No. of Shares.	Dividend.	Arrears of Dividend.	Date of Receipt.		SIGNATURES.
				1865.		
Chas L. Somers,	100	$40		June	15	*Chas. L. Somers.*
Thos. C. Smith,	50	20	$20	"	16	*Thos. C. Smith.*
Jos. T. King,	200	80				
Philip S. Hall,	150	60				

BOOK ACCOUNTS.

Entries of transactions should be made at or near the time of their occurrence.

The time to make a charge against a purchaser is when the goods are ready for delivery.

Entries, to be admissible as evidence, should be made by a proper person, and be without erasure, alteration, or interlineation.

Mistakes should be corrected by marking the erroneous entry *void*, and then making a correct entry; or, if the entry has been transferred to other books, by making another entry in explanation.

Items and particulars should be specified, as a general charge cannot be supported by this kind of evidence. The entry must be made for the purpose of charging the debtor; a mere memorandum for any other purpose is insufficient.

As a general rule, copies of all important papers, such as letters, orders, accounts current, and account sales, should be kept, as they may be required for proof or reference; but, usually, a copy is not a voucher, and nothing but the original paper will answer.

To collect a debt on the evidence of a book account, from a person in a distant place, a copy of the account should be made out, and accompanied with an affidavit in the usual form, setting forth:—1st, that the above copy of account is correctly taken from the book of original entries; 2d, that the charges were made at or about the times of their respective dates; 3d, that the goods were sold and delivered at or about the time the charges were made; 4th, that the charges are correct and the account just; and, 5th, that the person named is not entitled to any credits. This affidavit should be sworn to before a magistrate or commissioner, and will save the trouble of producing the books.

BILLS, INVOICES, AND STATEMENTS.

A Bill is a written description of particulars or items.

A Bill of Goods, or Bill of Parcels, is a description of the quantity and price of goods sold, with the time of the transaction and the names of the purchaser and seller.

An Invoice is a full account of goods or merchandise, in which the marks, numbers, contents, and value of each package are described, together with the charges for commission, insurance, packing, &c.

A Statement is a synopsis of an account, or a brief enumeration of bills which have been purchased within a certain time. Some mercantile houses send statements monthly, or at other regular periods, to their customers who purchase on credit, that a comparison of account may be made, and, that if any error exists, it may be remedied in time.

FORMS OF BILLS.

1. *Bill ——, unreceipted.*

Rochester, *March 18, 1867.*

Mr. Henry L. Stone,

Bought of George S. Thompson.

10 lbs. Java Coffee,	@	.40	4	00
5 " Green Tea,	"	1.20	6	00
12 " Brown Sugar,	"	.14	1	68
25 yds. Muslin (Wamsutta),	"	.23	5	75
17 " Flannel,	"	.45	7	65
1 doz. Linen Hdkfs.,			3	00
12 yds. Mous. de laine,	"	.20	2	40
			$30	48

2. *Bill receipted by Firm.*

NEW ORLEANS, *December 26, 1866.*

MR. J. J. BIBB,

To B. H. FENTON & Co., *Dr.*

To 48 yds. Muslin,	@ .22		
" 12 " Drilling,	" .18		
" 10 " Gingham,	" .35		
" 20 " French Chintz,	" .40		
" 7 " Broadcloth,	" 3.25		
" 2 doz. Spools Thread,	" .75		
" 1 " Linen Napkins,	" 2.00		
" $3\frac{1}{2}$ yds. French Cassimere,	" 1.90		
		$	

Rec'd payment,

B. H. FENTON & Co.

3. *Bill receipted by Clerk.*

{ Shipped at buyer's risk. }

CHICAGO, *Feb. 19, 1867.*

MESSRS. H. H. APPLEGATE,

TERMS, *Note at 60 days.* *To* JAMES HARRIS SON & Co. *Dr.*

25 boxes Cheese, 820 82 738,	@ .12	$88	56
10 bags Flaxseed, 1206 — 11 = 1195 lbs. $21\frac{19}{56}$ bus.,	" 3.00	64	02
2 bbls. Eggs, 141 — 6 = 135 doz.,	" .25	33	75
3 kegs Butter, 295 — 31 — 6 = 258 lbs.,	" .35	90	30
5 tierces Leaf Lard, 1620 — 271 = 1349 lbs.,	" .21	283	29
		$359	92

STAMP

Rec'd payment,

JAMES HARRIS, SON & Co.,

per L. M. WILSON.

4. *Bill receipted by Clerk.*

PHILADELPHIA, *11mo., 7, 1867.*

MR. SETH W. OSBORN,

O. B. 55, page 150. *Bought of* J. M. & T. H. SAUNDERS.
TERMS, *4 months.*

Packages	Nos.				$	cts.
365	20	2 doz. Men's Blk. Cassr. Hats,	@	$24.00	$48	00
"	16	6 " " " Wool "	"	18.00	108	00
"	12	3 " Boys' Drab " "	"	15.00	45	00
"	21	3 " Child's Fancy Wool Hats,	"	15.00	45	00
"	17	3 " Men's White Canton Hats,	"	13.50	40	50
1320		60 prs. Women's Calf Pegged Boots,	"	2.25	135	00
1350		96 " Misses' " " Balmorals,	"	1.15	110	40
1216		36 " Women's Morocco Welt "	"	2.10	75	60
1301		36 " Child's Kid Pump Boots,	"	60	21	60
		2 Cases,			1	50
					$630	60

STAMP

Received payment,
J. M. & T. H. SAUNDERS,
per J. L. GURNEY.

5. *Bill paid by Note.*

PLEASE EXAMINE PACKAGES CAREFULLY FOR MISSING ARTICLES.

NEW YORK, *January 13, 1867.*

MESSRS. GEO. W. MCWILLIAMS & CO.,

O. B. 4, page 75. *Bought of* FISHER & COLLINS.

		$	cts.
7	Doz. Edg'd Muffins, $\frac{2}{1.00}$, $\frac{4}{1.20}$, $\frac{1}{1.35}$,	8	15
2	Sets W. Gran. Tea Sets, 46 ps., @ $8.50,	17	00
2	Doz. Mocco. Pitchers, $\frac{1}{4.50}$, $\frac{1}{7.00}$,	11	50
6	" Table Tumblers, @ 1.25,	7	50
50	" W. Gran. Dishes, $\frac{10}{50}$, $\frac{15}{1.00}$, $\frac{10}{1.50}$, $\frac{10}{2.00}$, $\frac{5}{3.00}$,	70	00
20	Sets " Teas, @ 1.10,	22	00
$1\frac{1}{4}$	Doz. Edg'd Bakers, $\frac{\frac{1}{2}}{2.00}$, $\frac{\frac{1}{2}}{4.50}$, $\frac{\frac{1}{4}}{6.00}$,	4	75
	Crate, $^{2.00}$ Box, ^{25} and Porterage, ^{50}	2	75
		$143	65

STAMP

Rec'd payment by Note at 4 mos.,
FISHER & COLLINS.

Bills for Services, &c.

6.

WORCESTER, *July 7, 1867.*

MR. JAMES L. RUSHTON,

To FREDERICK T. STONE, *Dr.*

1867. Jan.	7	For Professional Services in Family,	$10	00
"	20	" 5 visits to son, Charles Rushton,	5	00
May	10	" 3 " " " Henry L. Rushton,	3	00
			$18	00

7.

BUFFALO, *August 19, 1866.*

MR. JOHN H. WAGNER,

To WM. H. TURNER, *Dr.*

1867. May	11	For Repairing House, as per Contract,	$25	00
"	"	" 800 feet Pine Boards, @ $8,	6	40
"	"	" Lock and Key for door,	2	25
"	"	" Nails, Hooks, &c.,	1	00
			$34	65
		Received payment, W. H. TURNER.		

8.

CHICAGO, *July 3, 1866.*

MR. OWEN T. JONES,

To HENRY G. LANGDON, *Dr.*

		For Instruction of son, William T. Jones,			
		in English branches, 3 mos.,	$15.00		
		in Latin, "	20.00	$35	00
		" Instruction of daughter, Louisa J. Jones,			
		in English branches, 3 mos.,	$15.00		
		in Music, "	15.00		
		" Use of Piano,	10.00	40	00
		" Books and Stationery furnished during the Term,		3	50
				$78	50
		Received payment, HENRY G. LANGDON, per S. Y LANGDON.			

9. *Items of an Account.*

MECHANICSVILLE, *Jan. 1, 1867.*

MR. S. B. MOREHOUSE,

To O. TOMPKINS & Co. *Dr.*

1866.					
Apr.	5	To 5 bbls. Genesee Flour, extra,	@ $15.00	$75	00
May	9	" 10 lbs. Pearl Starch,	" .18	1	80
June	16	" 20 " English Breakfast Tea,	" 2.25	45	00
Sept.	14	" 2 bbls. Prime Pork,	" 17.50	35	00
				$156	80
		CR.			
May	5	By 17 yds. English Broadcloth, @ $3.00,	$51.00		
"	10	" 25 " French Chintz, " .40,	10.00		
July	11	" 12 " English Beaver Cloth, " 3.00,	36.00	97	00
		Balance due,		$59	80
		Settled by due-bill,			
		O. TOMPKINS & Co.			

INVOICES—DRY GOODS.

CINCINNATI, *Jan. 17, 1867.*

MESSRS. LEONARD & CURTIS,

Bo't of JOSEPH CUSHING & Co.

Terms, 3 mos. Note to your own order.

L. & C.	304	2 cases Merrimac Prints, 80 ps., 2804 yds.,	@ .17		
"	312	1 case Satinets, 450 yds.,	" .78		
	540	5 ps. Extra Black Cassimere, 120 yds.,	" $2.75		
	17	10 " Satin Stripe Muslin, 200 "	" 1.30		
	137	40 Check Square Shawls,	" 2.13		
	15	6 Imperial Long "	" 11.00		
	801	3 ps. Solferino Opera Cloth, 90 yds.,	" .85		
	4267	12 Ladies' Mourning Long Shawls, 60 × 120,	" 9.00		
	No. 1	2 ps. Taffeta Ribbons,	" 1.50		
		5 " Buff Chambrays, 155 yds.,	" .42		
	142	2 " Printed Plaid Flannel, 90 yds.,	" .52		
E. C.	46	15 " Plain Mousseline de Laines, metres 674.1 = 730¼ yds.,	" .28½		
		Rec'd payment,			
		JOS. CUSHING & Co.,			
		per L. R. TAYLOR.			

Invoice of TWO *packages of Merchandise purchased by* W. B. LONGWORTH & CO., *and forwarded to* B. G. BABCOCK, *Liverpool, for shipment per "Kangaroo" S. S., bound for* NEW YORK, *for account and risk of* MESSRS. HOMER, COLLADAY & CO., *Philadelphia, and to them consigned.*

Mark	No.	Description	Qty.	Price	£	s.	d.	£	s.	d.
⟨A⟩H										
※ 30	7743	16/4 Fancy Wool Long Shawls,	70	24/–	84					
		" " " "	18	17/–	15	6				
		" " Square "	12	9/–	5	8				
	100/1244	100/734 Broche Borders, yds.	200	1/–	10					
	2301	" "	200	10½*d.*	8	15				
	2302	" "	200	8*d.*	6	13	4			
		Cases, Packing, Oil-Cloth, &c.				19	10	131	2	2
※ 31		16/4 Fancy Wool Long Shawls,	72	23/–	82	16				
		" " " "	48	12/–	28	16				
		Case, Packing, &c.				19	6	112	11	6
								243	13	8
		Discount on £241 14*s.* 4*d.*, @ 2½,						6		10
								237	12	10
		Charges, Cartage, 1/6, Commission 1½ per cent., £3 11*s.* 4*d.*,						3	12	10
		Cash, 1st Sept. 1866,						£241	5	8
		E. E.								
		GLASGOW, 11th August, 1866.								
		W. B. LONGWORTH & CO.								

Other invoices may be found under PROFIT AND LOSS.

MONTHLY STATEMENT.

Monthly Statement.

BOSTON, *Jan. 31, 1867.*

MESSRS. B. H. BRADFORD & CO.,

To A. A. LAWRENCE & CO. *Dr.*

1867.			$	cts.
Jan.	4	To Mdse., as per Bill rendered, @ 3 months,	$75	00
"	17	" " " " " 3 "	132	00
"	26	" " " " " 60 days,	318	00
"	29	" " " " " 3 months,	123	75
			$648	75

BILLS OF LADING.

A **Bill of Lading** is a formal receipt subscribed by the master of a ship, or other common carrier, acknowledging the receipt of goods intrusted to him for transportation, and binding himself, under certain exceptions, to deliver them, in like good condition as received, at the place and to the person named in the bill, or his assigns, for a remuneration or freightage. The bill of lading is the evidence of shipment and the title to the goods shipped, and may be indorsed or transferred to other parties.

Three sets are usually made out: one to be sent to the person to whom the goods are consigned, one for the person shipping the goods, and a third to be retained by the carrier, or master of the vessel. The bills of lading contain a description of the packages shipped, including their number, marks, weights, &c.

Common Carriers are those who hold themselves out to carry all goods intrusted to them, or all goods of a particular kind. They are of two kinds,—inland carriers by land or water, and carriers by sea. They are answerable for all losses which do not fall within the excepted cases of inevitable accident and the acts of the public enemies of the country. The carrier may limit his responsibility by agreement with his customer; but he cannot exempt himself by notice or agreement from responsibility for *actual negligence.* He has a lien on the goods carried, and may retain them until he has been paid his freight.

Primage is an allowance made for loading the goods. The term "Average" refers to general or marine average, in which, if loss arise during the voyage, the cargo is required to bear a proportionate share.

A **Manifest** is a list containing the marks, description, and number of packages of the ship's cargo, together with the names of the shippers and consignees, and must be certified by the master of the vessel before the collector of customs, or the consul.

A **Consul** is an officer appointed by Government to reside in a foreign country, for the purpose of protecting the commercial interests of the subjects of his own nation. Documents of any kind attested by the consul, under his hand and seal of office, are admitted as evidence in courts of justice.

BILL OF LADING, SIGNED BY MASTER OF VESSEL.

Shipped, In good order and well-conditioned, by **B. Gallaway, Jr.**, as Agent, in and upon the good ship called the Kathleen, whereof is Master for this present voyage, **U. E. Roberts**, and now riding at anchor in the river Thames, and bound for **Philadelphia**, via Falmouth, **Eighteen Bales Merchandise**, being marked and numbered as in the margin, and to be delivered in the like good order and well-conditioned, at the aforesaid Port of **Philadelphia** (*the act of God, the Queen's enemies, fire, and all and every other dangers and accidents of the seas, rivers, and navigation, of whatever nature and kind soever, excepted*), unto **Mr. Porter Morgan, Philadelphia**, or to his assigns, he or they paying freight for the said goods, £5 11*s.*, in full. Primage and Average accustomed.

P.M.
P.

18 Bales.

℅ 1/18.

In Witness whereof, the Master or Purser of the said Ship hath affirmed to **three** Bills of Lading, all of this tenor and date, the one of which Bills being accomplished, the others to stand void.

Rate 20/–.

	£	*s.*	*d.*
Freight,	5	5	9
Primage,		5	3
	£5 11*s.*		

Weight and contents unknown; and not accountable for leakage, breakage, or rust. Freight payable at the current rate of exchange on the day the ship enters at the Custom-House.

Dated in London, this 23d day of Dec., 1865.

Contents unknown.

U. E. Roberts,
Master.

BILL OF LADING SIGNED BY CLERK OF R. R. CO.

Camden & Amboy Railroad and Transportation Company.

Philadelphia, Feb. 24, 1866.

Received, of Messrs. Barclay & Barclay,
30 casks Linseed Oil,

Marked:—H. L. T.—℅ 1 to 30.

To be transported to New York, and delivered to
Mr. H. L. Turner, or order, upon the following

TERMS:

[Here the conditions are inserted.]

W. P. Murphy,
For the Company.

STEAMBOAT BILL OF LADING.

Received by the **Wilmington Steamboat Line**, in apparently good order, from H. Y. Heald, marked and entered as below (contents unknown), which we promise to deliver at Wilmington (breakage and leakage excepted), and not being responsible, if lost, stolen, or damaged, beyond the value of Fifty Dollars per package.

1 Case Merchandise.

Marked :—George Danby,
Wilmington, Del.

Philadelphia, Jan. 19, 1867. P. T. Simpson, *Agent.*

FREIGHT BILL.

FORM No. 69.—SERIES B.

No. 12118. *Philadelphia, Nov. 8, 1866.*

Mr. *Robert B. Stewart,*

To PENNSYLVANIA R. R. CO. Dr.

For Freight from .... *Mill Creek* .... *on*

	Weight.	Rate.	Freight.		Expenses.		Total.	
3 boxes Apples,	1935	56	10	83		57	11	40
4 " Mdse.,	1450	60	8	70		50	9	20
							$20	60

Rec'd payment for the Company,
Thos. Y. Murray.

WAREHOUSE RECEIPT.

Syracuse, June 18, 1867.

Delivered to **John Cottrell & Co.**, in good order, for which they have paid the charges thereon.

Marks.	Articles.	Quantity.	Charges.	
J. C. & Co.				
X. L.				
※ 1 to 20	Oswego Flour, extra,	20 bbls.		
※ 20 " 30	Corn Starch,	10 "		
	Freight from Oswego,		1	50
	Drayage, Storage, &c.,		3	00
			$4	50
	T. & L. Mosier.			

ACCOUNT SALES.

An **Account of Sales** is a detailed statement of goods sold and the charges incurred thereon, and is made for the purpose of showing the net proceeds of sales. When goods have been sold on commission, the agent or commission merchant makes out an account sales, to be sent to the consignor, or person for whom the goods were sold.

Account Sales are made out in various forms; that form being used which is most convenient for the branch of business in which it is used. Sometimes they are made out in the form of a ledger account; the quantity of goods sold, with their marks, prices, &c., being entered on the credit side, and the various charges on the debit side. The difference between the two sides exhibits the net proceeds, and is entered on the smaller side, to produce a balance.

Another form, and the one which is generally adopted, is to enter the sales, with all the particulars, first, and the charges underneath.

When the goods are not all sold, a minute of those still on hand should accompany the account sales.

To make out an account sales, turn to the consignment account in the ledger, and from thence to the original entries, to obtain all the items affecting the account. When the goods are sold for cash, or when the consignor guaranties the sale, it is not necessary to give the names of the purchasers; although this is frequently done.

A *del-credere* commission, or guaranty, is a commission charged for becoming responsible for the debts of those who purchase the goods on credit.

Account Sales are averaged to find the date when the proceeds may be paid without loss of interest to either party. (See AVERAGE OF ACCOUNTS.)

Sales of {200 bus. Wheat, 150 bbls. Flour,} *received per Barque* AURORA, *for Account of* JAMES T. HOYT, *Berlin, Md.*

		To whom sold.	Description.		Price.		
1866.							
Dec.	19	Jefferson Andrews,	25 bus.	Ohio Wheat,	1.15	$28	75
1867.							
Jan.	5	R. J. Long,	50 bbls.	Elm Grove Fam. Flour,	9.50	47	50
"	8	Chas. S. Brown,	100 bus.	Kentucky Wheat,	1.20	120	00
"	13	L. S. Harris & Co.,	20 "	Ohio "	1.18	23	60
"	"	"	75 bbls.	Oregon Fam. Flour, Ex.,	8.50	637	50
"	25	Henry G. Stone & Co.	55 bus.	Ohio Wheat,	1.10	55	00
"	"	"	25 bbls.	Flour, Grant's Mills,	11.00	275	00
						$1187	35
		——— CHARGES. ———					
		Freight and Drayage,			$45.00		
		Insurance on $1000, @ 1¼ per cent.,			12.50		
		Storage and Labor,			7.25		
		Commission and Guaranty, 5 per cent. on 1187.35,			59.37	124	12
		Net Proceeds due per average, ———, 1867,				$1063	23
				LEONARD B. HUDSON.			
		NEW YORK, Jan. 28, 1867.					

Account Sales of 75 Bales of Wool received per Pennsylvania Railroad, and sold for Account of MESSRS. SMITH & WILLIAMS, *Salem, Columbiana Co., Ohio.*

1866.					
Nov.	10	Three-quarter blood Merino Fleece, Net 9238 lbs., @ 60c.,	30 days,	5542	80
Dec.	15	Half-blood Merino Fleece, Net 2638 lbs., @ 55c.,	"	1450	90
"	"	Unwashed Merino Fleece, Net, 240 ⅓ discount, 80 160 lbs., @ 55c.,	30 days,	88	00
1867.					
Jan.	5	Common and quarter-blood Fleece, Net 985 lbs., @ 50c.,	30 days,	492	50
				$7574	20
		——— CHARGES. ———			
		Freight and Drayage,	$192.33		
		Commission, including Insurance, Storage, and Labor, 2 cents per lb. on 13,101 lbs.,	262.02	454	35
		Net Proceeds due Dec. 22, 1866,		$7119	85
		E. E. THAW & WALKER.			
		PHILADELPHIA, Jan. 10, 1867.			

ACCOUNTS CURRENT.

Accounts Current are statements in detail of accounts which have been open or running from one time to another. They are usually made out twice a year, or whenever circumstances require, by the parties desiring settlement.

The object of an Account Current is to furnish the person to whom it is sent a statement, that he may know the extent of his dealings, and what balance may be due from him to settle his account.

Accounts Current are drawn from the accounts in the Ledger, with which they must agree, and should contain a description of every transaction, with date, items, and amounts, as expressed in the books of original entry, allowing for the difference of style. When particulars are not supplied, reference should be made to the entries or papers in which they may be found. Interest is allowed, or not, according to custom or the understanding between the parties. The time for which interest is calculated is counted from the date when the amount is due, or equivalent to cash, to the date of settlement. For the different methods of calculating the interest, see INTEREST ACCOUNTS. Accounts Current are sometimes averaged as in Average of Accounts.

If there are errors in an Account Current received, it should be objected to within a reasonable time, or it becomes an Account Stated, which does not require a proof of items.

The letters E. E. and E. O. E., appended to invoices and accounts, are for the purpose of intimating the right of correcting errors or of supplying omissions.

For additional Accounts Current, see pages 47 and 49; and for finding interest on English Accounts, see INTEREST IN ENGLAND.

FORM OF ACCOUNT CURRENT.

MESSRS. H. S. MOREHOUSE & CO. *in Account Current and Interest Account with* S. D. DOUGLASS & CO. *to January 1, 1867.*

Date.		Amt.	When due.	Days.	Int.	Date.		Amt.	When due.	Days.	Int.
1866. July 7	To Mdse., as per bill rendered, at 3 mos. . .	1250 00	Oct. 7	86	17 92	1866. Aug. 15	By Inv. of Sugar @ 60 days,	950 00	Oct. 14	79	12 51
" 15	" Mdse., as per bill rendered	1540 00	" 15	78	20 02	Sept. 5	" Your Draft on Gray & Bro. at 30 days . . .	250 00	" 12	81	3 38
Aug. 10	" Mdse. (Net), as per bill rendered	1300 00	Aug. 10	144	31 20	Oct. 17	" R. Hunter & Co.'s Draft on Commercial Bank at sight	1500 00	" 17	76	19 00
" 15	" Net Proceeds of Wheat, as per your Account Sales	3800 00	Sept. 10	113	71 57	" 15	" Your ½ Net Proceeds of 1500 bbls. Flour, as per Acct. Sales rendered	3800 00	Nov. 3	59	37 37
" 20	" Our Drft. on L. T. Adams at 30 days	425 00	" 19	104	7 36	1867. *Jan. 1*	" *Balance of Interest* . .				*75 81*
		8315 00			148 07			6500 00			148 07
	Add Bal. of Interest, .	75 81				" "	" *Balance*	*1890 81*			
		8390 81						8390 81			
1867. Jan. 1	To Bal. due us	1890 81									

E. E.

S. D. DOUGLASS & CO.

PITTSBURGH, Jan. 1, 1866.

ORDERS.

An Order is a written request to deliver money or goods to some person mentioned, or to his order, or to the bearer, on account of the person signing the request. It is used by the person receiving it as a voucher that the person signing it is responsible, and that the thing or things mentioned have been delivered. Orders may be made negotiable; but the persons on whom they are drawn are not under obligation to pay them unless they have been accepted.

ORDERS FOR MONEY.

Lancaster, Aug. 16, 1867.

Mr. James T. Fordley,

Please pay to M. B. Brown, or order, One Hundred Dollars, and charge to our account.

$100. *Jas. W. Andrews & Co.*

Messrs. Alfred Slade & Co.

Gentlemen:—Please pay to Thomas Brown, or order, Thirty Dollars, due on my account, and oblige

Yours, respectfully,

Philada., Aug. 12, 1866. *Robert H. Jenkins.*

ORDERS FOR GOODS.

Baltimore, Feb. 19, 1867.

Mr. William B. Linden,

Please pay to Andrew B. Jones, or bearer, Sixty Dollars in Goods from your store, and place to account of

Henry W. Wilkins.

Albany, Mar. 25, 1867.

Mr. Charles Riqua,

Please send me, per bearer, Ten Barrels Flour, Genesee Extra, and oblige

Yours truly, *Henry Burnham.*

Dayton, O., August 16, 1866.

Messrs. L. A. Tiers & Son,
New York.
Dear Sirs:
Please send immediately Five (5) Half-Chests Imperial Tea, Hugo & Otto, ※7, as per sample sent us, and oblige
Yours, truly,
Corbin & Walworth.

St. Louis, Jan. 3, 1867.

Messrs. E. C. & J. Biddle,
Philadelphia, Pa.

Gentlemen:—Please send us, per Adams Express,

60 Crittenden's Book-Keeping, C. H. Edition.
25 do. do. H. S. do.
30 Lynd's Class-Book of Etymology.
12 Cleveland's American Literature.
16 Alsop's Algebra.

Upon receipt of your Bill, with Goods, we will remit by Draft or Express, as you may direct.

Respectfully, yours,
A. B. M. Thompson & Co.

CHECKS.

A Check is a written order or request, addressed to a bank or banker, by a person having money deposited, requesting the payment, on presentment, of a certain sum of money to a person therein named, or to his order, or to the bearer.

When drawn payable to a person *or bearer*, it is transferable without indorsement, and the holder is entitled to payment; when drawn payable to a person *or his order*, it must be indorsed by the person to whom the check is made payable; when made payable to a person without the words "or order," or "bearer," or to a particular person "only," it is not negotiable.

As checks made payable to a person's order compel the payee to indorse them, they are, when drawn in this form, often used in lieu of receipts.

The drawer of a check may countermand its payment at any time previous to its payment or acceptance by the bank.

A check received from others should be presented without unnecessary delay, as the drawer will not otherwise be responsible for its payment in case of the failure of the bank.

Every holder of a check is liable to every subsequent holder only for the time for which he would be held if originally liable.

A post-dated check is payable on the day of its date; but, as circumstances may arise that will render void a check which is payable in the future, some prefer dating the check with the day on which it is drawn, and stating in the body of the check the day when it is to be paid.

When made payable on a future day mentioned, different from that of the date, they have been treated as bills of exchange, and as such are entitled to days of grace, and require revenue stamps, the same as bills of exchange.

The amount of a check should always be written out in words. The amount in figures is placed in the corner, that the sum for which the check is drawn may be seen at a glance, and also as a precaution against any alteration which might be made.

CHECK PAYABLE TO BEARER.

STAMP. No. 7. Cincinnati, Aug. 16, 1867.

First National Bank,

Pay to Samuel Wallace, or Bearer,

Three Hundred $\frac{50}{100}$ Dollars.

$300 $\frac{50}{100}$. Hugh Graham.

STAMP. No. 127. *Baltimore, Nov. 22, 1865.*

The National Bank of Baltimore,

Pay to .... *James S. Brown,* .... *or Order,*

.... *One Hundred and Seventy* .... $\frac{38}{100}$ *Dollars.*

\$170$\frac{38}{100}$. *Wm. H. Grant.*

CHECK PAYABLE AT A FUTURE TIME.

STAMP. No. 173. *New York, Mar. 13, 1867.*

National Park Bank,

Pay to .... *John H. Hope,* .... *or Order,*

Eight Hundred *Dollars,*

on the 27th inst., without grace. Acceptance waived.

\$800. *Robert R. Andrews.*

CERTIFIED CHECKS.

A certified check is one for the payment of which the bank becomes responsible, upon being certified, or marked "good" by the paying teller, with his signature attached. Certified checks are used to prevent the inconvenience and risk of withdrawing and counting sums of money that are to be immediately paid to others. They are also used instead of drafts for making remittances to distant places.

STAMP. No. 122. *Philadelphia, April 6, 1867.*

Philadelphia National Bank,

Pay to .... *Hugh Graham,* .... *or Order,*

One Thousand .... *Dollars.*

\$1000. *M. E. Bradford & Co.*

Good when properly indorsed. W. H. Wells, Teller.

CERTIFICATES OF DEPOSIT.

Certificates of Deposit are used when money is temporarily deposited, and no regular bank account is kept. When made payable to another person's order, they are frequently employed for making remittances, in the same manner as certified checks.

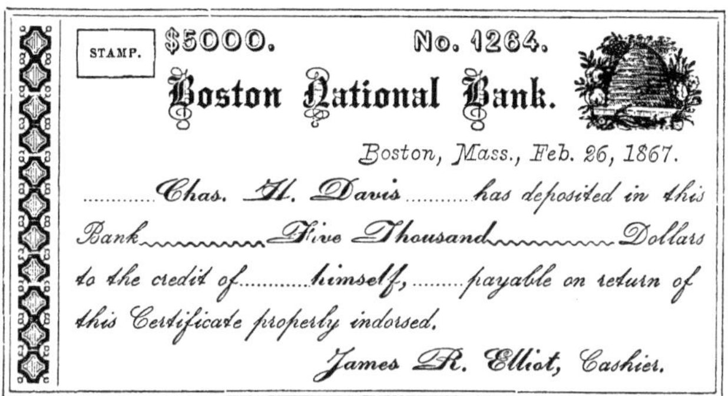
STAMP. $5000. No. 1264.

Boston National Bank.

Boston, Mass., Feb. 26, 1867.

............Chas. H. Davis..........has deposited in this Bank Five Thousand Dollars to the credit of............himself,.........payable on return of this Certificate properly indorsed.

James R. Elliot, Cashier.

TRANSACTIONS WITH BANKS.

Banks are organized institutions for the employment of capital. Banks of "circulation and deposit" have the use, under certain restrictions, of the capital paid in by the stockholders, the money belonging to depositors, and the notes of their own circulation. The National Banks are required to deposit with the Treasurer of the United States interest-bearing bonds of the United States, in proportion to the capital stock paid in. All bonds so deposited are held exclusively as security for the circulating notes delivered to the banks depositing the bonds. The following suggestions may be found useful to those who have dealings with banks:—

Make your deposits in the bank as *early in the day as you conveniently can*, and never without your bank-book.

For your own security, it is well to have ONE PARTICULAR

PERSON to do your business at the bank, who shall be competent to take charge of the money and papers you intrust to his care, and sufficiently intelligent to understand and properly deliver the messages and explanations you may have occasion to make; also, that you write or stamp OVER YOUR INDORSEMENT, upon all checks which you send to be deposited to your credit in the bank, the words "FOR DEPOSIT TO OUR CREDIT," which will prevent their being used for any other purpose.

Always use the deposit tickets furnished by the bank, and examine the date and indorsement of every check. When checks are deposited, the banks require them to be indorsed by the depositor, whether drawn to his order or not.

Keep your check-book, when not in use, under your own lock and key. Make it a rule to give checks only out of YOUR OWN CHECK-BOOK.

Draw as few checks as possible. When you have several sums to pay, draw ONE CHECK for the whole, and take notes of such denominations as will enable you to distribute the amount among those you intend it for.

Do not allow your bank-book to run too long without being balanced, and when returned by the bank compare it with your own account, and examine your cancelled checks without delay. If you wish to preserve your cancelled checks, deface or destroy the signature as soon as returned, in a manner that will prevent their being copied, and place the checks out of the reach of others.

In filling up checks, do not leave space in which the amount may be increased. It has been decided that when a check is so carelessly drawn that an alteration may be easily made, the loss arising from the alteration, if any, must be borne by the drawer.

Write your signature with your usual freedom, and never vary the style of it.

Offer notes for discount or collection in good season. Do

not put off the offering of notes for discount until the last day of your need. When notes are discounted or collected for you, hand your bank-book to the clerk, that they may be entered in it to your credit.

COUNTERFEIT BANK-NOTES.

A *counterfeit* note is a *fac-simile* of the genuine, or as nearly like it as it can be made. A *spurious* note is made up of designs different from the genuine, and calculated to pass where the genuine is not known. An *altered* note is one altered from a lower to a higher denomination; or one on a broken or bogus bank, on which the name or locality is changed for that of a bank in good standing.

RULES FOR DETECTING COUNTERFEIT NOTES.

Examine the vignette or picture at the top of the note: see if the faces have a lifelike expression; if the eyes are well defined, showing the pupil distinctly, the white clearly; see if the drapery or dress fits well, looks natural and easy, and shows the folds distinctly —if the whole figure harmonizes. See if the sky is clear, or transparent, or soft and even, and not scratchy, and if the different objects have a finished appearance. In the genuine, small figures in the background are always exceedingly well executed.

Examine the medallion rulings and circular ornaments around the figures, &c.; see if they are regular, smooth, and uniform. When there are two medallions on a bill designed to be alike, they are exactly alike, being from the same original die. This work is done by a geometrical lathe, a machine of immense cost, and which produces fine and ornamental circles of such uniformity and exquisite perfection that it is almost an impossibility for the counterfeiter to produce a good imitation.

Examine the letters and figures; see if they are perfect in every respect,—all perfectly true and uniform and regular. In counterfeits the round handwriting is seldom well executed. Carefully study the hair-lines and curves, the shade or parallel ruling on the face or outside of the letters; see if they are without breaks or flaws, and have a finished, graceful appearance. Examine the engraver's signature or imprint; see if it is clearly and beautifully engraved; if the letters are all of one size and one slant; if the distances apart and the thickness of stroke are equal.

Examine the President's and Cashier's signatures. In some counterfeits the signatures are lithographed *fac-similes*, inked over with a pen, which gives them a stamped appearance, the stroke a dead color and a rough edge, and sometimes the pen does not follow the hair-stroke curve correctly; while the genuine signatures, which are written with a pen, have rather a glossy appearance, and the stroke a smooth edge.

Bank-notes altered by what is termed the "pasting process" may be detected by holding them to the light, when the parts pasted on will be discovered. When the alteration has been made by substituting figures or letters for others which have been extracted, the denomination in the centre of the note, when examined letter by letter, will be found to be poorly formed and blurred, and the parallel lines irregular and imperfect. The texture of the paper between the letters is very often destroyed,—a defect which may be discovered by comparing the paper between the letters with that immediately above and below; the ink of the altered part is also sometimes different from the rest of the note.

Avoid all hurry and confusion when taking money, as much of the bad money passed is passed under such circumstances.

DESCRIPTION OF NATIONAL CURRENCY.

NATIONAL BANK-NOTES.

UNITED STATES and title of bank on each of the different denominations.

1s.—Two females standing in front of an altar, one of them pointing upward. A large 1 on the left end, on which is, "Secured by Bonds," &c.

Reverse Side.—Landing of Pilgrims, in large oval; ONE, eagle in shield; ONE, on right; ONE, arms of the State; ONE, on left end.

2s.—Large 2, extending almost across length of note; United States, &c., on upper part, and 2 on lower part, on left end; female seated holding American flag, on which is a wreath.

Reverse Side.—Sir Walter Raleigh erect, smoking pipe; six men and a boy grouped around him at a table. 2, eagle and shield, on right; 2, arms of the State, on left end.

5s.—Columbus introducing America to Europe, Asia, and Africa, —the countries represented by female figures. Columbus discovering America; four men. 5 on right end, FIVE on left end.

Reverse Side.—Landing of Columbus and men. Spread eagle on right; arms of the State on left; FIVE and 5 on each end.

10s.—Female seated on spread eagle in clouds. Franklin drawing lightning from clouds with a kite; boy seated; 10 on right, TEN on left end.

Reverse Side.—De Soto on horseback, with his army, discovering the Mississippi. Spread eagle; arms of the State; 10, 10, on each side.

20s.—On right, allegorical representation of Loyalty; figure of Liberty in foreground, bearing national flag; farmers, artisans, &c., rallying around the flag. On left, battle of Lexington. 20 on each end.

Reverse Side.—Baptism of Pocahontas. Eagle and shield; arms of the State; 20 on the right, XX on left end.

50s.—Allegorical representation of Victory: three figures in a cloud; soldier kneeling. Washington and men in a boat crossing the Delaware. 50 on each end.

Reverse Side.—Embarkation of the Pilgrims. Eagle and shield; arms of the State; 50 and L on each side.

100s.—Female with wings, seated—allegorical representation—maintenance of Liberty and Nationality. Men in a row-boat in foreground, two vessels in background. 100, C, on right end; C, 100, on left end.

Reverse Side.—Signing Declaration of Independence. Eagle in an oval; arms of the State; 100 on right, C on left side.

TREASURY NOTES, OR GREENBACKS.

1s.—UNITED STATES. A long oval portrait of Hon. S. P. Chase on left end. A strip of lathe-work between signatures. 1 in green and 1 in fancy die. Oval in the lower centre, in which the rays converge to the number showing the denomination of the note, which is on a white ground.

2s.—A side view of Alexander Hamilton in lower left centre. Two strips of lathe-work. II in green die; 2 on each end in fancy die. Oval in lower centre, with rays similar to the "ones."

5s.—FIVE DOLLARS. 5 on a strip of lathe-work; right end, male portrait; 5 above; left end, female erect, with sword and shield.

10s.—Upper centre, eagle on a shield. 10 in green die each side. Right end, female erect by pedestal, holding tablet, &c.; left end, portrait of President Lincoln.

20s.—Centre, female erect, with sword and shield; figure 20 and green die each side. TWENTY DOLLARS across each end in green die-work.

50s.—Side view of Alexander Hamilton in oval die. Treasury die in pink on right of vignette. 50 on die on each end of note.

100s.—Large spread eagle on a rock. 100 in green die on right; 100 in black die in right upper corner; 100 in black die in lower left corner.

500s.—In centre, portrait of Albert Gallatin in round green die. 500 on each end. FIVE HUNDRED DOLLARS on a strip of lathe-work below.

1000s.—In centre, portrait of Robert Morris in green round die. M, with 1000 across it, on each end. ONE THOUSAND DOLLARS on a green strip of lathe-work below.

DUE-BILLS.

A **Due-Bill** is a simple acknowledgment of a debt, in writing. It is not payable to order, nor is it assignable by mere indorsement. *Bouv. L. D.* It is subject to all the off-sets and equitable rights between the original parties, and action must be brought in the name of the original obligee. Due-bills do not draw interest unless specified.

DUE-BILL FOR MONEY.

$125. *Philadelphia, July 10, 1866.*

Due Henry W. Chase, for value received, One Hundred and Twenty-Five Dollars, with interest.

DUE-BILL FOR GOODS.

Due, New York, August 9th, 1866, to H. Y. Bennett, for value received, Sixty-Five $\frac{50}{100}$ Dollars, in goods from my store.

$65\frac{50}{100}$. *Geo. W. Hanson.*

PRODUCE NOTES.

A **Produce Note** is a written engagement to deliver specific articles to a specified amount. Like due-bills, produce notes are not assignable by mere indorsement. The maker of the note must be able to prove that he was ready at the proper *time and place*, and continued ready, to deliver the articles, or he may be compelled to pay their value in money.

PRODUCE NOTE.

37\frac{25}{100}$. *Lebanon, July 2, 1866.*

For value received, we promise to pay to Thos. J. Stewart, on demand, Thirty-Seven $\frac{25}{100}$ Dollars, in goods at our store.

R. B. Painter & Co.

FORM OF ASSIGNMENT OF A PRODUCE NOTE.

(*To be indorsed on the back of the Note.*)

For value received, I assign the within Note to A. J. Gordon, without (*or with*) *recourse, this 17th day of July, 1866.*

Thos. J. Stewart.

PROMISSORY NOTES.

A **Promissory Note** is a written promise to pay, unconditionally and at all events, a specified sum of money. Promissory notes are either *negotiable* or *non-negotiable.*

A note is negotiable when the promise is made not only to the person named in it, but to his *order* or *bearer*, and may be collected by whomsoever may be the holder of the note at the time of its maturity.

If a note be made payable to Jas. Graham, or *bearer*, it may be collected by Jas. Graham, or by any one who may hold or bear it, and is negotiable by mere *delivery.*

FORM OF NOTE PAYABLE TO BEARER.

$500. *Portland, July 3, 1866.*

Three months after date, I promise to pay to James Graham, or bearer, Five Hundred Dollars. Value received.

Chas. J. Raymond.

A note made payable to James Graham, or *order*, may be collected by any one to whom James Graham may order it to be paid. The order is commonly written upon the back of the note, and is called an indorsement. If James Graham simply wrote his name on the back of the note, it would be an indorsement in blank, and is equivalent to "Pay to bearer," and would then be negotiable by delivery. (See INDORSEMENTS.)

NOTE PAYABLE TO A PERSON, OR ORDER.

$1000. *Troy, June 29, 1866.*

Thirty days after date, for value received, we promise to pay to James Graham, or order, One Thousand Dollars.

J. R. Flannigan & Co.

A note made payable to James Graham, or James Graham only, is not negotiable, and is payable only to the party named.

NON-NEGOTIABLE NOTE.

$300. *Worcester, June 10, 1866.*

Sixty days after date, I promise to pay to James Graham Three Hundred Dollars. Value received.

Henry J. Gordon.

A custom prevails in the mercantile community of drawing notes payable to the maker's own *order*, with his indorsement, for the purpose of facilitating their transfer without requiring the holder to indorse them.

NOTE TO ONE'S OWN ORDER.

$1800. *Pittsburgh, September 20, 1866.*

Four months after date, I promise to pay to the order of myself Eighteen Hundred Dollars, without defalcation. Value received. *Philip T. Wharton.*

In Pennsylvania, the words "*without defalcation*" must be inserted in the note in order to render it negotiable. In New Jersey, "*without defalcation or discount;*" in Missouri, "*negotiable and payable without defalcation or discount;*" in Indiana, the words "*without any relief whatever from valuation or appraisement laws*" are inserted.

The words "value received" imply a consideration, which is necessary to make a promise binding on the maker of it.

The person who promises to pay is called the *promisor*, *maker*, or *drawer;* the person to whom the note is made payable is called the *payee;* the person who writes his name upon the back of the note is called the *indorser;* and the person to whom it is transferred by indorsement is called the *indorsee.*

All the parties who have written their names on a note are liable for the amount due, but only one satisfaction can be recovered.

A note given on Sunday is void; so is a note founded upon fraud, or when the consideration is illegal. Any material alteration in a note—as, for instance, in the date, or amount, or time of payment—discharges all parties who have not consented to such alteration.

If a person at the time of taking a note has notice that it is void through fraud or upon any legal grounds, he places himself in the position of the payee. A note as a gift is void from want of consideration.

Notes made payable at a fixed time are allowed three days after the expiration of the time expressed for payment. These three days are called "days of grace."

Demand for payment must be made upon the last day of grace; or, if that falls on Sunday, or on a leading holiday, such as the Fourth of July, Thanksgiving, Christmas, New Year, and, in Pennsylvania, Washington's Birthday, demand must be made on the day previous.

If a note is given by a person who cannot write, it is important to have a witness who can testify to the genuineness of his mark.

Promissory notes do not bear interest until after maturity, unless so specified.

If a note is paid before due, and afterwards comes into the hands of a *bona fide* holder for value, he can still claim full payment from the maker at maturity.

A note after it is dishonored or over-due is not negotiable, but subject to all the equities which the maker may have against the original payee; and no more can be collected than the original payee could have recovered.

A note given by a minor is voidable at the election of the minor; and, until ratified by him after his arrival at full age, it is of no effect.

If no time is fixed for payment in the note, it is payable upon demand; if payable to a fictitious person, it is payable to bearer.

If a promissory note, or bill of exchange, has been lost or destroyed, payment must be demanded and notice given as if the note was still in possession.

The amount of a negotiable or non-negotiable bill or note which has been destroyed by fire or other accident, may be recovered upon sufficient proof.

Payment of a non-negotiable note which has been lost may be enforced; but if a note or bill negotiable and transferable is lost, it is held in some States that a suit at law may be maintained against the maker; in others, that it cannot; and, again, in others, that the holder may recover upon sufficient security and indemnity being given.

The amount of a note should always be written out in words; it is usually written in both words and figures. When the sum in figures differs from that expressed in words, the latter is taken as the amount of the note.

PRESENTMENT FOR PAYMENT.—The presentment of a bill of exchange or promissory note should be made on the day of its maturity,—that is, on the last day of grace,—and *not before*, and must be made personally, either by the holder or his authorized agent, and cannot be made by a written demand sent to him through the post-office.

In order to charge an *indorser*, if the bill or note is payable at a particular place, a bank for instance, it must be presented there for payment on the very day it becomes due; if no place is mentioned, the demand must be made at the maker's place of business during business hours, or at his dwelling-house within reasonable hours. If the note is given by joint makers, it must be presented to them all. In case of the death of the maker, it should be made to the executor or administrator, if they have been appointed; if not, at the dwelling-house of the deceased. When the maker has absconded, no presentation is necessary.

A **Notary,** or **Notary Public,** is an officer authorized by law, whose business it is to attest documents or writings of any kind to give them the evidence of authenticity.

A **Protest** of a promissory note or bill of exchange is a formal declaration made by a Notary Public under hand and seal, at the request of the holder of a bill or note, for non-acceptance or non-payment. This declaration is a protest to the drawer and all other parties to the bill against any loss which may be sustained by the payee or holder. (See BILLS OF EXCHANGE.)

It is not necessary, to fix the liability of the *maker* of a note, that there should be demand, protest, or notice; but *notice of non-payment*, either verbal or written, but well authenticated, *to the indorser, is necessary to hold him liable.*

The notice should be given on the same day on which the note falls due, or the next day thereafter; otherwise the indorser will be discharged.

The notice should state that the bill or note was duly presented, and that payment was refused, and should contain a correct description of the note, so that there can be no mistake in regard to its identity; it should also contain a declaration that the person to whom the notice is sent will be looked to for payment and indemnity.

It is advisable, when a note is not paid by three o'clock on the day of its maturity, to place it in the hands of a notary for protest, as the protest is evidence that the note was properly presented for payment and that payment was refused.

An **Accommodation Note** is one for which the maker receives no consideration, but which he makes for the purpose of lending his credit to the payee to enable him to raise money. The party for whom such an accommodation was made, cannot recover from the maker; but if it is indorsed for value to a third person, although he may have notice that it is an accommodation note, and no consideration was given for it, that third person can nevertheless recover from the original maker. An accommodation note is drawn in the ordinary negotiable form, and is either made payable to the party accommodated, or passed by the payee to the credit of the drawer.

A **Collateral Note** is one given with stocks or other property as security, empowering the payee to sell if the note should not be paid when it becomes due.

A **Joint Note** is one which is written thus, "we promise to pay," &c., signed by two or more persons, or written "we promise to pay," and signed "A. B., principal, H. T., security." The words *principal* and *security* only show the relation of the makers to each other; they do not affect other parties.

When a note is written "we jointly and severally promise," or "I promise," &c., and signed by two or more persons, it is a **Joint and Several Note.**

The promisors of a joint note must be sued jointly, while either promisor of a joint and several note may be sued alone.

A release of the maker, or of one joint maker, by the holder, is a discharge of all the indorsers.

If a seal is added to a promissory note, it is not debarred or cut off by the Statute of Limitations, but it then becomes non-negotiable, and can be transferred only by assignment.

A **Judgment Note** differs from a common promissory note in having a seal appended, with a power of attorney to confess judgment.

The maker, by this power of attorney, authorizes the payee to have judgment entered, which is a lien against his lands or estate, and authorizes the issuing of an execution without resort to a suit by the ordinary course of law.

An agent is personally liable on the contract he makes, if he makes himself so expressly, or transcends his authority. (See AGENCY.)

If an agent exceeds his authority in signing the name of his principal to a note, the note will be void as to the principal, even in the hands of a *bona fide* holder. A general authority to transact business, even if it is expressed in words of very wide meaning, will not be held to include the power of making the principal a party to negotiable paper.

If an agent having authority gives a note beginning "I promise," &c., and signed "A. for B.," it has been decided that this is the note of the principal, and not of the agent.

If an agent of an incorporated company makes a note beginning "I promise," &c., and signs it "A. B., agent for —— Company," the company, and not the agent, is liable on the note.

FORMS OF NEGOTIABLE NOTES.

$600. *New York, July 17, 1866.*

Three months after date, I promise to pay to George H. Morehead, or order, at the Metropolitan National Bank, Six Hundred Dollars. Value received. *Samuel H. Stewart.*

$675. *Philadelphia, August 8, 1866.*

Sixty days after date, we promise to pay to Edmund A. Souder, or order, Six Hundred and Seventy-Five Dollars, without defalcation. Value received. *L. H. Burton & Co.*

$3500. *Trenton, N. J., August 9, 1866.*

Thirty days after date, for value received, I promise to pay to Geo. L. Bower, or bearer, Three Thousand and Five Hundred Dollars, without defalcation or discount.

Robert H. Turner.

NOTE WITHOUT DAYS OF GRACE.

$250 $\frac{75}{100}$. *New Orleans, April 4, 1867.*

Ten days after date, without grace, I promise to pay to Samuel G. Milburn, or order, Two Hundred and Fifty $\frac{75}{100}$ Dollars. Value received. *Philip S. Chester.*

ONE FORM OF ACCOMMODATION NOTE.

$500. *Lancaster, March 13, 1867.*

Sixty days after date, I promise to pay to the order of John D. Laverty Five Hundred Dollars, at the Lancaster National Bank, without defalcation. Value received.

Credit the drawer,
John D. Laverty. *S. F. Powell.*

NOTE BEARING INTEREST.

$290. *Albany, August 16, 1866.*

Six months after date, I promise to pay Charles Riqua & Co., or order, Two Hundred and Ninety Dollars, with interest. Value received. *John L. Brown.*

A JOINT NOTE.

Montgomery, August 11, 1866.

Three months after date, we jointly promise to pay to Walter L. Vaughan, or order, Three Hundred and Fifty Dollars. Value received.

$350.

William H. Tracy,
Darwin L. Hunter.

A JOINT AND SEVERAL NOTE.

Montpelier, October 11, 1866.

Sixty days after date, we jointly and severally promise to pay to the order of John B. Felshaw Seven Hundred and Thirty $\frac{50}{100}$ Dollars, without defalcation. Value received.

730\frac{50}{100}$.

Henry A. Tyson,
James C. English.

NON-NEGOTIABLE NOTE.

Harvard, Ill., April 9, 1867.

Thirty days after date, I promise to pay to A. D. Groesbeck One Thousand Dollars. Value received.

$1000.

Charles J. Fisher.

JUDGMENT NOTE.

SIXTY DAYS *after date, I promise to pay to* AUGUSTUS H. ROBINSON, *of Buffalo, or order, One Thousand Dollars, with interest, for value received.*

AND FURTHER, *I do hereby authorize any attorney of any Court of Record in Pennsylvania, or elsewhere, to appear for me, at any time after the above note becomes due and remains unpaid, and after declaration filed thereupon, to confess judgment against me for the above sum, with costs of suit, release of errors, &c.*

WITNESS *my hand and seal, at Cincinnati, this 17th day of August, in the year one thousand eight hundred and sixty-six.*

Signed, sealed, and delivered
in the presence of
ORLANDO BARNES,
HENRY F. FOSTER.

JOEL F. HARRISON. [Seal.]

A NOTE PAYABLE BY INSTALMENTS.

$1200. *Baltimore, September 10, 1866.*

For value received, I promise to pay to Charles M. Williamson, or order, Twelve Hundred Dollars, with interest, in the manner following, viz., Two Hundred Dollars two months after date, and the balance in instalments of Two Hundred Dollars each, payable every two months thereafter, until the whole amount shall be paid. *James L. Bennett.*

FORM OF NOTE USED BY MANY WHOLESALE HOUSES.

$150. *Philadelphia, May 19, 1867.*

Four months after date, I, the subscriber, residing in Massillon, Stark Co., State of Ohio, promise to pay to the order of Young, Moore & Co. **One Hundred and Fifty Dollars,** *for value received, negotiable and payable without defalcation or discount, and without relief from any valuation or appraisement law, with current rate of exchange on Philadelphia, Pa.*

No. 89. Due Sept. 19/22. *Jas. A. Jackson.*

INDIANA PARTNERSHIP NOTE.

JAS. J. HUMES, CHAS. J. LINN.

100\frac{75}{100}$. *Indianapolis, June 16, 1864.*

Four months after date, we, the subscribers, of Blue River, county of Johnson, State of Indiana, promise to pay to the order of Hunter, Simons & Co.

(without any relief whatever from appraisement or valuation laws, with the current rate of exchange)

One Hundred $\frac{75}{100}$ Dollars, without defalcation, for value rec'd, payable and negotiable at the State Bank of Indiana.

Samuel Hunter, *Humes & Linn.*
Alfred Simons,
William Smith.

COLLATERAL NOTE.

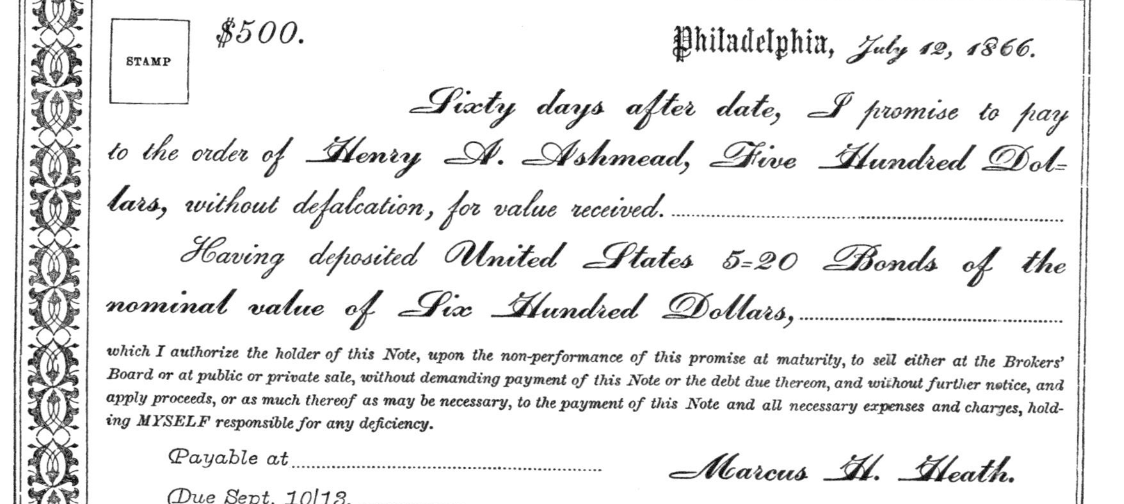

STAMP

$500.

Philadelphia, July 12, 1866.

Sixty days after date, I promise to pay to the order of Henry A. Ashmead, Five Hundred Dollars, without defalcation, for value received.

Having deposited United States 5-20 Bonds of the nominal value of Six Hundred Dollars, which I authorize the holder of this Note, upon the non-performance of this promise at maturity, to sell either at the Brokers' Board or at public or private sale, without demanding payment of this Note or the debt due thereon, and without further notice, and apply proceeds, or as much thereof as may be necessary, to the payment of this Note and all necessary expenses and charges, holding MYSELF responsible for any deficiency.

Payable at ....

Due Sept. 10/13, ...

Marcus H. Heath.

DRAFTS AND BILLS OF EXCHANGE.

A **Draft** or **Bill of Exchange** is an order, or open letter of request, for a sum of money, addressed to a person in a distant place.

A Bill of Exchange must be for the payment of *money*, and also payable absolutely at all events, and must not depend upon any uncertainty or contingency.

When the order is addressed to a person residing in a foreign state or country, it is called a *Foreign Bill of Exchange.*

When addressed to a person residing in the same State or country as the drawer, it is called a *Draft*, or an *Inland* or *Domestic Bill of Exchange.*

The different States of the United States, in law, are foreign to each other: so that a bill drawn in Pennsylvania upon a person in Illinois is considered a foreign bill.

There are, however, no essential differences between foreign and inland bills, except that the rights of proceeding and remedies thereon are governed by different rules and regulations in different countries; and in the case of foreign bills, when acceptance or payment is refused, *a protest is indispensably necessary.* This instrument is admitted in foreign countries as a legal proof of the refusal.

A protest is not absolutely required to entitle the holder of an *inland bill* to recover from the drawer or indorser when acceptance or payment has been refused. *Due notice*, however, must be given of the non-acceptance or non-payment.

Drafts, or bills of exchange, are used for safety in making remittances. They are drawn payable to the order of the person to whom sent, and are, therefore, not to be paid until indorsed by him.

Their use avoids the expense and trouble of sending coin

or currency, and as they are left in the hands of the person making the payments, they thus become vouchers to prove that the money has been properly paid.

Bills of Exchange may be made payable at sight, that is, on presentation; or a certain time after sight, or on demand, or a certain time after date.

They are sometimes drawn at *usance*, which is the usual time allowed by custom or law in the place where they are made payable, and varies from *fourteen days* to *three months.* The *usance* of England is *sixty days after sight*, with three days of grace; of France, *thirty days.*

If made payable in so many days *after sight, or demand*, they should be presented for acceptance, in order to fix the period of payment; but if the bill is payable *on demand* or at *sight*, or a certain number of days *after date*, it need not be presented merely for acceptance, but only for payment. It is usual, however, and advisable, to present all bills except those drawn payable at sight, or on demand, for acceptance.

If the bill contains the words "*as per advice*," the drawee may wait for further directions or advice; and if he accepts or pays without doing so, he does it at his own peril.

Bills of Exchange are usually collected through the medium of banks or bankers, and, when desired for the purpose of making remittances, may be purchased from them, generally, at a small premium or discount on the amount of the bill.

The person who writes or draws the bill is called the *drawer.* The person to whom it is addressed is called the *drawee.* The person to whom payment is made is called the *payee.* If the *drawee* agrees to pay the money signified in the bill, he does it by writing his name across the *face* of the bill, and is then said to *accept* it, and is called the *acceptor.* If the person to whom the bill is made payable assigns it to another person, he does it by writing his name upon the *back* of the bill, and is then called the *indorser.*

Accepting a bill binds the acceptor the same as signing a

note of the same tenor. Every indorser, as well as the acceptor, is security for the bill, and if protested for non-acceptance or non-payment, they and the drawer are liable to the holder for the principal sum, the interest, and the expense incurred by the dishonor,—such as cost of protest, broker's commission, and rate of exchange. Most of the States of the Union have provided by statute a certain fixed sum or percentage in lieu of damages and re-exchange. The parties to a bill are liable to the holder according to the law of the place where they entered into their respective contracts; the drawer, according to the law of the place where the bill is drawn; the acceptor, according to the law of the place of acceptance; and the indorsers, of the place where the indorsements were made.

When a person draws a bill of exchange, he subjects himself to the payment of it should the person on whom it is drawn refuse either to accept or pay, if the holder of the bill gives him due notice.

If acceptance is refused, or if payment is not made on the day when the bill becomes due, notice should be given, *without delay*, to each party liable, that they may be held.

The holder should give notice to the other parties to the bill, if the acceptance is in part, or qualified, or not in full, if he intends having recourse to them in case of non-payment when due.

The acceptor, who is the party originally held bound, may be allowed whatever indulgence or delay the holder pleases, short of the time allowed by the statute of limitations.

A DRAFT OR INLAND BILL OF EXCHANGE.

No. 37. STAMP

$1000. Rochester, Nov. 24th, 1865.

........................At Ten Days' Sight, Pay to the Order of ....CHARLES McCLINTOCK......................

................ONE THOUSAND DOLLARS,..............

Value received, and charge to Account of

To Duncan & Sherman,
New York.

Thomas Perrins.

ACCEPTED DRAFT.

STAMP

$250 $\frac{75}{100}$ Dover, Dec. 8th, 1865.

Ten Days after Sight, Pay to the Order of ....THOMAS W. MOORE..........................

..........Two Hundred and Fifty............$\frac{75}{100}$ Dollars,

Value received, which place to Account of

To R. R. Robinson & Co.
Wilmington, Del.

James Merrell.

Accepted Dec. 12, 1865.
R. R. Robinson & Co.

Drafts are sometimes accepted in the following form:—"Accepted Apr. 4th, 1867, payable at the City National Bank, Charles Ennis."

FOREIGN BILLS OF EXCHANGE.

Foreign Bills of Exchange are usually drawn in Sets, called the First, Second, and Third, etc. of Exchange, all of the same tenor and date, and so worded that when one is paid the others are rendered void. They are sent by different mails or conveyances, as a precaution against loss or inconvenience arising from accident or miscarriage. *Sola* is the name given to a single bill.

FIRST OF A SET OF EXCHANGE ON LIVERPOOL.

Exchange for £1000. Boston, Apr. 30, 1867.

At Sixty Days' Sight of this FIRST *of Exchange (Second & Third of same tenor and date unpaid) Pay to the Order of* ....PETER WALKER............

One Thousand Pounds Sterling

for Value received, and place the same to account of

To Brown, Shipley & Co.,
Liverpool, Eng.

1

George Peabody.

SECOND OF A SET OF EXCHANGE ON PARIS.

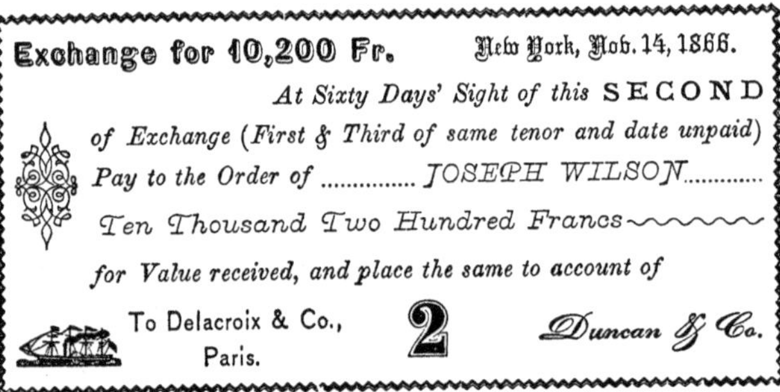

Exchange for 10,200 Fr. New York, Nov. 14, 1866.

At Sixty Days' Sight of this SECOND *of Exchange (First & Third of same tenor and date unpaid) Pay to the Order of* ....JOSEPH WILSON............

Ten Thousand Two Hundred Francs

for Value received, and place the same to account of

To Delacroix & Co.,
Paris.

2

Duncan & Co.

THIRD OF A SET OF EXCHANGE ON FRANKFORT.

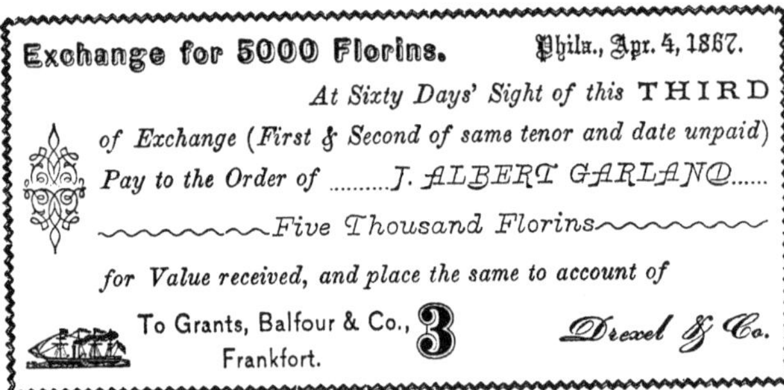

Exchange for 5000 Florins. Phila., Apr. 4, 1867.

At Sixty Days' Sight of this THIRD *of Exchange (First & Second of same tenor and date unpaid) Pay to the Order of* ....J. ALBERT GARLAND......

Five Thousand Florins

for Value received, and place the same to account of

To Grants, Balfour & Co.,
Frankfort.

3

Drexel & Co.

INDORSEMENTS, ACCEPTANCES, &c.

INDORSEMENTS.

The word indorsement signifies a writing on the back of a bill or written instrument; but it is well settled that this is not essential in order to charge a person as an indorser. The indorsement may be on any part of the note, or on a paper annexed to it, and in ink or pencil; but it is better that the signature should be in ink, to prevent erasure.

When a note or bill is drawn payable to a person or his order, it is properly transferable only by indorsement; nothing else, in law, will hold the parties to a note directly liable to the holder.

FORMS OF INDORSEMENTS.

1. INDORSEMENT IN BLANK.

John S. Barton.

2. INDORSEMENT IN FULL.

Pay to Jas. Jones, or order.
John S. Barton.

3. QUALIFIED INDORSEMENT.

John S. Barton,
Without recourse.

4. RESTRICTIVE INDORSEMENTS.

Pay Robert Hunter, for my use.
John S. Barton

Pay to Chas. Harrison only.
John S. Barton.

5. CONDITIONAL INDORSEMENT.

Pay George Gray, or order, the within, unless before due he receives the amount from my agent.
John S. Barton.

6. INDORSEMENT BY AN AGENT.

John S. Barton,
Agent for Howard Chester.

7. A GUARANTY ON A NOTE.

For value received in cash, I hereby guaranty the payment of the within Note.
John S. Barton.

1. A blank indorsement makes a note transferable by mere delivery only, and by it the indorser is made liable for the payment of the note. If the note or bill is lost after such

blank indorsement, any person who should become the holder of it, in good faith, for a valuable consideration, without notice, would be entitled to receive the amount thereof.

2. Indorsements in full prevent a subsequent *holder* from recovering against the antecedent parties, unless he can deduce a regular title to the bill from the person whose name stands as first indorser.

If all the subsequent indorsers are in blank, the holder may make himself the immediate indorsee of any one of them, or he may deduce his title through them all in succession.

If some of the subsequent indorsements are in full and some in blank, then he must make a regular deduction of title through them all, or make himself the immediate indorsee, under some prior blank indorsement.

Persons taking a bill or note subsequently to a blank indorsement may transfer it, either by delivery or by indorsement.

3. A qualified indorsement is one which affects the liability of the indorser, but not the negotiability of the note. If the holder of a note wishes to transfer it without being held liable for its payment, he can do so by writing his signature and adding "*without recourse,*" or other words to that effect.

4. The holder who has absolute property in a bill or note has the power of limiting payment to whom he pleases. A restrictive indorsement will not, however, be presumed from equivocal language, as restrictive indorsements tend to impair the negotiability of bills and notes.

5. If the payee or indorsee of a bill or note annexes a condition to his indorsement, *before acceptance,* the drawee who afterwards accepts it is bound by the condition. If the terms of the condition are not complied with, the property in the bill reverts to the payee, and he may recover the sum payable in an action against the acceptor.

6. An agent should expressly indorse as agent, or write the name of his principal; otherwise the indorsement would

be inoperative. When an agent is compelled to indorse notes or bills over to his principal, to avoid responsibility, he should use a restrictive form of indorsement.

In Pennsylvania, a factor who remits a bill to his principal, in payment of goods sold on his account, and indorses the bill, does not thereby become *personally responsible to his principal*, if he receives no consideration for guaranteeing and does not expressly undertake to do so. 4 *Rawle*, 384–389; 5 *Whart.* 288.

An indorsement in the form of *A. B., Treasurer of —— Company*, has been held not to render the agent liable as an indorser, but considered as intended only to pass the paper, and as equivalent to an indorsement "without recourse."

7. An indorsement implies a contract to pay the note if dishonored, if due notice is given of dishonor, and not otherwise; whereas a *guaranty* implies a contract, if due notice is given of dishonor *within a reasonable time.*

The guaranty should contain words importing consideration, and, *unless made expressly negotiable*, is good only to him who first takes the note and advances money upon it. If the guaranty is upon a separate paper, it should describe the note with sufficient distinctness.

If, upon proper presentation, payment of a note or bill is refused, the holder must give prompt notice of such refusal to each indorser whom he wishes to hold for payment, and inform him that he will be held for the payment of the same; otherwise the indorser will be discharged. If the holder could delay, he might injuriously affect the indorser, and his remedy against other persons.

The holder of a note or bill may commence suit against any of the indorsers, or against all of them at once.

When there are several indorsers, each is liable to those after him, and should give notice to all parties indorsing prior to himself.

Each indorser may require any one whose name precedes

his own to make good to him the loss he may sustain, provided he gives notice of his intention to do so on the day he receives his own notice, or the day after.

This notice may be given by any person competent to serve it; but a notary public is usually employed for the purpose.

ACCEPTANCES.

An Acceptance is an engagement to comply in whole or in part with the terms of a bill. When the drawee engages to pay according to its terms, it is called a *general acceptance;* when he agrees to pay with some qualification or condition different from the bill, it is called a *conditional* or *qualified acceptance.*

When a bill is presented for acceptance, the drawee is entitled to twenty-four hours, if he desires it, to decide whether he will accept it or not. In New York and Missouri, if the bill is not returned within twenty-four hours, it is deemed by law to be accepted.

Acceptances are usually written across the face of the bill, and, for distinctness, in red ink.

Any words not refusing its request, or the signature of the acceptor in blank, is *prima facie* evidence of acceptance; and when not otherwise provided for by law, the acceptance may be either verbal or in writing,—a written acceptance, of course, being more easily susceptible of proof.

In New York it is held that no person shall be charged as an acceptor of a bill of exchange unless the acceptance be in writing, and every holder may, on presentation of the bill, require that the acceptance be written on the bill, and if such acceptance is refused, the bill may be protested for non-acceptance.

The holder may assent to a qualified acceptance, and it will be good as far as it extends; but he takes it at his own risk, and he must give notice to the antecedent parties, or they will not otherwise be held bound by it. The condition of the acceptance should appear upon the face of the acceptance in writing, as any subsequent holder for value, without notice, would not be bound by verbal conditions.

The holder is not bound to take any but an unqualified or unconditional acceptance; and when refused, if he wishes to maintain a claim against the other parties, he should treat the bill as dishonored, unless they assent to the proposed conditional acceptance. If the holder declines the conditional acceptance, it will be a waiver of all right to hold the drawee.

Form of Conditional Acceptance written across the face of a Draft.

"Accepted if in funds from consignment shipped us on 3d instant. ROGER B. GRAY.

"NEW YORK, Oct. 17/66."

AGENCY.

An **Agent** is a person having power to act for another, who is called a principal.

A man may do by his agent whatever he can lawfully do himself, and his agent can do for him.

A *General Agent* is one appointed to transact all the business of his principal, or all his business of a particular kind.

A *Special Agent* is appointed for a specific and particular purpose.

A **Broker** is an agent employed to negotiate between other parties, and is presumed to act in the name of his principal.

A **Factor** or Commission Merchant is an agent to sell goods for his principal, but who acts for several persons in that capacity. He differs from the broker in having actual possession of the goods. A Factor may buy and sell in his own name as well as in the name of his principal.

An Attorney is an agent acting in behalf of his client.

The authority of an agent may be constituted in three ways: by deed under seal, by a writing without seal, or by mere words.

The authority of an agent may be revocable or irrevocable. It is irrevocable when an interest in the subject-matter is conveyed to the agent, or the authority is given for a valuable consideration; it is revocable when no interest is conveyed, in which case the principal can revoke the authority at his pleasure, subject in some cases to a claim for damages.

An agency may be revoked by the operation of law, by expiration of time, by changes producing incapacity to act, by the extinction of the subject-matter or its complete fulfilment, or by the death of the principal. A power of attorney to sell goods or stocks ceases with the life of the principal, and upon his death may become valueless.

Where the conveyance or any act is required to be under seal, the authority to execute it must be under seal also.

Verbal authority, ordinarily, is sufficient; but an agent ought, for his own security, to act under written authority, and to disclose his character whenever he executes a contract. In signing his name, the mere use of the word "agent" is not sufficient; the name of the principal must also appear. Instead of writing "Henry Grant, Agent," it should be "R. Brown, per Henry Grant;" or, "R. Brown, by his attorney, Henry Grant."

If an agent does an act or makes a contract unauthorized by his principal, though in the name of the principal, he is personally liable; but if the principal, with the knowledge of all the facts, adopts or acquiesces in the acts done under an assumed agency, he cannot afterwards impeach them under the pretence that they were done without authority, or even contrary to instructions. If the principal does not dissent and give notice of it within a reasonable time after being informed of what has been done, his assent and satisfaction will be presumed.

"An agent is personally liable if he makes himself so expressly, or if he transcends his authority or departs from its terms and directions, or if he conceals his character as agent, or if he purposely conceals the name of his principal, or, perhaps, if he does not actually state the name of his principal."

It is the duty of the agent to follow implicitly his instructions, and to keep his principal fully and promptly informed in regard to the business intrusted to him.

An agent is liable for interest if he has made it on the money in his hands, but not if it has lain idle.

As a general rule, an agent cannot appoint a substitute, or delegate his authority to another. But a power of substitution may be expressly given, or it may be inferred from the nature of the act to be performed, or where there is a known and established custom of substitution.

POWER OF ATTORNEY.

A Power of Attorney, or Letter of Attorney, is a written instrument, usually under seal, by which authority is given to one person to perform some lawful act for another.

Authority to execute a deed must be given under seal, and be acknowledged by both husband and wife, and must be done in the name of the principal.

Upon the death of the principal, the authority delegated by power of attorney ceases, and all subsequent acts under it are void.

The authority intended to be conferred should be expressed in clear and intelligible terms, and be properly executed, attested, and acknowledged.

FORM OF POWER OF ATTORNEY.

Know all Men by these Presents, That I,
of , County of , and State of , have made, constituted, and appointed, and by these presents do make, constitute, and appoint
, of , County of
and State of , my true and lawful attorney, for me, and in my name, place, and stead, and in my behalf, to (here insert the things which the attorney is to do); giving and granting unto my said attorney full power and authority generally to do and perform all and every act and thing whatsoever requisite or proper to effectuate all or any of the premises, with the same powers, and to all intents and purposes with the same validity, as I, if personally present, could (giving and granting, also, unto my said attorney full power to substitute one or more attorney or attorneys under him my said attorney in or concerning the premises, or any part thereof, and the same at his pleasure to revoke; and) hereby ratifying and confirming whatsoever my said attorney (or his substitute or substitutes) shall and may do by virtue hereof in the premises.

In Witness whereof, I have hereunto set my hand and affixed my seal, this eighteenth day of September, in the year of our Lord 18

Signed, sealed, and delivered [Seal.]
in the presence of
Henry R. Linden,
Wm. H. Moult.

N.B.—By omitting the words in brackets, no power to appoint a substitute is given.

SHORT FORM.

Know all Men by these Presents, That

do make, constitute, and appoint
true and lawful Attorney for and in name

with power, also, an attorney or attorneys under for that purpose to make and substitute, and to do all lawful acts requisite for affecting the premises; hereby ratifying and confirming all that the said attorney or substitute or substitutes shall do therein by virtue of these presents.

In Witness whereof, have hereunto set hand and seal the day of , in the year of our Lord one thousand eight hundred and [L.S.]

Signed, sealed, and delivered
in the presence of

POWER TO TRANSFER STOCK.

Know all Men by these Presents, That I, K. W. Y., of Oswego, County of Oswego, and State of New York, do make, constitute, and appoint Leonard D. Gray, of the same place, my true and lawful attorney, for me, and in my name and behalf, to sell, transfer, and assign unto Hosea W. Hunter, of said Oswego (or, any other person or persons), One Hundred Shares in the capital stock of the Syracuse National Bank, in Syracuse, State of New York, standing in my name on the books of said corporation; and to do all necessary acts and to make the necessary acquittances and discharges to effect the premises (add, if desired, and I do further empower him to substitute any person or persons under him, with like power); hereby ratifying and confirming all my said attorney (or his substitute or substitutes) shall lawfully do by virtue hereof.

In Witness whereof, &c.

POWER TO RECEIVE DIVIDEND.

Know all Men by these Presents, That I, H. Y. Bell, of Oswego, County of Oswego, State of New York, do constitute and appoint Hiram Howell, of Meridian, Cayuga county, to receive from the Cashier of the Oswego National Bank the dividend or dividends now due me on all stock standing to my name on the books of the said bank, and to receipt for the same; hereby ratifying and confirming all that by him may lawfully be done by virtue hereof in the premises.

Witness my hand, etc.

Signed and delivered in presence of, &c.

CONTRACTS.

A contract is an agreement, upon sufficient consideration, to do, or not to do, some specified thing.

A consideration may be *any benefit to the party promising, or some trouble or injury to the party receiving the promise.*

In general, an offer or proposal becomes a contract as soon as it is accepted, and acceptance may be made before the expiration of the time limited, or at any reasonable time before knowledge of a retraction of the offer.

In the majority of the United States, no action can be brought against a person upon an agreement not to be performed within one year from the making of it, unless some note or memorandum of the agreement be signed by the party to be charged, or his lawfully appointed agent.

Persons under twenty-one years of age, married women, and insane persons, are incompetent to make a contract. A minor, however, may contract for necessaries; so, also, may a married woman when her husband, without good reason, refuses to make suitable provision for her.

The subject-matter of the contract must be possible; it must also be lawful. A contract founded upon fraud, or to do an illegal or immoral act, is void. A contract in total restraint of the exercise of a man's trade or profession, would not be enforced by the courts, because it is against public policy; but a contract restraining him in any particular city or place is valid.

Care bestowed in clearly expressing the contract in plain and unambiguous language, may be the means of preventing lawsuits and the loss of friendship as well as the loss of money. "Three things should be attended to in writing a contract. 1st. Weigh well your words, and ascertain their exact import or value. 2d. Use enough of them to express all that you mean or intend by the contract. 3d. Arrange them in such a manner that they have but one meaning, and that the meaning you intend."—HON. JOEL JONES.

Verbal evidence may be admitted to explain, but not to change, the original contract.

Contracts of Sale.—A sale is a contract for the transfer of property for a valuable consideration. The subject-matter and the price must be certain, or capable of being made so, to constitute a sale. The subject-matter should be perfectly identified, ascertained, and designated, so as to be distinguished from every thing else. In the several States, excepting Louisiana, no contract for the sale of any goods is binding, when the price is above a certain sum, unless the buyer shall accept part of the goods so sold and actually receive the same or give something in part payment, or unless some writing of such bargains be made and signed by the party to be charged. The sum required in Massachusetts and New York is $50; in Vermont, $40; in Connecticut, $35; in New Hampshire, $33.33; and in New Jersey, $30.

MERCANTILE LETTERS.

1. Offering Goods.

New York, Feb. 15, 1867.

Messrs. T. L. Morton & Co.,

Baltimore.

Gentlemen:

We take the liberty of enclosing a few samples of Black Taffetas, just received per Steamer Niagara. They are in patterns of about 14 yards, full 24 inches wide, at $3.15 per yard. Should you need any of them, we shall be happy to receive your order.

Yours, respectfully,

A. W. Colton & Co.,

pr. Jas. T. King.

2. Declining to Purchase.

Messrs. L. H. Alward & Co., Milwaukie, November 1, 1866.
Philadelphia.

Gentlemen:—We are in receipt of your favor of the 30th ult., and have likewise received the samples of Poplins, but, having as many goods of this description as we require for our present sales, we must decline handing you an order from samples forwarded.

Respectfully, yours,
Chandler & Co.

---

3. Order for Goods.

Memphis, Tenn., August 10, 1866.

Messrs. Marshall & Howland,
New York.

Gentlemen:—You will please ship us at your earliest convenience Three (3) Half-chests Imperial Tea (Andreas, #257), same as in last bill; also, Two (2) Half-chests of *best Imperial* (Queen of the North, #9, or something better). Ship by Great Western Dispatch, and mark goods as follows:

J. M. Orwig & Bro., *Memphis, Tenn.,*
Care Gould & Linton, *Cincinnati, Ohio.*

Please write across Bill of Lading, "Insured in consignees' open policy in the Globe Insurance Co. of Cincinnati," and send Gould & Linton the amount of Invoice, that they may enter on our policy book. Your early shipment will much oblige

Yours, very truly,
J. M. Orwig & Bro.

---

4. Enclosing Invoice and Bill of Lading.

Per "Wyoming." Philadelphia, March 17, 1867.

Messrs. L. M. Seaton & Co.,
New Orleans.

Dear Sirs:—We confirm our last letter of 12th inst., and hand you herewith enclosed B. of L. and Invoice of Cases E, H, #632 and 633, ordered by your Mr. Carlton, which we have shipped this day on board Steamer Wyoming. Amt., $1250.50/100; due June 17th.

Should you need any of our qualities of Cassimeres, we shall be pleased to fill your orders on the best terms possible.

Yours, truly,
Wells, Fisk & Co.

5. Advising Receipt of Invoice.

Mr James L. King, *Boston*. St. Louis, April 5, 1867.

Dear Sir:

Your favor of March 29th, with B. of L. and Invoice, was received in due time. The goods are all that we desired; and for your promptness and care in filling our order, accept our thanks.

Enclosed find in payment Holmes & Bros.' Draft on First National Bank of Boston, at sight, for $1875.\frac{50}{100}$. Please acknowledge receipt per return mail, and oblige

Yours, respectfully,

Thos. L. Smith & Co.

---

6. Consigning Goods to be sold on Commission.

Messrs. Samuel G. Porter & Co., Cincinnati, May 11, 1867.

New York.

Dear Sirs:—Your favor of 7th inst. is at hand. We enclose you Invoice and Bill of Lading of 100 bbls. Mess Pork and 50 firkins of Butter, shipped this day per Merchants' Line, to be sold for our account, as per agreement. We request you not to sell for less than Invoice price, and if you succeed in disposing of this lot satisfactorily, you may be almost sure of receiving further consignments from us. We have drawn on you at ten days' sight, through Phœnix Bank, for One Thousand Dollars. Awaiting your advices, and hoping soon to hear from you, we remain,

Very truly, yours,

M. Johnson & Co.

---

7. Enclosing Account Sales.

Messrs. M. Johnson & Co., New York, June 10, 1867.

Cincinnati.

Dear Sirs:—Enclosed we send you Account Sales of Pork and Butter shipped us on May 11th. The Net Proceeds, $1750.62, due per average July 2d, we have placed to the credit of your account; the result, we hope, will be satisfactory.

We shall be pleased to receive further consignments from you, and will endeavor to dispose of them on the most advantageous terms.

Thanking you for past favors, we remain,

Truly, yours,

Samuel G. Porter & Co.

8. Enclosing Account Current.

Mr. Henry T. Morris, Sandusky, O., Jan. 1, 1867.
Nebraska City.
Dear Sir:

We respectfully call your attention to the enclosed Account Current, with interest calculated to this date, showing a balance in our favor of $3275.$\frac{50}{100}$. If you find correct, please remit us a Draft at sight for the amount, and oblige

Yours, respectfully,
D. Rundel & Co.

---

9. Enclosing Remittance.

Messrs. J. T. Anthony & Co., Savannah, January 21, 1867.
Manchester, Eng.
Gentlemen:

Your favor of 2d inst., covering statement of account, is at hand, and upon examination we find it correct. Enclosed please find Richardson & Cowden's 1st and 2d of Exchange on Brown, Shipley & Co. for Two Hundred and Sixty Pounds 7/5, in settlement of account to 1st inst.

Please acknowledge receipt, and oblige

Yours, very truly,
B. F. Moore & Co.
per D. B. Martin.

---

10. Another.

Messrs. A. L. Watson & Co., Trenton, April 10, 1857.
Philadelphia.

Dear Sirs:

Enclosed find my Check on First National Bank of this city for Twenty-Two Hundred and Fifty Dollars, in payment of Bills of

July 21	1262.10
" 25	872.00
" 28	115.90
	$2250.00

Please acknowledge receipt, and oblige

Yours, respectfully,
James Anderson.

11. Acknowledging Remittance.

Buffalo, Jan. 12, 1867.

Received from Messrs. George H. Jackson & Co., Five Hundred and Fifty $\frac{25}{100}$ Dollars on account.

$550.$\frac{25}{100}$. H. D. Clinton & Co.

Messrs. George H. Jackson & Co., Buffalo, Jan. 12, 1867.
Utica, N.Y.

Gentlemen:—Above please find receipt for remittance contained in yours of 10th inst., for which we are obliged. We find in your statement a variation in two items, those of December 6th and 19th. Can you favor us with an explanation, as we have no credits reducing the amount of $35 to $25.$\frac{50}{100}$, or $675.$\frac{35}{100}$ to $654.$\frac{75}{100}$?

Waiting your reply, we remain,

Respectfully, yours,
H. D. Clinton & Co.

---

12. Another.

Messrs. Thos. M. Young & Co., Albany, Nov. 13, 1866.
Syracuse.

Gentlemen:—We have the pleasure to acknowledge the receipt of your esteemed favor of 10th inst., containing your Notes dated

Sept. 1, at 3 mos., for 425.66,
" 15, " " 425.66,
Oct. 1, " " 425.67,

Amounting to Twelve Hundred and Seventy-Six $\frac{99}{100}$ Dollars, which we have placed to your credit in settlement of your account.

Please accept our thanks, and, requesting the favor of your future orders, we remain,

Very truly, yours,
Chas. L. Riqua & Co.

---

13. Asking for Settlement.

Mr. Henry G. Sanders, Worcester, May 25, 1867.
Concord.

Dear Sir:—We respectfully call your attention to our statement of account rendered April 3d, a settlement of which at your earliest convenience will much oblige

Yours, very respectfully,
Horace Boyd & Co.

14. Another.

Mr. H. Y. Henderson, Wilmington, April 5, 1867.

Dover, Del.

Dear Sir:

Enclosed please find our usual monthly statement, amounting to $375.$\frac{25}{100}$, for which, if found correct, we shall be pleased to receive remittance by 30th inst.

Should we receive no remittance by that time, we propose to draw on you at sight for the amount, unless in the mean time we are otherwise advised.

Yours, respectfully,

James S. Smith & Co.

---

15. Advising of Draft.

Mr. H. T. Hawkins, Cleveland, June 3, 1867.

Harvard. Ill.

Dear Sir:

As we are in want of funds, we take the liberty of drawing on you at 5 days' sight for bills of

Jan. 10th,	$575.00
Feb. 12th,	300.00
	$875.00

which please protect, and much oblige

Yours, truly,

Brown & Worthington.

---

16. Enclosing Notes for Collection.

Cashier First National Bank, Philadelphia, July 29, 1866.

Cincinnati.

Dear Sir:—Enclosed find for collection,

Note J. Smith, due Aug. 3/6,	810.20
" J. Jones, " " 8/11,	600.00
Acceptance Morton & Co., due Aug. 10/13,	920.62
	$2320.82

If paid, please remit Draft for proceeds.

Yours, very respectfully,

George V. Maus.

INSTALMENT RECEIPT.

No. 13. INSTALMENT RECEIPT.

$2500. **200 Shares.**

WASHINGTON R. R. COMPANY.

Received, Washington, Apr. 11th, 1867, of S. J. Andrews, Two Thousand Five Hundred Dollars, being Twenty-Five Dollars per share, and the Third Instalment on Two Hundred Shares of the Capital Stock of the **WASHINGTON RAILROAD COMPANY**; *for which said shares a full Certificate will be given upon payment of all instalments due thereon, and the surrender of this Certificate.*

Leonard R. Cushing, *Daniel E. Eveland,*
Secretary. *President.*

Copy of an Exchequer Bill issued in the reign of Queen Anne.

£12 10*s*. "EXCHEQUER.

A 28/24. Purſuant to an Act of Parliament, Anno 1709, for enlarging the Capital Stock of the Bank of England, &c. This Bill entitles the bearer to twelve pounds, ten ſhillings, with intereſt at a farthing a day. To be received in all aids, taxes, loans, and payments whatſoever to Her Majeſty, and to be paid to the bearer by the Governor and Company of the Bank of England, from time to time, as the ſame shall be paid into the exchequer by any receivers or collectors of Her Majeſty's revenue, aids, taxes or ſupplies; and be thence reiſſued and at all times by ſuch receivers or collectors out of any public money in any of their hands, as directed by the ſaid Act."

BANK DEPOSIT TICKET.

Deposited, April 8th, 1867, at the

MECHANICS' NATIONAL BANK.

By Brown, Butler & Co.

	Dollars.	Cts.
Bank Notes, 5's and upwards	675	00
" " 1's and 2's	25	00
Specie	50	00
Checks, as follows	325	75
	465	50
	$1541	25

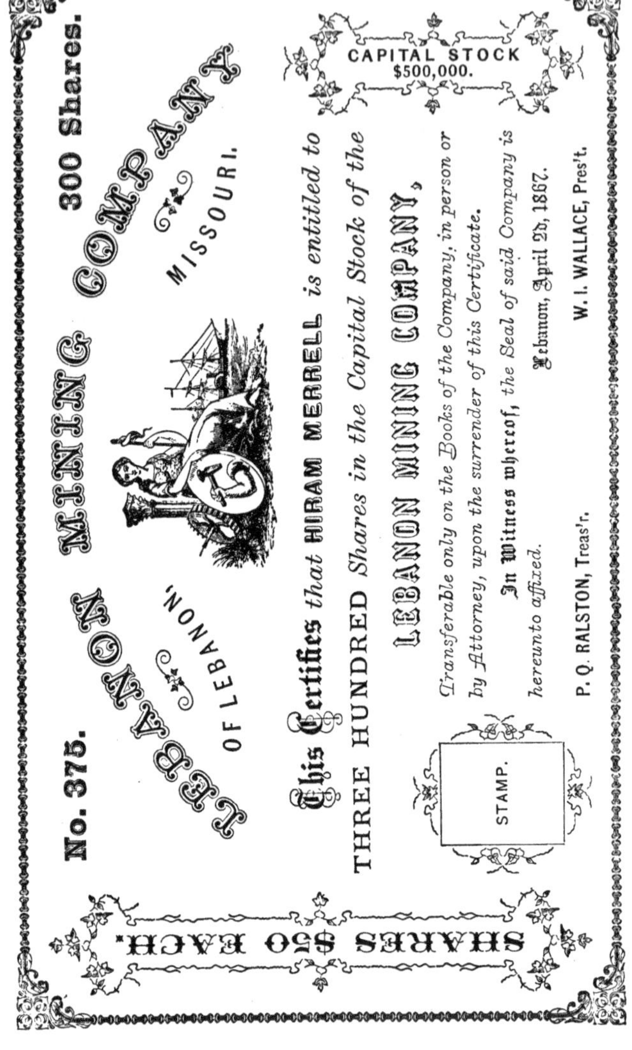

No. 375. 300 Shares.

LEBANON MINING COMPANY

OF LEBANON, MISSOURI.

This Certifies that HIRAM MERRELL is entitled to THREE HUNDRED Shares in the Capital Stock of the

LEBANON MINING COMPANY,

Transferable only on the Books of the Company, in person or by Attorney, upon the surrender of this Certificate.

In Witness whereof, the Seal of said Company is hereunto affixed.

Lebanon, April 2d, 1867.

P. Q. RALSTON, Treas'r. W. I. WALLACE, Pres't.

STAMP.

CAPITAL STOCK $500,000.

SHARES $50 EACH.

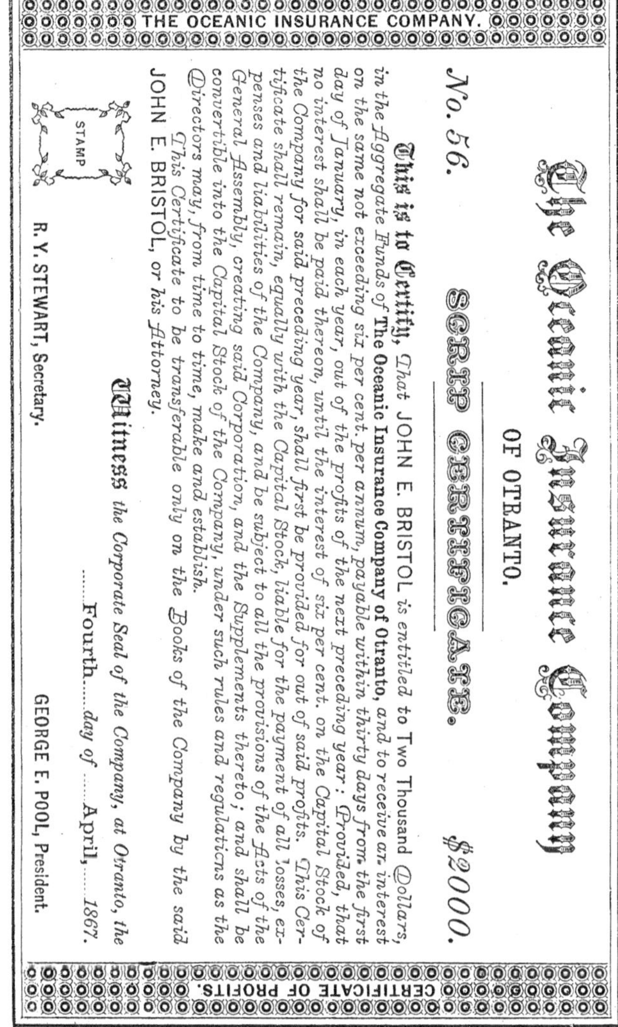

THE OCEANIC INSURANCE COMPANY.

The Oceanic Insurance Company

OF OTRANTO.

No. 56. **SCRIP CERTIFICATE.** *$2000.*

This is to Certify, *That* JOHN E. BRISTOL *is entitled* to Two Thousand *Dollars, in the Aggregate Funds of* **The Oceanic Insurance Company of Otranto,** *and to receive an interest on the same not exceeding six per cent. per annum, payable within thirty days from the first day of January, in each year, out of the profits of the next preceding year: Provided, that no interest shall be paid thereon, until the interest of six per cent. on the Capital Stock of the Company for said preceding year, shall first be provided for out of said profits. This Certificate shall remain, equally with the Capital Stock, liable for the payment of all losses, expenses and liabilities of the Company, and be subject to all the provisions of the Acts of the General Assembly, creating said Corporation, and the Supplements thereto; and shall be convertible into the Capital Stock of the Company, under such rules and regulations as the Directors may, from time to time, make and establish.*

This Certificate to be transferable only on the Books of the Company by the said JOHN E. BRISTOL, *or his Attorney.*

Witness *the Corporate Seal of the Company, at Otranto, the* ......Fourth......*day of* ......April,......*1867.*

STAMP

R. Y. STEWART, Secretary. GEORGE E. POOL, President.

CERTIFICATE OF PROFITS.

Treasurer's Department. | Register's Office.

1000 No. 60247. | No. 60247. 1000

IT IS HEREBY CERTIFIED THAT

The United States of America

Are indebted unto

S. Hodges Crittenden,

or Bearer, the sum of ONE THOUSAND DOLLARS, *redeemable at the pleasure of the United States after the 30th day of April, 1867, and payable on the 30th day of April, 1882, with interest from the 1st day of May, 1862, inclusive, at Six per cent. per annum, payable on the first day of May and November in each year, on the presentation of the proper coupon, hereunto annexed. This debt authorized by Act of Congress, approved Feb. 25th, 1862.*

Entered............E. I. S.

Recorded...........M. R.

Redeemable after Five Years,
and Payable Twenty Years from date.
Loan of Feb. 25, 1862.

Washington, May 1, 1862.
L. E. CHITTENDEN,
Register of the Treasury.

Six Months' interest, due 1st May, 1882, payable with this bond.

30 Act of Feb. 25th, 1862. 30
The United States of America
Will pay the bearer
THIRTY DOLLARS,
for Six Months' interest, due Nov. 1, 1881, *upon Bond* 60247. L. E. CHITTENDEN,
$1000. *Reg. U. S. Treas.*

30 Act of Feb. 25th, 1862. 30
The United States of America
Will pay the bearer
THIRTY DOLLARS,
for Six Months' interest, due May 1. 1881, *upon Bond* 60247. L. E. CHITTENDEN,
$1000. *Reg. U. S. Treas.*

30 Act of Feb. 25th, 1862. 30
The United States of America
Will pay the bearer
THIRTY DOLLARS,
for Six Months' interest, due Nov. 1, 1880, *upon Bond* 60247. L. E. CHITTENDEN,
$1000. *Reg. U. S. Treas.*

www.ingramcontent.com/pod-product-compliance
Lightning Source LLC
LaVergne TN
LVHW011208110826
845150LV00006B/1362

* 9 7 8 1 4 2 5 5 1 8 3 7 0 *